In the News

2nd Edition

In the News

The Practice of Media Relations in Canada

William Wray Carney

2nd Edition

 The University of Alberta Press

Published by
The University of Alberta Press
Ring House 2
Edmonton, Alberta, Canada   T6G 2E1

Copyright © William Wray Carney 2008

Library and Archives Canada Cataloguing in Publication

Carney, William Wray, 1950-
In the News : The Practice of Media Relations in Canada / William Wray Carney. – 2nd ed.

Includes bibliographical references.
ISBN 978-0-88864-495-4

1. Public relations–Canada. 2. Mass media and business–Canada.
I. Title.

HD59 C37 2007 659.2'0971 C2007-904992-3

The University of Alberta Press is committed to protecting our natural environment. As part of our efforts, this book is printed on Enviro paper: it contains 100% post-consumer recycled fibres and is acid- and chlorine-free.

In the News is published with financial support from MarketWire, which the Press gratefully acknowledges. The University of Alberta Press gratefully acknowledges the support received for its publishing program from The Canada Council for the Arts. The University of Alberta Press also gratefully acknowledges the financial support of the Government of Canada through the Book Publishing Industry Development Program (BPIDP) and from the Alberta Foundation for the Arts for its publishing activities.

  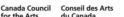

This book is dedicated
to Gilbert Thomas Carney and Dorothy Nema Bayley Carney
Together again

Content

Preface

The idea for this book came to me several years ago, when I was preparing to teach a class in media relations at the University of Alberta's Faculty of Extension. I received the standard form for instructors that asked, among other things, if I had a textbook I required students to use for the course.

As always, I ticked the box that said "No," then wondered why such a book wasn't available. A number of trade books on media relations have been published, but they tend to be overly specialized (e.g., media relations for small business, how to write a news release), too theoretical (media as part of the militaristic machine) or simply too personal (recitations of old media war stories, long on personal experience but short on the considerable research that has been done on news media in North America and the world).

In looking at the stack of photocopying I had prepared for the University to hand out to the students, and the amount of research I had collected over the years, it dawned on me that there was a need for a basic text on media relations. Such a book would provide an introduction to media relations, grounded in both experience and research, and would reflect current media and communications practices. While primarily intended for students in university and college communications programs, it would also be of benefit to practitioners and aspiring practitioners of media relations in the private, public and voluntary sectors. It would also be of interest to those who are concerned about the role of media and communications in society, particularly in the last two chapters.

This book is an attempt to meet those needs. It is drawn from many sources, including my experience in journalism and communications, and my studies and teaching. It also incorporates a good deal of research that I have come across in the past several years as part of my daily work life and teaching at the University of Alberta, University of Regina and Concordia University College of Alberta.

Acknowledgements

Many people have been kind enough to review this book in draft and provide helpful advice and input. I want to thank Randy Kilburn, Joy Adams Bauer and Wendy Campbell for their attention to the manuscript, and give special thanks to Kimberly Kratzig and Lyn Brown ABC, for their meticulous read of a very rough draft. James Murphy QC of Ogilvie LLP reviewed the section on media law, and Judy Hutchins of Marketwire contributed reference material for the section on the mandatory requirements for disclosure by companies listed on the Canadian stock exchanges.

I am particularly grateful to Marketwire, formerly CCNMatthews, for its continued sponsorship and support.

I would like to recognize the support of staff at Carleton University School of Journalism's Resource Centre, the library of Grant MacEwan College in Edmonton, the University of Alberta Library and the Regina Public Library. The comments of the academic reviewers, Albert S. Deyell and Evelyn Ellerman, were most helpful, as was the careful editing of Leslie Vermeer of the University of Alberta Press, who also contributed to the sections on magazines and the new media. I appreciated the careful help of Gladys Wasylenchuk in reviewing the final proofs of the first edition, and to Tyler McMurchy for the proof of the second editiion. I would like to thank Dave, Ruth, Sarah and Parker, for putting up with an eccentric house guest while the first draft of this book was being written, and to Paul Tymchuk of Sudbury, Ontario, who always believed that this book would see the light of day. Finally, I'd like to thank two significant mentors during my career, John Gibson, APR and Dr. James Howell.

I have quoted extensively from three major sources in this work, all of which have provided copyright clearance to allow their material to be used as a reference in this book. The Canadian Press has allowed material from *The Canadian Press Stylebook*. Nelson Education (formerly Harcourt Canada) has given permission to use material from *The Canadian Reporter, News Writing and Reporting*, second edition, by Catherine McKercher and Carman Cumming. Finally, Angus Reid Canada (now Ipsos Reid) allowed me to use their original research into news editors' practices and beliefs throughout the text (more on Ipsos Reid research can be found at their website, *http://www.ipsosreid.com*).

While many people have been involved in the making of this book, and their contributions have been noted, the final decision on what appears and how it appears is mine, as are any errors or omissions. In the furtherance of the profession, I would be glad to hear other views and practices on media relations, and other research that I may have overlooked. Please send me a note at wwcarney@hotmail.com or contact the publisher. I hope that future editions of this book will be strengthened by additional research and reflections on current practice.

Given my comments in the later chapters about lack of editing being a significant weakness affecting the quality of new media, particularly the blogosphere, I would again like to point out that this edition is much stronger than my earlier drafts, thanks to the thoughtful review and edits provided by Dr. Karen Wall of Athabasca University, and Michael Luski of The University of Alberta Press. As with Leslie Vermeer's edit of the first edition and Zanne Cameron's edit of the second edition, the editors deserve much credit for the value and quality of this book. Any opinions expressed here are mine, as are any errors, though it is hoped the second edition has rounded them all up and corrected them.

Students, please do not e-mail me asking for answers to the assignments your instructors have given you. As a professor, I will direct you to your instructors to answer any questions you may have. If, however, you wish to share your experiences or perspectives on media relations I will be glad to read them.

A Note on Resources

The student or reader who lacks media experience should read and refer to three essential works on media in Canada. The first, which is needed by the experienced practitioner as well as the novice, is *The Canadian Press Stylebook*, fourteenth edition, edited by Patty Tasko (Toronto: The Canadian Press, 2006), which is the reporter's standard reference for technical, professional and ethical practices. (You should note that there are other media guides in Canada, such as CanWest Global and CBC's. However, journalism and communications students routinely start with the CP guide, and for that reason we will use that as our common reference point on style guides.)

The second is *The Canadian Reporter: News Writing and Reporting* by Catherine McKercher and Carman Cumming (Toronto: Harcourt Brace & Company, 1998), which is the standard text for student journalists and provides a good deal of theory about how reporters are supposed to gather and report on news.

The third is *A Guide to Canadian News Media* by Peter Desbarats, second edition, (Toronto: Harcourt Brace Jovanovich Canada, 1996), which gives a good sense of both how the media work and what issues drive a good many reporters.

All three of these resources are available from their publishers or from the bookstore of a university or college offering programs in journalism or communications. Please see Chapter 17 and the bibliography for additional resource materials.

For the second edition, specific website URL's may have changed since originally accessed.

Lastly, the information on ownership, particularly on broadcasting, reflects the publication date of 2008. For updates on media changes in Canada, please refer to my blog: http://mediarelationsincanada.wordpress.com.

Introduction

Media relations is one of the mainstays of the communications business. With the proliferation of news media in the past decade (all-news television channels, all-news radio stations, a second national newspaper), more opportunities exist than ever before for being "in the news" and using news media as a means to communicate your issues to the public at large or to very targeted groups.

In the past, most communicators who specialized in media relations came from a media background: former reporters who by experience and instinct knew how the media worked, what they needed and what they responded to. As with journalism itself, however, more communicators are coming to the profession through the academic route, taking formal degree and certificate programs offered by universities and colleges. In Canada, about 100 such programs exist, often as a part of the same faculty, such as the School of Journalism and Communications at Carleton University in Ottawa.

What students of communications lack is a standard textbook on media relations that meets academic standards, is research-based and provides both a practical and a philosophical guide to dealing with media and reporters. Trade books on media relations have been written, but they are of varying quality or focus on specific aspects of media relations (e.g., for business,[1] for advocacy groups,[2] or on how to write a news release[3]). The experience practitioners bring to the field is valuable, and much of this book is based on my experience and that of my colleagues. However, wherever possible in this book, experience will be supported by research, and in the case of conflict, research will get the nod. For example, in his book *Making the News,* Mike Ura advises, "Have as full a press kit as possible."[4] However, a survey of editors and reporters by Angus Reid in 1993 shows that their biggest dislike of such kits is that they are too bulky and lengthy.[5] Experience counts, though, and will be acknowledged; Ura's advice on when to call a news conference is fundamentally sound and will stand until proven otherwise: "Rule of thumb: If you can send out a news release, don't call a news conference."[6]

A further distinction of this text is that it has passed academic review—that is, it has been scrutinized by academics in the field of communications and found suitable to be used as a textbook in a post-secondary setting. While it is intended primarily as an introductory textbook for communications students, I hope it will be equally useful to the aspiring practitioner of media relations, who may lack formal education or experience in media relations but still needs to work with media.

As noted, a variety of good books are targeted to specific groups or aspects of media relations, and they will be cited throughout this text. This book, however, seeks to take a broader perspective, touching on all major aspects of the trade. It is also intended to be of use for all groups and individuals who wish to practice media relations, from non-profits to advocacy groups to business (big and small) to government. While some common principles and practices apply to all, from time to time some of the unique aspects that limit or enhance a particular group's ability to practice media relations will be discussed. For example, governments have clear and precise legal limitations defining what information they can release or must not release to the media; advocacy groups have much greater licence in terms of what they can give to the media. This cross-industry information can be valuable whatever your own background. You may find yourself working in different sectors at different points in your career; and equally, you may need to be aware of the limitations of the sectors you don't typically work with and be able to respond to or compensate for them.

A final group might also find this book of benefit: reporters and journalism students. More research and publishing has been done on media than on communications, and communicators know far more about how media work than reporters know about how communications works. The relationship between the working reporter and the working communicator can be complex and ambivalent: some reporters swear by communicators who consistently provide reliable, accurate and comprehensible information; others swear *at* communicators who seem to be more of a barrier than an entry point into an organization and its issues. (A more detailed description of this relationship can be found in Chapter 3). There are certainly different schools of thought on how media relations should be practiced, and those ideas will be discussed here in the hope that the relationship between reporter and communicator becomes more transparent, and of more value to both.

In addition to providing a standard text for the practice of media relations, this book also hopes to complement the more theoretical texts on the media in general and its role in society. A variety of schools of thought on mass media have developed since Marshall McLuhan (the medium is the message) and Noam Chomsky (manufacturing consent), attained a high public profile and added idioms to the language; others are known only within academic circles. This book hopes to provide a practical grounding to the philosophical debate on the nature of media. I encourage you to delve into this issue in greater depth and develop a more philosophical understanding of the media. A number of excellent scholarly and non-academic texts exist, many of which you will find discussed in the Further Reading section in Chapter 17.

I also hope to provoke deeper thought about the ongoing debate on the nature of news and the future of newsgathering and reporting. Different schools of thought express different points of view on the current nature of news. For example, the Freedom Forum Media Studies Center at Columbia University (New York) identified two broad schools of thought on the future of news: declinists and neo-Pollyannaist.[7] Declinists take a pessimistic view of the state of news coverage, noting an obsession with trivialities and flash, instead of substantive, in-depth news stories. They point to short, insubstantial stories and the management of news by spin doctors. Neo-Pollyannaists cite the Internet as a great enabler, allowing the consumer easier access to quality media, such as the *New York Times,* and more direct access to source material, instead of having to rely on media coverage. (The federal budget, for example, is posted on the Internet as it is delivered in the House of Commons, providing Canadians who have Internet access immediate, complete information about the budget, and not requiring the intervention of a journalist to summarize and interpret it).

For both fields of philosophical inquiry, this book hopes to provide some practical grounding. In the last two chapters, this text will change from the practical applications of day to day media relations and connect to the larger discussion of the role of communications and media in shaping public opinion and public policy.

Nevertheless, this book and the author have their own perspective on news and media. In the interests of disclosure, the point of view of this book can be summarized as follows:

· News media are various and express different points of view;

· Marketing drives most news media more so than public interest, although media also act in the public interest and according to their own tradition;

· Media relations does not involve "spin doctoring."

We live with a multiplicity of media, each with its own qualities and point of view. At one time, particularly in the 1950s and 1960s, it was easier to define "mass media," connoting a consistent, monolithic point of view. In that era, most towns and cities had only two television stations, a handful of radio stations and one or two daily newspapers. Today, niche media, targeted to specific audiences and tastes, have generally replaced mass media. In television, most viewers can't count the number of channels they receive, let alone the number available to them by cable or satellite. In addition to local newspapers, two national newspapers have emerged to provide many Canadian communities with a choice among four dailies. And radio, supposed to have been made obsolete by television, continues to multiply and offer listeners many different choices in programming.

Edmonton, a medium-sized Canadian city, provides a good example of the multiplicity and diversity of news media. With a market of about 1,000,000, including the surrounding areas, it supports six television stations, four daily newspapers, 26 radio stations and a host of specialty weekly newspapers. (Please see Chapter 4 for a detailed discussion about how the media work in this market).

The second premise of this book is that marketing, not public interest, drives most news media. However, the successful communicator needs to bear both approaches in mind. Most news outlets are keenly aware of their audience and want to provide news that is relevant and interesting to them. This is seen most clearly in radio. Edmonton's 26 radio stations, for example, are either targeted to age groups (12- to 34-year-olds, 50-plus) or interest groups (all-news, gospel, ethnic communities). News about pension plans, for example, is more likely to be carried on CFRN-AM (target audience 50 years and older) than on Joe FM (CKNG-FM), home of contemporary music targeted at 12- to 34-year-olds.

Market-driven media exist more as a matter of degree than as an absolute. News has traditional values, taught in journalism schools and practiced daily, that we will explore in the course of this book. News also occasionally has a pronounced ideological bent that buttresses the outlet's marketing efforts with its audience. For example, Toronto's four daily newspapers each have a different philosophical approach to what is newsworthy and how it should be covered. More overt ideology exists in media such as the former *Western Standard,* which consistently and explicitly presents its news from the perspective of fundamental Christianity and Prairie populism. The fiscally and politically conservative views of Conrad Black could be seen in the news choice and coverage of the *National Post* before he sold it to the Asper Group. Other, more overtly leftist media also present news from an ideological perspective: *This Magazine* (Toronto), *Prairie Dog* (Regina) and *Canadian Dimension* (Winnipeg).

Notwithstanding tradition and ideology, all news media, including CBC TV and educational stations, now rely heavily on advertising, sponsorships or subscriptions to survive. Their editors' choice and presentation of news is heavily focussed on meeting the needs of their defined market and target audience. That perspective–that of the target audience–will be maintained throughout this book, since it underlies one of the key issues for every communicator: who are you trying to reach and why?

The third premise is that professional media relations does not involve "spin doctoring." Spin is discussed at greater length in Chapter 3; however, the basic distinction is that spin is better equated with propaganda than with traditional communications. Spin is most often practiced by highly partisan entities, such as political parties, unions and industry/issue advocates. Too often, spin ignores reality. A good example of spin can be seen after a leaders' debate in an election campaign. As soon as the debate ends, functionaries from all parties fan out to convince reporters that their candidate won the debate. It's difficult in a five-party debate for all five parties to claim victory, but spin doctors attempt to do just that—usually unsuccessfully (subsequent polls always determine who the public thinks won the debate).

Before getting into the specific issues of dealing with the media (writing a news release, conducting an interview, etc.), we need to cover a few larger, preparatory issues from the communicator's perspective, in order to better understand the media experience. First, we'll examine the issue of dealing with the media at all, and consider what alternatives exist. Then we'll look at some basic principles, followed by an analysis of how media and reporters work in their day-to-day routines. The approach emphasized here is that of the traditional communicator: media relations should be part of a planned process, in which all communications efforts are co-ordinated and coherent. We will also discuss some sample media plans. After exploring the intricacies of dealing with the media, including a section on the complex relationship between communicator and reporter and a review of ethical and professional guidelines for both parties, the book explores the different types of media you can become engaged with, and spends some time looking at that most critical element of media relations, the interview. By the conclusion of the book, you will have had a basic overview of the major principles and practices of media relations.

This book provides theories and principles of media relations, the practice of the craft of media relations, and extends to a larger discussion of the role that both media and communications play in society by helping to inform and shape public opinion. You will benefit most from it by taking the information, applying it and discovering for yourself not only what works in your field but what your own approach is to dealing with the media. The book provides a starting point from which you can develop and carry out your own media relations plan. It's also a guidebook, a reference to check in with from time to time to confirm your understanding, refresh your ideas and renew your energies.

In the best of all possible worlds, you will be able to use the information in this book to meet not only your own needs but also those of your employer/client, your target audience, the public and the media. Along the way, I hope you have fun. Dealing with the media can be many things, from frustrating to fulfilling, but it is almost never boring.

THEORY AND PRINCIPLES ON MEDIA RELATIONS | ONE

Why Media, Why News

Getting into the news is one of the mainstays of communications. News means not only the journalistic presentation of events but also opportunities for public discussion and debate (on talk shows and call-in programs, for example).

It also includes opinions, whether put forward in anonymous newspaper editorials or in the high-profile columns of featured names such as Jeffrey Simpson. News can be light or serious, fact or feature. The news media encompass not only television, radio and newspapers, but also the Internet, magazines, newsletters and more. Being "in the news" can range from a 15-second story item on radio to a multi-part documentary series on national TV.

Business and community groups, social advocates and politicians, athletes and actors, labour and professional groups all want to get their message out to the world, or to key target audiences, through the news media. From the beginning, communications has been typified by its efforts to communicate to key audiences and the public at large through the news media. Indeed, the very earliest term for a communicator was "press agent," denoting someone whose agency was required for news to get into the press.

A number of alternatives to media also exist, notably advertising; media relations is just one avenue for reaching the public or a target group. Before you even begin to consider practising media relations, you need to consider why you would want to choose news and the news media as a means of communications at all.

Why Choose Media as a Means of Communications?

News media have a number of strengths and weaknesses as a communications vehicle, which will be explained below. Why deal with media at all, given the number of alternative means of communications that exist and that afford you greater control? Here are a number of issues to consider.

Because you must

Most governments (federal, provincial, municipal), government-funded agencies (crown corporations, schools, universities, health districts) and judicial bodies (federal and provincial courts, labour boards, commissions of inquiry, zoning boards, etc.) are established to serve a public purpose. They also tend to have a higher degree of accountability to the public at large, and to the media, than do individuals or voluntary/advocacy groups. Companies listed on the stock exchanges have an obligation to report on their business; privately held businesses don't. While governments and companies may face legal restrictions on what type of information they can and cannot release (the next chapter outlines some of these restrictions and obligations), nevertheless there is an expectation that they will be open and accessible to the public, and that includes openness to the media.

The public has a high expectation that governments and government agencies in particular will be forthcoming and open, and indeed governments often exhibit a higher degree of commitment to the philosophy and practice of media relations than do many businesses. That they often do so in a unique environment of partisan politics should not obscure the fact that one of the major relationships between media and communicators is at the government level.

Because you should

It could be argued that individuals and groups share some of the same obligations as government to account for their actions: because they are part of society and enjoy the benefits of society. It is a legitimate purpose of media relations to practise it not for the tangible benefit it may deliver but for its own sake as part of living in a democratic society. Such practice should take into consideration that an individual has greater rights to privacy than does a government; but news for its own sake is a valid reason to deal with media.

On the corporate side, there is a new sense of accountablity and responsibility called Corporate Social Responsibility (CSR). Particularly after scandals such as Enron and WorldCom, there is a public expectation that corporations have more to do than just make money for shareholders: they have a responsibility to society to help improve that society. Better communications with the public and media can be argued as part of CSR.

On a more pragmatic basis, individuals and groups should be more active in practising media relations so that, in the event that one day they are exposed to the public and the media, they will be known to both and an existing relationship of trust will help the individual or group get through an unanticipated crisis. This will be expanded in the next chapter in the section Five Principles of Communications.

Because media will help you achieve your purpose

Most people practise media relations for a specific purpose, which is often a part of a larger plan of communications. That purpose may be to raise awareness for a cause, promote a business or social issue, counter criticism or something similar. However, identifying this purpose is also one of the main themes of this book: have a good reason to deal with media so you can practise media relations in a planned and organized fashion.

Because media have strengths that other forms of communications lack

As we will discuss in the next section, media offer advantages that other means of communications don't. (Getting a message out through the media can be instantaneous and can reach either a very large audience or a very targeted audience, depending on which media send the message). Equally, media come with disadvantages, which we will also discuss. (Media can distort or ignore your message; a subject may lose its subtlety or sophistication if it comes out in a 30-second news story).

Because you'll be in the media anyway

Business and governments often know in advance that there will be a public hearing, community consultation on bylaw change, licence renewal, protest or similar reaction to a given event or announcement. These types of public events are often marked by a need to communicate with communities, boards and key stakeholders, and this communication is often achieved through the media.

Business in particular can generally predict when it will be in the news and can develop media relations strategies to prepare for it. For example, in 1999, the federal Minister of Transport waived some of the competition legislation, which allowed the struggling Canadian Airlines to talk to its rival, Air Canada. Both airlines, then the Onex Corporation, quickly developed business plans and went through a high-profile public and media debate over the future of the airline industry, characterized by heavy involvement with news media and advertising. Although the debate occurred in public and in the media space, behind the scenes an intense, planned and strategic effort was unfolding; an attempt to win public and government support to each side of the issue. In addition to proactive communications, such as advertising, which could be planned in advance, both parties needed to be able to respond instantly to get out their messages in a volatile, quickly evolving media storm.

Because you may be in a crisis and need to be prepared

Most Canadian municipalities are required to have a crisis plan in the event of natural disaster (e.g., flood, severe weather) or industrial accident. Similarly, many businesses—particularly high-risk industries such as pipelines, refineries, railways and chemical companies—devote considerable resources to developing plans in the event of a disaster. Integral to all these plans is a communications strategy, and crisis communications has become a subspecialty of the communications industry. Media relations is a key component of crisis communications, as will be discussed at length later in this book.

Advantages and Disadvantages of Media

If by this point you have decided that you should or would like to deal with media, you need to be aware of the relative strengths and weaknesses media and reporters bring to communicating an issue. These qualities need to be considered before you communicate with the media. At the same time, if other options are more effective, you should pursue them as well, even if your agency has an obligation to communicate with media. For example, a utility communicating a rate increase must answer media inquiries and may have in place a sophisticated media plan that includes satellite tours, editorial briefings and so forth. However, that company should also be communicating directly with its customers, either through a printed insert with the monthly bill or through major advertising—or perhaps both, depending on the nature and extent of the increase.

First, let's look at media strengths as a means of communications.

Advantages

Media relations offers some distinct advantages for the communications practitioner, as it is often superior to alternative means of communications. Media can be a quick, efficient, relatively low-cost way to reach your target audience, whether it's tightly focussed or wide-ranging. Regardless of the issue, you should always consider news media as a potential means of communication, carefully weighing their advantages against their disadvantages.

Raising awareness   Being in the news raises your profile, and that of your organization or cause, considerably. A simple mention in a local newspaper or television broadcast can end up being carried literally around the world, if a news wire or news channel picks it up. I was responsible for media relations for a high-profile child welfare case in Saskatchewan that received national media attention in 2000. A few months later, while briefing a visiting South African delegation on communications, I was stunned to learn that they were familiar with the case: they had seen it on CNN International.

Awareness by itself, though, doesn't mean that anyone will be convinced of the value of your argument or cause; it just means many people know about it. Awareness does not even imply accuracy; it simply means people are aware that something is going on.

If you are hoping to persuade people of your point of view, awareness-raising is an essential step, but it is only the first step. Consider the following standard marketing process, which shows the stages of thought and motivation a consumer goes through before deciding to purchase a product or service:[1]

1. Awareness

2. Knowledge

3. Liking

4. Preference

5. Conviction

6. Purchase

In marketing terms, the "purchase" at the end of this process may be the literal purchase of a product or service, or it may be the support of a particular point of view, or it may be a behaviour change. Mothers Against Drunk Driving (MADD), for example, gained excellent media attention early in their organization's history. As the movement matured, MADD began active lobbying, which led to legislative change to reduce drunk driving and a shift in public attitude that driving drunk was socially and legally unacceptable. The practitioner should consider what his or her ultimate "purchase" is and what other elements of the communications/marketing mix are required to meet it.

Impact   The news can move people. Terry Fox is a prime example: he started his Marathon of Hope with only CBC radio providing national coverage, and only local coverage until he hit Ontario. Relying solely on news coverage, he had an enormous impact on fund-raising for cancer research, and the annual Terry Fox Run continues to be a significant event today, more than twenty-five years later.

Cost   Advocacy groups in particular love the news. They devote enormous amounts of energy to getting into the news, simply because they can't afford any other types of communications, especially advertising. For instance, Greenpeace started out as a small group of anti-nuclear and environmental activists, relying solely on news. Greenpeace is now a multinational, multi-million-dollar environmental organization that has branched out from advocacy to research, policy development and political lobbying. For smaller agencies and volunteer groups, news coverage costs nothing except time. Media relations can still be expensive, however, if you choose options such as media tours, video news releases, open houses, sophisticated public-opinion research, extensive media monitoring and other big-ticket items.

Audience   Media can give you a huge audience, or a targeted audience, but media stay in business by reaching people. If you need to reach as many people as possible across the country, getting your story on the CTV National News or in an item by Canadian Press that runs in every news outlet across the country is enormously effective. Conversely, media can be equally effective in reaching smaller but more targeted audiences. If you're trying to reach prairie farmers, for example, one story in the Western Producer, the bible of the western farmer, will get you into almost every farm household in Western Canada.

Legitimacy/credibility   Every day, editors and reporters have to choose among hundreds of possible news stories they come across, from news releases, faxes, items coming from wire services and professional news services, leads from their own reporters, tips from the public and regular sources such as police scanners, contacts and communicators. From this they can pick only a few. For example, to make the queue for the six to ten minutes allowed for local news in a suppertime television newscast, a story must stand out in some way to the people making the selection. By choosing your story, the reporter or editor has determined that you and your issue are legitimate items of interest to their audience—and to society at large.

A 1999 study found that only 15 per cent of Canadians have much respect for journalists.[2] Yet, despite such limited support for reporting and news-gathering techniques, the news is read, watched and listened to for a reason: people want to know what is going on, and they rely on media to tell them. A 1988 study in the United States affirmed high levels of trust in the media per se.[3] Where criticisms and distrust arise is the dubious and sometimes insensitive means of newsgathering. A classic example occurred in Ottawa in December 1999. A prominent physician felt forced to resign after he had a discussion with an undercover police officer in a prostitution snare; the report was widely—and sometimes salaciously—reported on radio and television and in the papers. The physician, a pillar of the community, received a massive outpouring of support from the public, and attention focussed instead on the police and media handling of the incident. (People are often critical of the media when they cover issues of particular concern to the public, as we will discuss in more detail in the next chapter).

Part of the reason media have credibility is that, unlike other forms of communications, such as advertising, media are perceived to possess a degree of objectivity. A study on the use of video news releases (VNRs) showed that "viewers were found to give more credibility to a VNR-based message within a news program than to a similarly structured advertising message...."[4] (You should note, however, that media do not accept VNRs without question and generally prefer the B-roll footage that usually accompanies them).[5]

The media, therefore, must be considered as a credible means of communicating information to the public, and thus you may gain an advantage when the media cover your issue.

Building public support   The example of many advocacy groups shows how the public may change its views on social issues in large part because of how the media cover them. The media can be vital to building public support. For example, Greenpeace started with a handful of activists in Vancouver who couldn't agree on what was more important, the environment or nuclear disarmament; they ended up merging two groups into one: Greenpeace. With little money, the new organization created highly successful stunts that drew media attention to its causes, such as challenging whalers at sea and cruising into nuclear testing zones. With this early media attention, Greenpeace was able to generate funds and support to help it become a respected multinational entity. Today, Greenpeace mounts legal challenges, provides original environmental research, develops green alternatives and acts as a powerful advocacy group.

Whether the media build public support for an issue as a matter of conscious choice (the National Post, for example, is a consistent supporter of tax cuts over social spending) or merely act as a monitoring device, intuitively picking up public trends at their earliest stages, is open to debate. Nevertheless, using the news media is one way to build support for a cause or an issue.

Disadvantages

For every strength the media offer, there is a weakness, and a risk, that practitioners need to take into account. Here are some of the key disadvantages to media coverage.

Lack of control   This is the most important issue most practitioners and organizations need to consider. At the end of the day, the reporter will write the story the way she feels is best. You do not get to see it before it is sent to the wire; you won't know what it looks like until it runs. Even if you have a good relationship with the reporter, an editor may choose to take a different angle on your issue, or at least your organization's perspective of it.

Some professions perceive control as a major value (for instance, physicians and nurses, engineers, police and security, managers), and many traditional government and business organizations retain tight control on their image and messages. Having to deal with media can be enormously frustrating for such bodies, because they can't control the media. These professions, and this sort of personality, should look at other alternatives if they want to communicate. For example, advertising may be a better route for someone in a very controlling agency, because the agency can review the ad before it runs, edit it as much as it wishes, conduct extensive market research, request additional drafts if necessary and otherwise control the presentation, tone and image.

Of course, controlling organizations or personalities should also consider changing that stance, if an opportunity to do so emerges. If an organization chooses to work with media—or suddenly finds it must work with media—it will have to develop a more flexible attitude. It will have to acquire the understanding that sometimes the final delivery of a message is out of its hands.

Practitioners also need to consider whether they have the personality and the perspective to work in an environment where, despite all their skills and best intentions, the story they want to tell can be told differently by the media. Flexibility is a key to practising media relations, as is an ability to work in some degree of ambiguity.

Accuracy Entirely apart from the fact that reporters and editors may interpret a fact differently than you do, they also make mistakes. A study done by the Columbia School of Journalism found that just under 19 per cent of stories were viewed by the reporters who wrote them to be defective either because the headline was inaccurate or because errors had occurred in the editing process.[6] Not only do journalists make errors, they are also very reluctant to concede them. Another Columbia School of Journalism study of US newspapers found that media are loathe to run corrections and do not like admitting they are wrong.[7] The communications practitioner needs to do everything possible to ensure information is kept simple and, preferably, documented, before releasing it to the media.

A study on the accuracy of quotes on the 1980s trial of Colin Thatcher, compared to the verbatim transcript, showed that "Discrepancies were found in 883 quote paragraphs, nearly 57 per cent of the total sample. Of these, 56 per cent were classed as minor and 44 per cent as major. Overall, therefore, major discrepancies occurred in the quote paragraphs."[8]

Brevity of impact   Yesterday's news goes right into the recycle bin. Unless your organization or issue is a standing item in the news (e.g., the Gomery Inquiry, Air India), the 15 minutes of fame promised by Andy Warhol comes and goes quickly, and so does the news media's effectiveness in communicating your message. Advertising agencies use frequency (how often the message gets out) and reach (who gets the message) as markers of ad effectiveness. Effectiveness works much the same way in media: unless your story gets out often, it will not penetrate the clutter of daily-changing news stories to reach its intended audience.

If you hope to convince the public of your point of view, or if you are trying to develop a media relations program for a government or business, you need to develop a long-term approach that will get you or your message into the news often enough that you are effective, but not so often that you become boring or irritating to either the public or the media.

Lack of depth   One of the common complaints about news media is that they are superficial in their coverage. It's often, but not always, true: documentaries, features and talk shows allow for deeper exploration and explanation of an issue. (The CBC and specialty cable channels such as the Discovery Channel or BNN, for example, can offer more extended coverage of issues). However, the basic rule for most news stories is that they be brief: a 30-second radio or television spot will often summarize a 300-page technical document in a few words—perhaps less than a single sentence. A major achievement, something that has taken many people years to complete, may be summarized to the point of trivialization.

Some media are so poorly supported, with one or two young reporters scrambling madly to fill space or airtime, that the very medium makes in-depth reporting unlikely (for example, small-town private-sector radio, community newspapers). This lack of resources can sometimes work to the advantage of the practitioner: community newspapers in particular will look for appealing local stories and tend not to be too critical of what they receive. However, it can work the other way as well: the outlet may print or broadcast news verbatim from a source in conflict with you, without bothering to get your side of the issue. (This is a long-standing problem, for example, in labour relations, in which both management and unions accuse media of not bothering to check with the other side in their haste to get out the news).

Desire for conflict   Conflict is a major element of news.[9] The traditional news beats of the courts, the police, politics and sports are typified by two sides in dispute, with media positioned as objective observers, noting the main points of each side.

The search for conflict and the desire to demonstrate objectivity mean that the media will seek out other points of view and present them as opposing. The question is, do you want to take the risk that media will put you in a position of conflict, particularly when you don't want to be in that position? Some organizations, such as government-funded community agencies, must take great care that their media relations don't jeopardize their other relationships, particularly with a key funder. On the other hand, if you are indeed in conflict with somebody, your chances of finding media coverage are significantly higher than if you are in agreement.

Dramatization Dramatization is often referred to as sensationalism, which may exist both in the tabloid press and in high-profile instances such as the Paul Bernardo trial. The media, however, do not like to view themselves as sensationalist, as the following directive from *The Canadian Press Stylebook* explains:

> Everything that we do must be honest, unbiased and unflinchingly fair. We deal with facts that are demonstrable, supported by sources that are reliable and responsible. We pursue with equal vigour all sides of a story.[10]

This noble goal, however well intended, is balanced by a need for drama, excitement and human interest, as *The Canadian Reporter* states:

> But the ultimate obsession for journalist is to get as close as possible to capturing what has actually happened [emphasis provided in original text]. Life itself is full of interest, full of drama. The task of arranging material so that it actually transmits the drama to readers can be intensely creative.[11]

The good reporter will balance CP's dicta of fairness, accuracy and completeness with the journalism textbook's expectation of liveliness and drama. Sometimes the desire for drama can dominate a story and turn it into something the practitioner did not present. In handling a large and complex story, the media will sometimes focus on the dramatic, letting the emotions of a story overwhelm the logic and the facts behind it. In those cases, the practitioner can fairly argue against such media coverage, using CP's directive on how to cover a story as a support.

Bad press Just as media can be helpful in building support for a cause or issue, they can also turn against it. Former Prime Minister Brian Mulroney was consistently vilified in the media at the end of his term of office, for reasons too complex to go into here. Readers of newspapers were constantly reminded that more Canadians believed Elvis was alive than believed Mulroney was a good prime minister. The bad press Mulroney received contributed to the Progressive Conservatives winning just two seats in the House of Commons in the subsequent 1993 election.

On a smaller scale, it is possible for columnists and editorial writers to take hostile positions against you or your organization, and individual reporters may develop points of view that simply can't be changed. When this happens, there are a limited number of options you can choose (complaining to the publisher, provincial newspaper association or ombudsman, or legal action if appropriate; see Chapter 15). More often, practitioners try to use other means of communications with their audience, such as advertising or direct mail, to counter negative media coverage.

Alternatives to Media

Not only are there disadvantages of media, there are also times when the public simply doesn't pay attention to it. In July 1999, for example, Saskatchewan Social Services received very positive newspaper coverage on the occasion of the first anniversary of a new social program for low-income working families. Articles appeared in Saskatchewan's three major daily newspapers: the *Regina Leader Post, Saskatchewan Star Phoenix* and *Prince Albert Daily Herald*. A strongly supportive editorial appeared shortly afterwards in the *Leader Post*. One of the articles noted that the program was under-subscribed and that people could call a 1–800 number to find out if they qualified. The call centre braced for a major increase in calls.

None came. In reviewing the coverage, managers and staff noted that the target audience had young children, were working in low-income jobs while trying to get off social assistance and either didn't have time to read a daily newspaper or couldn't afford a subscription. A successful direct mail and word-of-mouth campaign that later went ahead to reach this audience attained full subscription into the program.

When media coverage doesn't work, you have to consider alternatives. The list below suggests alternatives for finding an audience. It is by no means comprehensive (the limitations are really only your imagination and budget), but it highlights major means of communication, other than media relations, that you can choose to use to get out your message.

Advertising

Television (including cable)

Radio

Newspapers (daily, weekly, specialty)

Magazines and newsletters

Billboards

Transit (bus and subway ads)

Internet (e.g., banner ads, pop-ups)

Publications

Catalogues

Directories

Programs

Mass mail

Direct mail

Cheque inserts

Newspapers inserts (flyers)

Brochures

Reports, annual and special

Posters

Newsletters (yours and others')

Comics

Audio/Visual

Films

Slide tape

Compact discs

New Media

Websites

Blogs

E-mail

Podcasts

RSS feeds

Chat rooms

Social Networking (e.g. Facebook, My Space)

Video Sharing Websites (e.g. YouTube)

Displays

Stand-alone exhibits

Conferences/trade shows

News Media (more details in Chapters 8, 9, 10)

News release

News backgrounder

News conference/scrum

TV/radio talk shows

TV cable channel programs and regular programs

Local cable television

Newspaper columnists

Editorial boards

Public service announcements (PSAs)

Personal approaches

One on one/door to door

Small-group presentations/seminars

Conferences/annual general meetings

Attendance at special events (Canadian National Exhibition, Pacific National Exhibition)

Word of mouth

Sales Techniques

Multimedia presentations

Sponsored programs

Promotional letters/flyers

Coupons, stamps, redeemables

Premiums

Novelties [12]

Events/demonstrations

Point-of-purchase (POP) programs

Incentives/rebates/discounts

Contests

Free samples

Affinity cards

Dealers' sales contests

Sales force bonuses and contests

Rallies

Finder's fees

Telemarketing

Guerilla marketing

Viral marketing

Other Methods

Talking Yellow Pages

Voicemail and dial-up programs

Community events (e.g., barbecues, bingos, dances)

Associations, societies, churches, service clubs

To determine when to select one of these techniques over others, start with the audience and their attitudes, behaviours and media preferences. For example, teenagers and seniors tend to be frequent users of transit (bus and subway); accordingly, communications aimed at those audiences typically make transit advertising part of the campaign (if the community is large enough to have a transit system).

The more narrowly defined the audience is, the more likely you are to succeed in reaching it. The general public is a difficult audience to reach unless you have a major budget for advertising (national television campaigns cost millions in media production and broadcast time). However, if your audience is Vietnamese residents in central Montreal, you can easily reach them through flyers in the neighbourhood and low-cost ads in Vietnamese newspapers.

Once you've defined your audience, simply match your audience with the communications medium they will likely respond to best. To do this, you must spend some time researching the target audience. You will also need to do some research if you are emphasizing media relations, that is, if media are a means of reaching your target audience. You'll need to find out who your audience is and what they are watching and reading.

Statistics Canada, the local library, the Internet and your own experience can provide you with a great deal of information about your target audience. For example, Statistics Canada reported that 72 per cent of families headed by a senior have a VCR; only 26 per cent of those same families have a CD player.[13] This kind of information is helpful in determining what communications tool to use, for example, to promote winter vacations to senior couples.

Media relations is generally practised as part of an overall communications strategy; other parts of the strategy may include advertising, direct mail and other kinds of campaigns. You can find out more about communications planning in other publications and in the literature describing advertising, marketing, research and sales, which is available in most libraries and bookstores.[14]

In general, before embarking on a media relations exercise, you should consider the pros and cons of using news media as a means of reaching the public; define a reason for using the media (even if only for simple accountability purposes); and look carefully at the other options available to you. You then need to consider some basic principles before starting out and develop a basic understanding of how media work. With all this in mind, you can work with media, and the experience will be of as much value to them as you hope they can be of value to you.

Basic Principles of Media Relations

A few basic principles underpin the practice of media relations and the relationship between communicator and journalist. These principles should be embedded in your practice of day-to-day media relations.

Principle One: Good Communications Cannot Overcome Bad Judgement

On June 23, 1972, President Richard Nixon met with one of his closest advisors, H.R. (Bob) Haldeman, to discuss how to handle the discovery of burglars at their opponent's headquarters in the Watergate complex during the presidential election. Both knew the burglars were part of a larger set of illegal, covert actions on behalf of the Nixon campaign. Their solution to head off the scandal? A "PR offensive."[1] This is the old-style definition of public relations: putting a nice spin on things until you get what you want. It didn't work for Nixon; within a year Watergate was a major scandal, and a year later Nixon would resign to avoid being impeached for his role (and had to be pardoned to avoid criminal charges). Haldeman would be convicted and serve jail time for his part.

If a company, person or government makes a bad decision, all the sophisticated, strategic, expensive communications in the world will not help them. Effective communications is based on sound judgement, and one of the first questions a practitioner needs to ask his or her client is, "Are we doing the right thing?" You can worry later about the messages and means of delivering them—they will follow quite naturally from your judgement.

One of the risks communicators face in the field is that, like reporters, they are rarely as expert as the people they work with. For example, communicators work for health organizations, law firms, accounting societies, engineering firms and such, yet they rarely have the same education and experience as their colleagues. You will often have to rely on your colleagues' professional judgement; but, as communicators working for organizations as diverse as Enron or Bre-X have found, that judgement can sometimes be flawed.

Practitioners in the field can help themselves and their organizations by trying to learn as much about the business they work in as possible. They can also help their colleagues when providing them with media training by constantly reminding them that if their judgement is sound, everything else is technique. Sound judgement should be the basis of every media encounter and every issue.

Principle Two: Provide Information from a Credible Source

Your odds of being successful (i.e., of getting your message relayed accurately) in a media encounter rise considerably if both the person and the organization releasing the information are credible, to media and to the public.

To the media, a credible source can be summarized as follows:

> Past suitability is one criterion: a source is more suitable if he or she provided good information in the past. Productivity is an issue: a source needs to provide a lot of information. Reliability is important: is the information any good? Trustworthiness is essential: the information cannot simply be self-serving. Authoritativeness is important: information from persons in position of authority. And finally articulateness: it helps if the source can "give a good clip."[2]

This explanation demonstrates in particular the importance of developing a relationship with media and of being someone who can be relied on for accurate, authoritative information when media need it.

To further increase the likelihood of being considered a good source, you must determine who in the organization is the best person to provide information to media. Within the specialized area of practice called risk communications, for example, research has been done to discover who the public believes to be reliable sources of information, particularly on health and environmental matters.[3] Annual surveys done by North American universities indicate the following people and agencies are perceived to be most reliable, in descending order:

Local citizens perceived to be neutral

Non-management employees

Nurses and doctors

Safety/emergency professionals (fire, police, ambulance)

Professors/educators, especially from respected local institutions

Non-profit, voluntary health agencies

Professional societies.

There follows a large gap in public acceptance, until the next lowest group of credible sources is defined:

Media

Environmental groups

Government (Canada only).

There is then another large drop, until we get to the least credible sources of information, as far as the public is concerned:

Industry officials

Government (US)

Environmental consultants from 'for-profit' firms.[4]

A number of reasons can be suggested for this hierarchy of credibility, one being that those at the top end tend to be perceived as acting in the public interest, with some degree of objectivity (health and education in particular) and commitment to public well-being (safety/emergency professionals). Industry and government are viewed less sanguinely, because they have track records of serious error (the Exxon Valdez, Enron) or have misrepresented the truth in the past (e.g., the tobacco industry claiming that cigarettes are not addictive and do not lead to lung cancer).

The above list is instructive when you decide who will actually deal with the media on behalf of an organization. The first question to consider is whether the communicator or the client should be the spokesperson. Communicators do not appear on the list at all, which should lead us to conclude that the client is better off being trained and supported as the spokesperson, rather than having the communicator speak on the client's behalf. However, this is not a perfect model, and thus you need a back-up plan. Communicators need to be available for action in case the client is unavailable for some reason. Under no circumstances should media calls be missed simply because someone is in a meeting or out of town; the media will simply go ahead without you, and only the opposition point of view will be covered. (In most cases, media will only call once. If no one from your organization responds, or you do not respond in a timely manner, the media will call other people, and you will lose an opportunity).

Of particular interest in this research is the high position of non-management staff. Although management often bears ultimate responsibility in an organization, the public prefers to hear the point of view of someone more directly involved in the matter at hand. Managers also tend to speak at a more abstract level than front-line staffers, and reporters are trained to seek the concrete over the abstract.[5]

Just the same, generic research has its limitations. Doctors found guilty of malpractice will not be credible no matter what the research indicates, and some politicians — Ronald Reagan and former Alberta Premier Ralph Klein, for instance — had high credibility levels despite their status as politicians and the criticism they naturally faced. A good rule when seeking to be reliable is to know what you are talking about, be able to back it up, show some commitment to your task, be articulate and believe that your judgements and statements are sound.

Principle Three: Practise Media Relations Regularly

Too often, companies and bureaucracies wait for a major event to occur (e.g., a public hearing or emergency) before deciding to deal with media. Unless they have the luxury of knowing in advance when an issue that will attract media attention is going to arise, these organizations are caught by surprise and lack day-to-day familiarity with media, which impairs their ability to get news out. For example, in the 1980s the Alberta government announced that hospitals could charge user fees. This drew a lot of media attention, and calls came in to the Alberta Hospital Association (which at that time represented all the hospitals in the province) for a response. While the AHA had a policy on user fees, the body was so unused to dealing with media that it couldn't respond and in fact looked somewhat clueless. The AHA was otherwise a very capable organization; it just didn't have the day-to-day experience in media relations to give it expertise in dealing with a breaking news situation.

If you or your organization plans to deal with the media, seek opportunities to work with them in advance of a crisis, so that you will build up your skill and familiarity with essential media needs (timeliness, simplicity and accuracy are three of the most prominent).

Principle Four: Understand Legal Restrictions and Obligations

The practitioner should have a good sense first of overall media law, then of the laws affecting disclosure and release of information in the area he or she works in. For example, health, business and government are each governed by legislation outlining what information they can, must or cannot release to the public and the media.

There are a number of issues to consider in media law. I would direct you first to *Media Law*, by Robert Martin, Professor of Law at the University of

Western Ontario,[6] and second to legal counsel. However, as an introduction, here is a quick summary of key legal issues that affect media relations.

First and foremost, I assume you are practising media relations in Canada. Canada has no First Amendment rights, and our libel laws are more stringent than those of the US. Carleton Journalism Professor Stuart Adam notes:

> [journalists] believed they would benefit from the declaration in Section 2(b) of the Canadian Charter of Rights and Freedoms that says the freedoms of "thought, belief, opinion and expression, including freedom of the press and other media of communications" are funda-mental and guaranteed. But there was an unanticipated catch. Section 1 of the very same Charter qualifies the freedoms it guarantees by saying that they can be limited for strong reasons. Section 1 says that the rights and freedoms are "subject only to such reasonable limits prescribed by law as can be demonstrably justified in a free and democratic society."[7]

For the media, there is no absolute access to information; for the holder of the information, there is no absolute power to withhold it. Both are subject to a variety of laws respecting both the necessity for preserving individual and corporate confidentiality, and the necessity for accountability and the free flow of information in a democratic society. There is no easy summary. Just as most journalists are required to take a course in media law, so should all com-munications students.

A couple of examples will suggest the complexity of the issue. The first example is government, which possesses an enormous amount of informa-tion about individuals, in tax and health records and through licensing and funding programs. To ensure personal privacy is protected, the federal government and all provinces have passed Freedom of Information and Protection of Privacy acts, which attempt to strike a balance between protect-ing privacy and providing information. There are also other laws, particularly in health, which provide more detail about what can and cannot be made public. For example, at one time Alberta had 12 different pieces of health leg-islation defining private and public information (*Hospital Act, Public Health Act, Registered Nurses Act, Donation of Organs Act,* etc.).

A second example is business, although it tends to be less complex than government. However, publicly owned businesses (any company listed on a Canadian stock exchange where a person can purchase shares in the company) are both required and encouraged to release information about their compa-nies. Companies must abide by corporate disclosure policies set out by the Canadian exchanges they are listed on as well as by the Canadian Securities

Administrators (CSA). Shareholders and investors can make informed decisions about their investments when material information is disclosed to the public on a timely and broad basis.

For the sake of fairness, companies must not disclose material news selectively to analysts or insiders, and insiders must report all trading activities on companies in which they hold shares. The Canadian Investor Relations Institute offers model guidelines on disclosure for publicly listed companies. However, the investor still needs to view these disclosures with healthy skepticism (for example, some may recall the Bre-X saga of the late 1990s, the mining company whose gold was found only in its news releases). The business communicator must ensure not only that news releases are accurate and meaningful, but also that the released information is consistent with other communications efforts (such as annual and quarterly reports, websites, prospectuses, financial statements and analyst reports), as well as with the specialized needs of business media.

The importance of knowing both legal and professional standards in releasing information can be seen in the decision of the Ontario Securities Commission to fine Air Canada $1 million for releasing information improperly.[8] Air Canada released information to a few selected financial analysts instead of making it available to all analysts at the same time. Typically this would have been done by circulating a news release through one of the commercial news release services. Not only did this ruling cost the company a substantial fine, it also threatened its credibility with professionals, the media and the public at large.

While different rules for disclosure exist according to where you live and who you work for, nevertheless there also common legal issues that all communicators need to understand. Bear in mind you are open to libel or defamation charges if you issue information that is inaccurate, damaging or demeaning. Anything you say in a news release, ad, interview, letter to the editor or news conference is subject to provincial laws on libel and defamation:

> The common law protects every person from harm to their reputation by false and derogatory remarks about their person, known as defamation. In addition, all Canadian provinces have libel/slander legislation (defamation includes libel and slander, where slander is verbal defamation and libel is printed defamation). It is a tricky and slippery field of law, based on statutes, English common law and many defences. No wonder it has been called a "peculiar tort." And remember, defamation tort law protects your reputation, not your feelings.[9]

The subject of libel is complex and worthy of consideration in your practice of media relations. While you may have an argument of "fair comment," you should be able to back up your case with verifiable fact and you should not release information in such a manner that it could be interpreted as a personal attack intended to harm someone's reputation. While some areas, such as politics and union-management negotiations, have stretched the concept of fair comment, politicians and unions have been successfully sued for defamation for going too far.

And bloggers note: you too are subject to laws regarding defamation and libel. The number of libel suits relating to blogs is rising.[10] Bloggers can protect themselves by knowing the law, and by being willing to make changes to offensive material once they've been warned it may be defamatory.

Finally, you need to keep abreast of changes to the law and of new court interpretations. A useful source for the practitioner is the Canadian Bar Association's website; it has a section on national media and communications law, with recent developments on legislation affecting media and advertising.

As stated before, please refer to *Media Law* for a deeper understanding of the complexity of Canadian media law, or seek legal counsel. When you start work for a new employer or client, be sure to ask them about the legal parameters in their business.

Principle Five: You Cannot Manage the Media

While some practitioners may claim otherwise, you cannot manage somebody else's business.[11] Pierre Karl Péladeau manages media, as does the board of directors of Global Television: they own the media (or at least their particular segment of it) and can direct it any way they want. Assignment editors, news directors and producers manage media by selecting what stories will be covered and, if necessary, how they will be covered. They can also take the stories their reporters bring them and change them if they don't like them; you can't.

This principle relates to our earlier discussion of control, or lack thereof, in media relations. Mulroney had some of the best communicators in Canada working for him, and considerable ability to set the national agenda; yet he was frustrated by the media's determination to go their own way on issues like free trade and the GST. Prime Minister Stephen Harper is showing similar frustrations in his attempts to control the media. It will be interesting to follow this conflict between Harper and the media, and whether it will lead to bad press of the magnitude that Mulroney received. While it is possible for you to have a good deal of influence over media and how they present the news, at the end of the day you are relying on someone else to tell your story. If that is too much for you, you should look at different means of communications. Even if you are comfortable having the media tell your story, always have a few alternatives at the ready.

Philosophical Considerations

People who routinely deal with media need to be aware of two issues they will face regularly: their own ambivalence about dealing with media and their reaction to being called "spin doctors."

Media ambivalence

Chapter 1 noted that the public generally finds the media to be credible purveyors of news, with a few exceptions. One, as noted, was general aversion to media aggressiveness and insensitivity. The other is a peculiar, but verifiable, fact that while people are generally great followers of and believers in the news, they are less supportive when the news is about them or their issue.

A study done by the University of Wisconsin looked at samples of Americans in groups whose issues are frequently covered by the media (Republicans, Democrats, Roman Catholics, born-again Christians, African-Americans, Hispanics and labour unions).[12] In every group, coverage of another group's issues was generally described as "quite likely fair," while each group described coverage of its issue as "biased." The researcher

> attributed his results to two possible factors: errors and omissions in coverage of all groups that are most noticeable to knowledgeable persons; and, more often, the fact [that] as a people identify more strongly with a particular group or cause, they tend to reject information and opinion that disagrees with their beliefs.[13]

Another way of understanding this concept is that people take their own issues seriously and personally, and may be offended at the representation of these issues in the news, calling it shallow, misrepresentative or sensationalist. In fact, the issues are being treated in the same manner as every other story subject; the affected group simply feels it more closely.

Typical of the unease that many people have about dealing with the media is the experience of Ruth Sullivan, whose son Joseph was one of the models for the autistic adult Raymond in the film Rain Man. As an advocate, she wanted her son's story told and condition understood; as a parent she felt protective:

As an advocate for Joseph and others like him, I have learned over the years that in using the media to spread the word about autism, one must be ready to talk about one's child. You put information about your loved one in the hands of reporters, editors and other media people with widely varying sensibilities and interests in the subject. You hope they will be accurate and kind in their telling of your story. The cost of going public is the risk that the media will distort, demean, misrepresent, or even hurt the very one(s) you are trying to help.[14]

That same ambivalence can be felt by practitioners, no matter how experienced. On the one hand, we do our job, fully knowledgeable and aware of its risks and rewards; on the other hand, we too often see simple errors, confusion, over-simplification, and we and the people we work with take it personally. Working with media can be a volatile business. One day you can be elated that your story has received exactly the coverage you hoped it would, and the next day deflated when different media get the same story all wrong. Practitioners are advised to keep an even keel emotionally. Even for a seasoned practitioner, this can be easier advice to give than to live up to. Seeing an inaccurate, misrepresentative or one-sided version of your issue is legitimate cause for anger. Chapter 15, on the fine art of complaining about media, provides you with some options to obtain redress from bad coverage; just make sure that when you go back to the media to get a story straightened out, you do so in a professional manner and without the anger. Keep your eye on the reason that you are using media in the first place, and develop a thick skin. You are also advised to practise what you preach: you will often give this same counsel to your spokespersons, and must demonstrate it yourself if you are to have any credibility as a professional. However, if you and your client often feel ambivalent about dealing with media, it's perfectly understandable. You care about your issue and how it is discussed and promoted, while the media don't see promotion as part of their job: they are trying hard to stay neutral and objective.

A few words on spin

Spin has a short and dubious history.[15] The best definition I've seen is "deceptive misrepresentation short of lying, especially by pretentious word or deed, of somebody's own thoughts, feelings or attitudes."[16] This definition is provided in a book called *On Bullshit,* by Harry Frankfurt, and in my experience, "spin" can easily be substituted for "bullshit."

Spin has its roots in political communications and is generally understood as taking a partisan approach to an issue, aggressively arguing one side of it while denigrating the other, often on the grounds that there are two sides to every issue and both deserve equal merit. Thus, in the world of spin, a story noting that cigarettes cause cancer should have as much space devoted to the counter-evidence (even though there is none) as is given to the scientific evidence.

Spin can be effective, at least in the short term. For example, the PR firm of Hill and Knowlton was hired for a fee of $11.5-million by the Citizens for a Free Kuwait during the First Gulf War (after the war, it was revealed most of the funds came from the government of Kuwait). As part of Hill and Knowlton's strategy, a Kuwaiti girl testified to the US Congress that invading Iraqi soldiers had entered a hospital, taken babies out of incubators and left them to die "on the cold floor."[17] This enormously emotional testimony helped turn public opinion, and the US Senate, in favour of war. After the war, it turned out the girl was the daughter of the Kuwaiti Ambassador. Hill and Knowlton assisted with her testimony, and Amnesty International withdrew its earlier report condemning the alleged acts, saying it found "no reliable evidence" for this supposed heinous crime.[18]

Practitioners of spin still abound, mainly in political realms, and some are famous for being spin doctors (spokespeople who aggressively pursue media to convince them that the spin doctor's position is received wisdom and should be presented as such).[19]

Frankfurt's analysis cites the difference between lying and spin as the following: a liar knows something is false and makes a conscious choice to contradict reality; the spin doctor is simply oblivious to fact, and only wants to put out unsupported argument. "By virtue of this, bullshit is a greater enemy of the truth than lies are."[20]

There is a place for argument in communications, and I've always used the example of the legal profession to illustrate this. In court lawyers argue different points of view, often based on a common set of facts determined through a preliminary inquiry or examination for discovery. Each side will attack the argument of the other, challenge the evidence, using reason, and build up the strengths of their side. In the same manner, communicators on opposite sides of a public dispute can put their cases forward without having to stoop to spin and let the public make the final determination as to which side is correct, often through the perspective of an independent third party—media.[21]

Meanwhile, great tension exists between spin and public relations, and there is a difference in the practices, summarized as follows.[22]

	Traditional PR	Spin
Goals	Active, presenting story in best light	Reactive, "damage control"
Media	Traditional: speeches, print, television	New Technology: fax broadcast, cell phones
Clients	Mainly corporate	Mainly political
Tools	Traditional: news releases, conferences	Subversive: pressure on media, seduction, influence
Techniques	Counsel and support	Hands-on, in the line of fire
Public	Stresses "mutual interest"	Promotes client's side only
Appeal	Segmented to publics	Floods all media, particularly key media
Ethics	Practises a standard code	The truth is "liquid"
Self-image/ Self-perception	Respected as professionals	Prefers low visibility, disclaims "doctoring" image

Spin sometimes works, but its ethical base is, at best, dubious. Pragmatically, all reporters and a good deal of the public (which is more media-savvy than it is usually given credit for) can spot spin at first glance and are skeptical of it. For this book, the emphasis is on the traditional public relations model: I believe that spin is unprofessional and ultimately counter-productive. I am on public record as stating that spin is bullshit, and that perspective is reflected in this book.

You should bear these principles in mind throughout your communications practice, regardless of who your client is or what industry you're in. These principles and the issues of ethics and professionalism discussed in Chapter 3 should inform all your future media relations.

Professional Relations

3

Before we get down to the brass tacks of working with the media to get your message to the public, we need to consider the relationship between media and communications, and discuss the ethical boundaries each profession sets out.

Communicator and Journalist

One of the most problematic, conflicted and rewarding relationships in business is that between journalist and communicator. Yet, as we will see in later chapters, many story leads are the result of communications strategies, particularly news releases. The journalist relies on the communicator for basic information and access to expert authorities, while the communicator relies on the journalist to disseminate information and reach key audiences. Thus, the parties are locked in a relationship based on mutual need. Neither one, however, is fully comfortable with the other. As Brian Biggar notes:

> The two occupational groups have maintained a symbiotic relationship. To the journalist, PR practitioners can be valuable sources of information, providing news materials and story ideas. To the public relations professional, the news media represent a vital communications link to the public. The two groups have an ambivalent 'love-hate' relationship, fraught with conflict, sustained by professional interdependence and tempered through negotiation.[1]

The term *public relations,* or PR, is often used interchangeably with the term *communications.* Technically speaking, public relations is more concerned with communicating to the general public; communications implies more specialized communications (e.g., investor relations, internal communications). PR also carries the connotation of old-time glad-handing and schmoozing—for example, in old-style PR, the way to get a story in the media was to buy reporters plenty of drinks. Communications is the term preferred by today's practitioners for describing what they do.

If practitioners have an ambivalent attitude toward media, that ambivalence is reflected by journalists in their dealings with media relations professionals. On the one hand, the media fear being manipulated; on the other, they often see themselves as being outgunned by professional communicators, lawyers and lobbyists.[2] Biggar surveyed 58 Ontario editors and 105 public relations practitioners in 1995, asking both the same questions to determine where they stood on issues common to both. Some of the results underscore the media's feeling of ambivalence toward the PR practitioner.[3]

4. Public relations practitioners too frequently insist on promoting products, services and other activities which do not legitimately deserve promotion:

	Agree	Disagree	Neutral
Editors	67%	26%	7%
Practitioners	46%	43%	11%

...

6. Public relations practitioners often act as obstructionists, keeping reporters from the people they really should be seeing:

	Agree	Disagree	Neutral
Editors	71%	21%	8%
Practitioners	20%	71%	9%

...

9. Public relations material is usually publicity disguised as news:

	Agree	Disagree	Neutral
Editors	79%	18%	3%
Practitioners	26%	66%	8%

...

14. Public relations practitioners are people of good sense, good will and good moral character:

	Agree	Disagree	Neutral
Editors	26%	10%	64%
Practitioners	75%	4%	21%

On the other hand, the editors also reported positive feelings and experiences with public relations practitioners:

10. The public relations practitioner does work for newspapers or news broadcasters that would otherwise go undone:

	Agree	Disagree	Neutral
Editors	47%	43%	10%
Practitioners	73%	15%	12%

...

16. Public relations practitioners understand such journalistic problems as meeting deadlines, attracting reader interest and making the best use of space:

	Agree	Disagree	Neutral
Editors	76%	17%	7%
Practitioners	96%	3%	1%

...

21. Public relations practitioners help reporters obtain accurate news:

	Agree	Disagree	Neutral
Editors	48%	26%	26%
Practitioners	94%	4%	2%

Clearly, these professionals hold quite different opinions about their mutual efforts. One thing both parties agree on is that the relationship, however tenuous or adversarial, is generally not hostile:

18. Journalists and public relations practitioners carry on a running battle:

	Agree	Disagree	Neutral
Editors	31%	50%	19%
Practitioners	31%	57%	12%

Biggar concluded from his research that finding generally negative attitudes toward PR on the part of journalists, Canadian editors agree substantially with their American colleagues in their critical assessment of public relations. Nevertheless, evidence suggests Canadian practitioners may face a moderately less hostile, and in some respects, more appreciative news media than their counterparts in the U.S.[4]

Meanwhile, when media treat the public relations industry as a story, reporters tend to be more objective than when they are relating their personal experiences, as they did in the survey. Another study, *The Media's Treatment of the Public Relations Profession,* undertook content analysis on 200 articles about public relations.[5] It found that 85 per cent of news articles treated public relations positively in terms of tactics/techniques, quality/value, crisis management and greater use of PR. This objectivity in treatment often collapses when reporters and communicators deal with each other directly, however. Communicators try to pitch the media stories that favour the practitioner's interests, and reporters resist these efforts. Just the same, reporters rely on communicators to provide accurate information and good resources for interviews.

Thus, the best approach for you to adopt as a communicator is one of professional equilibrium. Don't get too high when the news turn out good, and don't get too low when it turns out bad. Maintain your professional poise at all times; work with reporters, but don't try to control them.

Reporters are aware of techniques used to manipulate them and are sensitive to avoiding manipulation, even if the source seems on the surface to be a grass-roots, salt-of-the-earth type fighting corporate or government injustice. In noting that even the most benevolent groups can stoop to dubious and unethical practices to get their message out, Ken Ringle of the *Washington Post* insists that reporters simply apply a basic rule of journalism:

> You guard against becoming a tool for lies by realizing that even in
> the best of causes, people try to use you. Both sides try to use you. You
> guard your neutrality. Apply equal skepticism to both sides. And if your
> mother says she loves you, check it out.[6]

In plainer language, Ernest Hemingway described this attitude as "having a built-in, shock-proof shit detector."[7]

On the other hand, media skepticism is a normal and expected part of the job for most communications practitioners: many are themselves skeptical of reporters who promise "a positive story" in exchange for information (feeling "that's my job, not theirs"). The line between skepticism and abuse is fairly clear, though, and communicators can reasonably expect that skepticism in the media will be civilly stated, just as reporters can reasonably expect a civil response to their inquiries.

Unfortunately, professionals on both sides of the relationship have their horror stories to tell: unethical practices, rude behaviour and deceptive techniques. Reporters are not inherently blessed with brains, civility or ethics; neither are communicators. Both can be wrong-headed, uncivil or simply

"TIMES CHANGE..."

obtuse. Unfortunately, both professions tend to judge each other by the worst of exchanges between them, forgetting that the day-to-day relationship is usually business-like and usually productive for both. However, at the end of the average day, reporters will gather together and discuss the most bone-headed communicator they dealt with that day (and they do exist); communicators will gather to discuss the most boneheaded reporter they dealt with that day (and they also exist).

Both professions have their stereotypes: the hard-drinking, truth-impervious reporter and the glad-handing, snake-oil salesman of the old school of communications. And like many stereotypes, these figures have some roots in historical behaviour. But today, both fields are well established and mature. Scholars, teachers and students study, research and analyze both professions, treating them both as worthy disciplines and valuable components of society, though moreso on the media side than the communications side, as we will see in later chapters. The old stereotypes have given way to higher standards of practice and professionalism on both sides. Fundamentally, the relationship between journalism and communications is a business relationship; we deal with each other to further our respective businesses. There's very little schmoozing in the modern relationship, no buying of drinks and slaps on the back. Do that with your friends; treat the other side as you would any other profession you deal with in your business. Nevertheless, as Aislin's cartoon indicates, times have changed for both occupations.

Every analogy has its limits, and the Aislin cartoon has three exceptions worth noting.

The first is quite simply that there should be two women in the cartoon, not men. Both professions are predominantly female, though not necessarily in the management ranks of either profession.

Secondly, they're clearly having a good day on the job. At some other time, they might be duking it out in the back parking lot of the same bar, the metaphorical equivalent of a defamation suit.

Finally, one nice thing about the cartoon is that you can argue they are both at the bar of public opinion, helping to shape that public opinion. However, the bar of public opinion is quite crowded. Politicians, advocates, religious leaders, business, labour, and academia are just a few of the other professions which try to shape public opinion.

Ethics

In the main, both journalism and communications are marked by professional attitudes toward their work. Professionals in both fields are always striving for higher standards (among other ways by teaching courses in journalism and communications) and trying to inculcate ethics and standards of practice in their students and colleagues. When it comes to ethics, both professions are limited by codes that define what is and is not acceptable practice.

Journalism and communications are unregulated professions, and both prefer to remain that way. Regulated professions (such as medicine, nursing, law and engineering) have professional codes of ethics and standards in addition to educational qualifications, and also have the ability to discipline and expel practitioners who do not meet the standard of ethical and legal behaviour. Given that neither journalism nor communications is likely to become regulated, they must police themselves. As the older profession, journalism has developed both ethics and ethical theory. Newspaper and television chains each have their own codes of standards and ethics, while several Canadian communications professions have voluntary codes of ethics. Standards of practice and ethics for most mainstream media can be found in their respective style manuals.[8]

What constitutes ethical behaviour in journalism can be a complex issue. For example, the obligation to be honest may need to be ignored when the journalist must misrepresent himself or herself to gain access to information on illegal behaviour. *Edmonton Sun* reporter Linda Slobodian gained access to a notorious drug house in inner-city Edmonton in this way, by pretending to be someone else; identifying herself as a reporter would have prevented her from gaining access.

The Canadian Reporter attempts to summarize some basic rules of ethical behaviour for journalists, which the media relations practitioner can cite when necessary. *The Canadian Reporter*'s guidelines are reprinted in full here:

- Admit error
- Protect your sources
- Don't in any cases distort, fabricate or plagiarize
- Don't accept favours, or appear to accept favours
- Don't let anybody else make your news judgements
- Stay away from the pack as much as you can
- Don't gratuitously harm people caught up on the fringes of events that are not of their own making

- Don't harm anyone unless you feel you have to do so
- Be reluctant to suppress news, even though there will be times when you'll find it essential to do so
- Don't lie, steal or misrepresent yourself except in extraordinary circumstances of a kind that would justify civil disobedience. When you do lie or misrepresent yourself, explain to your reader what you've done and why—and be then ready to take your lumps, including going to jail if necessary
- Where loyalty to your employer is concerned, be as faithful as you can without betraying the public trust
- Don't lose your sense of humanity
- Don't use your clout as a journalist to intimidate for personal ends
- Live up to your commitments
- Provide in your reporting the widest possible forum for opposing views
- Invade privacy only when you are certain it is in the public interest
- Don't take on outside work or causes that would undermine your actual or perceived independence
- Be careful to avoid doing careless or gratuitous harm to the least powerful sectors of society
- Avoid smearing people by innuendo or implying guilt by association
- Avoid thoughtless writing that reinforces racial, sexual or physical stereotypes. (In other words, think carefully about the meanings of the words you use and why you choose them)
- Protect the right to a fair trial of everyone, even those you hold in the most contempt
- Finally, respect the informing function—the obligation to supply people with the information you think they will need to respond intelligently to their environment.[9]

It should be noted that the Canadian Association of Journalists came up with a much more complete and thorough code.[10] *The Canadian Reporter* provides a good introduction to a complex field (both journalism and communications university programs tend to devote an entire course on ethics). As you go further in your career, look more toward the CAJ's code as one to rely on and to refer to.

One caution: criticizing other people for their behaviour leads to the expectation that equally ethical behaviour be shown by the critic. Do not expect that ethics is a one-way street; be prepared to defend your behaviour when you criticize others.

On the other side of the exchange, the Canadian Public Relations Society has established a code of professional standards for its members. Because the Society is a voluntary association, the standards are not binding across the profession, and there are some legal limitations on the application of such a code in a non-regulated profession such as communications:

- A member shall practice public relations according to the highest professional standards.

- A member shall deal fairly and honestly with the communications media and the public.

- A member shall practice the highest standards of honesty, accuracy, integrity and truth, and shall not knowingly disseminate false or misleading information.

- A member shall deal fairly with past or present employers/clients, with fellow practitioners, and with members of other professions.

- A member shall be prepared to disclose the name of their employer or client for whom public communications are made and refrain from associating themselves with anyone that would not respect such policy.

- A member shall protect the confidences of present, former and prospective employers/clients.

- A member shall not represent conflicting or competing interests without the express consent of those concerned, given after a full disclosure of the facts.

- A member shall not guarantee specified results beyond the member's capacity to achieve.

- Members shall personally accept no fees, commissions, gifts or any other considerations for professional services from anyone except employers or clients for whom the services were specifically performed.[11]

To these standards I would add a few more points, reflecting some of the issues and values that I discuss in this book, in the hope it will stimulate further debate about this crucial and evolving aspect of the business of media relations:

- Tell the truth.
- Release only information that you are confident is true and accurate.
- Answer all calls from the media, even from those reporters you do not like to deal with. (For some exceptions, see Chapter 15).
- Treat each encounter with an individual reporter as confidential.
- Live up to all commitments made to the media.
- If you know the source of information the media is looking for, send them there.
- Be civil when dealing with media, for its own sake and in the hopes the same consideration will be given to you.
- Understand the law as it affects communications and your industry.
- Try to find a balance between maintaining the privacy of information, particularly personal information, that you are privy to, and the media's legal and ethical access to it. Where appropriate, try to accommodate both (e.g., ask an individual for permission to release private information, while ensuring he or she is aware of the consequences of doing so).
- Protect your client's and your spokesperson's best interests when putting them in front of the media. Ensure they are well briefed, well supported and cognizant of all the risks and rewards they may face.

For the communicator, one of the difficult parts of living up to standards of practice is not dealing with the media but dealing with the client or employer. The experience of Wilma K. Matthews, ABC, author of *Effective Media Relations*, a manual for the International Association of Business Communicators, suggests some of the difficulties the ethical communicator faces in the field:

> I've been involved in media relations for more than 25 years. During this time I've ... counselled for prudence and been rewarded with threats of suing the media. I've shown bottomline measurement only to be asked about the number of clips. I've written concise, well-ordered and relevant news releases only to have them garbled by well-intentioned but nonwriter engineers, attorneys and casual passerbys. I've been told to stonewall, lie, evade and mislead by egoists who think they won't get caught, and I've taken the high ethical road in each case.[12]

Just as journalists can reasonably be expected not to engage in unethical behaviour, so can communicators and media relations practitioners.

Engaging in unethical behaviour with members of the media is not only wrong in itself, as it is with anyone else, it is also legally dangerous. The consequences of providing the media information or comment that is not factual, or that is defamatory, can be fatal to a reputation and a career.

As with all guidelines, a generic set of rules on ethical behaviour can only provide a general indication of what should and should not be done. Another measure is instinct—the feeling that a situation is not right. Experienced journalists develop this feeling and sense an ethically risky situation before they can articulate it. Communicators must develop this same intuitive sense of professional right and wrong to complement any set of ethical guidelines.

One thing to emphasize with both codes, and any code of ethics for either journalism or communications: they are voluntary and unenforceable. At times, as when one group calls the other unethical, they may even be illegal, and put the accuser at risk of being sued for defamation.

There are regulated professions (law, medicine, engineering) which are regulated by law and have formal bodies which can provide eduction, training and discipline. A physician who abuses a patient or a lawyer who cheats a client are both at risk not only of legal action, as is a communicator or journalist who defames, but also at risk of being banned from their professions for life. Neither journalism nor media have associations with that kind of power to curb abuse. Moral suasion (as discussed in chapter 15) is about all we have to work with. One wonders if at some point society will demand higher standards for journalists and communicators, as they did for lawyers, physicians and others.

Basics of Media: Who They Are

4

From foundational principles and professional considerations, it's time to get down to some specifics. This chapter provides an overview of the diversity of news media in Canada. Chapter 5 looks at how reporters decide what is newsworthy, gather news and present it. With this grounding, both theoretical and practical, we can then discuss how to practise the profession of media relations.

Types of Media

Before looking at the wide range of news media practising today, we need to define and differentiate among three different types of news, since most media provide each to varying degrees: hard news, soft news and opinion.

Hard news is characterized by its timeliness: something is happening now that the reader/listener/viewer wants to know about immediately. It is heavily focussed on the classic "five W's and an H" of journalism and curiosity: Who, What, When, Where, Why and How (Some reporters add a second H: How Much i.e. how much money does it cost?). It is usually brief and fact-filled (e.g., "City Hall cut taxes today; Sonja Smith has details.")

Soft news, sometimes called feature or human-interest news, is less timely and more in-depth than hard news. It looks more into the why of a news issue and probes its effect on people. ("The Jones family of Ourtown will not be celebrating the tax cut: Mr. Jones has lost his city job because of it. George Doe talks to the Jones family and finds out where they will go from here.")

Opinion news encompasses editorials, commentary, columns, open-line radio and talk shows. It is less about the news and its effects than about people's interpretation and opinion of it. ("Should George Jones be laid off so you can get a tax cut? Our lines are open, and we are joined in the studio by the Jones family and Her Worship the Mayor.")

Most media incorporate all three types of news in their coverage, although some—such as talk radio or CTV Headline News—specialize more in one form than another.

Further, in broad terms there are two types of media available to the communications practitioner: broadcast and print. For the sake of argument, the Internet will be defined as broadcast, even though, unlike traditional broadcast media, it is often print-based and printable.

Broadcast Media

Until recently, broadcast meant radio and television, and to a lesser extent film and video; today it includes the Internet. Both radio (except CBC) and television (including CBC and most educational channels) rely heavily on advertising for revenue. Cable specialty channels receive a fee from every cable subscriber as well as advertising revenue.

Radio

The advantage of radio news is its immediacy and frequency. Before 24-hour TV news stations and the Internet, radio was the quickest way to get news out. Generally speaking, most commercial radio news will be broadcast every hour on the hour, with longer news shows at 8 a.m., noon and 6 p.m.

Radio news, outside of CBC Radio, is more often purchased from a radio news service such as Broadcast News (associated with Canadian Press) than produced by the station itself. Most radio stations have only one or two reporters, responsible for everything in the news area. As a result, they tend to file as many local news stories as possible, and fill the remainder of their newscast with audio news supplied by Broadcast News or with copy supplied by Canadian Press or a news-release service such as Marketwire or Canada NewsWire.

Private stations focus more attention on radio personalities, particularly during the peak audience periods: the morning show (6–9 a.m.), noon show (noon–1 p.m.) and drive home (4–6 p.m.). These periods represent the highest listenership in radio; private stations compete to have the liveliest personalities on at this time, and entertainment is a key focus. Nevertheless, all these shows will from time to time address newsworthy issues either as a public service or because they know their audience will be interested (e.g., rural country-and-western noon shows will be glad to talk with someone about farm safety). There are also nationally syndicated special-interest radio shows, generally produced in Toronto or the US and purchased by individual radio stations across the country.

There are three exceptions to this type of radio broadcasting: CBC news, all-news stations and specialty stations such as ethnic or student radio. CBC Radio One (AM) broadcasts national news during peak hours and again later in the evening (10 p.m., midnight). Local news usually comes on the half hour, outside of longer shows such as CBC Radio One's national morning show. CBC pours considerable resources into these newscasts, and maintains French and English networks across Canada. And its ratings are up, from sixth place overall in 1998 to third in 2003.[1]

In addition to regular newscasts, CBC also has local morning, noon and drive home shows, which feature extended interviews and documentaries, as well as regular news, sports and weather. Nationally, CBC radio offers *Sounds Like Canada,* a national magazine show from 8:30 a.m. to noon, repeated (in a condensed form) in the evening, which also offers a range of features, interviews and documentaries. Another important CBC radio program is *As It Happens,* a daily (6:30–8 p.m.) call-out show on issues of the day. CBC has a popular Sunday morning program featuring original or in-depth documentaries; it also features specialized news shows during the week (e.g., the science program *Quirks and Quarks,* the political program *The House*).

All news, or talk, radio is just that. The station does not play music, but consists of open-line radio shows (local and syndicated), sports and entertainment shows, and extended news broadcasts, including live broadcasts of breaking news. Talk shows feature discussion between host and guest(s); open-line shows may have host and guest(s), but accept calls from listeners as well. Hosts of open-line shows can range from conservative to liberal; many are the most popular personalities on the station and in the market. For example, in Vancouver Rafe Mair attracts the most interesting and newsworthy guests because of his high ratings. Newfoundland also has a strong tradition of phone-in radio hosts, such as Anne Budgell of CBC Radio's *Radio Noon.*

The third exception to mainstream radio is the specialty station, such as student radio or ethnic radio. These stations focus on very narrow segments of the listening population. CBC French radio and television provide French-language service across the country. Not surprisingly, Vancouver boasts three ethnic radio stations, primarily Chinese. And within specialty stations, there can be programming directed to even smaller niche markets, such as *Gaywire,* a program targeted to gay and lesbian students, on CJSR, the University of Alberta's campus radio station.

Satellite radio was just coming on stream as this book was going to press, but has proven a great success in the United States. Check with satellite providers for their full range of broadcasting to determine if any are of value to you. However, the need to fill the airwaves for 24 hours a day, 365 days a year means in all likelihood that the satellite radio stations will be hungry for relevant content.

For more information on local and national radio shows (hosts, producers, times, audience and such), refer to Matthews Media Directories (commonly referred to as the Matthews list). Matthews Media Directories are published by Marketwire and are available at most public library reference desks or directly from the company.

Media directories are updated regularly because of high turnover in the news industry and are available by subscription (for more information, check the Marketwire website). Note that directories tend to focus on television, radio stations and daily newspapers, as well as magazines and trade journals.

Television

Television offers many of the same types of programming as radio, as well as different advantages. In terms of audience, there are roughly three times as many radio stations as television stations in most markets, and radio tends to offer smaller audiences (with exceptions like the above-noted Mr. Mair, who has a very large listenership in the lower mainland of BC); but these audiences tend to be more focussed. (Later in this chapter we will look at how radio and television break down their markets). Both commercial and CBC television news tend to follow the same patterns.

CTV and CBC both have national morning shows, heavy on features and entertainment, with cutaways to local news; private non-network stations also tend to have a morning show. Because, in general, very little has occurred since the evening news the night before, morning shows tend to supplement hard news with feature stories (human interest, public service) and longer interviews (three to five minutes live). The viewership is about half that of evening news. Morning shows have a much lower-key presentation, with warm hosts instead of authority figures, and they concentrate heavily on the weather. The news content (exclusive of interviews, weather and banter) can be summarized as follows:

- Fast-paced: two-thirds of stories under 45 seconds;
- Reactive: only two per cent of stories based on in-depth reporting;
- Glitzy: more pop-culture stories than other time slots;
- Cautious: more than 40 per cent of stories are about non-controversial events;
- Cheerful: more celebration, how-to and cooking segments than any other time slot.[2]

Noon news shows tend to be local and focussed on hard news, particularly the events of the morning. The supper-hour news is the major local television broadcast of the day. It is aired between 5 and 7 p.m. and runs half an hour or longer. This program normally has the highest local ratings of the day.

In the evening, usually at 10 or 11 p.m., the national (CBC, CTV, Global) news will run, as will news from independent stations. This may or may not be followed by a local wrap-up after the national news, which is essentially a re-cap of the six o'clock news and often repeats many of the earlier news items, including soft news on a slow day.

Mainstream television in Canada doesn't offer the opportunities for talk shows that radio does, or that the US does with its syndicated talk shows à la Oprah Winfrey, Jerry Springer et al. Nor does it offer much in the way of special-interest shows, although this trend will vary from market to market (consult with Matthews Media Directories or your local television guide to find out what shows are available in your region). CBC is unique in offering *The Journal,* a late-night news program that allows for longer documentaries and extensive interviews. Hour-long local supper-hour TV news will often offer the same type of programming in the second half of the show.

However, a whole new range of programming that didn't exist 10 to 20 years ago is now available thanks to specialty and cable TV channels such as Discovery Channel and Newsworld. Both CBC and CTV offer 24-hour news, although CTV's channel is more of a headline service that summarizes breaking news, while Newsworld offers a range of programming. Specialty cable channels (such as The Discovery Channel, Women's TV Network, Home and Garden TV, Food Network Canada, Outdoor Life Network and many others) offer specialized programming that reaches a limited but highly targeted audience. Again, given that these programs change each season, you must check a media directory, local listings or the websites of these channels for program updates, new shows or producer changes. (In television, the producer is the person who normally determines the content of the program, and hence the key person you want to pitch your story ideas to, as we will discuss in Chapter 8). Local cable companies also provide an opportunity for feature stories.

The Internet

The Internet has become a viable news medium and it provides some opportunities for communicating to news media. Its relation to news occurs in a couple of areas. First, most newspapers, radio and television stations, wire services and magazines have a website, on which they routinely post the stories that run in their normal medium. One of the most popular sites in Canada,

Canoe.ca, is a product of the *Sun* newspaper chain. As a communications practitioner, you need to be aware that if your story is posted it could attract attention well outside your intended audience, anywhere on the Internet. (The same thing can happen, to a lesser degree, when international broadcasters or news services pick up items from local news for worldwide distribution).

In addition to mainstream media sites on the Internet, there are also specialty sites that provide news solely for the Internet. These include the Drudge Report (drudgereport.com) and Bourque Newswatch. There being fewer standards on the Internet than in mainstream media, you are advised to be careful of what appears on these pages; many are simply repositories of gossip and chatter. However, Drudge achieved fame when it was the first of any media to point out the Monica Lewinsky-Bill Clinton connection. This aspect of news is still evolving; nevertheless, Internet news now stands as one of the major broadcast media and should be one avenue you consider when seeking media attention.

Another aspect of the Internet related to news is that anyone can set up a website or blog and become a broadcaster or publisher. Having a presence on the Internet may help you reach your audience, particularly if it is geographically fragmented. The success of a website depends on knowing your audience: many groups, particularly disadvantaged groups and seniors, don't have regular access to the Internet, so it can't be your only strategy. However, most public libraries offer free Internet service, and many communities and social groups offer low-cost Internet service. In 2001, 63 per cent of US homes have a computer, most with Internet access, so the Internet is becoming more of a media option for getting your message out.[4]

An Internet presence also allows you to practise media relations by giving the media access to your website and the data in it. Some organizations (e.g., TransCanada Pipelines) set up media rooms on their website, which contain news releases, media contacts, Frequently Asked Questions, background documents, original research and other information that media in particular may be interested in. Please see Chapter 10 for some advice on how to build and maintain a good media room.

Print Media

Print media primarily refers to newspapers and magazines. Newspapers are generally national, daily or weekly; magazines may be weekly, monthly, quarterly or irregular.

Daily newspapers

Most communities over 50,000 people have a daily paid newspaper; most communities greater than 500,000 have at least two (usually, but not always, a CanWest Global broadsheet and a *Sun* tabloid). Toronto has four dailies, as does Montreal, in English and French. There are a number of free commuter and specialty dailies in most major cities, such as *Metro* in Toronto, though they come and go with frequency (e.g. CanWest started a free daily targeted at youth called *Dose* in 2005; it didn't last a year).

In a daily newspaper, local news appears in the city section. In smaller dailies, the first section of the paper contains local, national and international news. Sports, entertainment and business sections are major parts of a daily newspaper; depending on the city, the paper may also have sections on lifestyle, computers, agriculture, food, religion and other specific interests.

Most dailies have columnists, who write either on specialized issues (sports, politics) or on general topics that appeal to them (response to current events, family life, humorous observations). Dailies also feature editorials, letters to the editor and an op-ed page (opposite the editorial page), where views from non-reporters and columnists are solicited. (We will discuss how to reach these different types of opinion in Chapter 10). Finally, in the news section, a large daily will have beat (specialty) reporters covering areas such as city hall, police, the courts, health, environment and so forth.

Tabloid dailies, particularly the *Sun* newspaper chain, reflect the same organization and areas of interest as the broadsheet (mainstream) newspapers, but are distinguished by their flash and their attention to stories focussed on crime, sex and sports. Despite their flash and hype, the papers in the *Sun* chain should not be confused with supermarket tabloids, which are classified as entertainment media, not news media. The *Sun* generally responds to ethical and professional issues as the other mainstream media do.

The advantages of daily newspapers are that they tend provide a wider audience than most other media, offer more comprehensive coverage of issues and contain more detailed information. Their major drawback is that fewer people have time to read them at all, let alone thoroughly, particularly with the advent of a second national daily.

Dailies are sold primarily through subscriptions or at newsstands; however, they depend on advertising for most of their revenue. A look through your daily newspaper will tell you the type of stories it prefers to cover, as well as its general approach to news.

National newspapers

Until recently, in Canada the term "national newspaper" meant the *Globe and Mail. The Globe* presented itself this way, although people living outside southern Ontario often felt the paper had (and has) a Toronto bias in its choice of news. However, in 1998, Southam (now CanWest) launched a second national, the *National Post,* using the former *Financial Post* as a platform.

The presence of competition at the national level had the same effect as competition at the local level: the new player forced the old player to upgrade its product. In the first year of operation of the *National Post, The Globe* added new sections, expanded the space available for news and added colour. Both papers tend to reflect the same organization and concerns as the local dailies, although both tend to do so from the business perspective (both *The Globe*'s Report on Business and the *Post*'s Financial Post sections tend to be separate newspapers under the cover of their parent daily).

It is now more possible than ever to get national news coverage of your issue. At one time, even into the 1960s, only the CBC (radio and television) and the Canadian Press (see below) could be considered national news media. Today, the two national papers add to the national exposure already possible through CBC, CP, CTV or *Maclean's* magazine. The downside of the national newspapers is that they tend to be politically right of centre (*Globe*) and far right of centre (*Post*) in their coverage of news; in some markets, such as Toronto, this presentation is balanced by left-of-centre (*Star*) and blue-collar (*Sun*) papers.

The long-term success of the *National Post* is still undetermined. It trumpeted its success after its first year, but in fact the first-year data on its readership were clouded by the fact that it gave so many newspapers away after its launch.[5] *The Globe* disputes the *Post*'s figures. (Such disputes are not uncommon. Newspapers, radio and television have outside agencies to measure their reach, but each will argue that it is number one, if not overall, then at least in specific time, location or demographic). Nonetheless, the *Post* appears to be established, and has increased the opportunities available for national news media relations with newspapers as well as broadcast media and *Maclean's*.

Weekly newspapers

Sometimes called suburban newspapers, community newspapers or controlled circulation newspapers, these publications can vary widely, from pure advertising vehicles that contain no news (called shoppers) to more traditional small newspapers (although the proportion of advertising is still high since, unlike dailies, they rarely charge subscriptions and have to earn all their revenue from advertising or inserted flyers).

The advantage of a weekly newspaper is that it usually stays in the home for a week, with the assumption that the residents will eventually find time to read it, which may not be the case for a daily. These papers also tend to be distributed geographically and can be a good means of communication when you are targeting specific areas for your message. They tend to have fewer, more general reporters than the dailies.

A study by the Canadian Community Newspaper Association shows that more people (69 per cent of respondents) read their community weekly than a daily (47 per cent).[6] Community newspapers should be on your media list and a significant target media.

Philosophically, it has been argued that the value and type of news in a community newspaper is different from that in a daily. Community news

> is shaped and frequently constrained by factors inherent to the small community. Editors and publishers believe it is their role to foster harmony, not create conflict. Community newspapers act as boosters for the local community, sometimes at the expense of analysis or criticism.[7]

We will examine how you can use this approach to relating to the community in later chapters.

Most provinces have a provincial weekly newspaper association that either issues a directory or allows direct access to weeklies for news releases. (See, for example, www.ocna.org, the website for the Ontario Community Newspaper Association). In most provinces, the weekly newspaper association will be listed in the Yellow Pages under Associations or Newspapers.

One more thought: although they're produced for students by students, don't forget college and university newspapers. Most campuses produce a weekly or semi-weekly paper, read by the majority of students and some of the staff. However, if your message needs to reach the 18-to-30-year-old demographic group, these papers are an excellent resource.

Magazines

In some ways, magazines reflect the newspaper world. There are national, local and specialty magazines, and they may be sold by subscription or delivered for free. Their editorial and design quality also varies. But magazines also differ from newspapers in a number of ways. People usually keep magazines longer than they do newspapers, sometimes even collecting them, and some magazines have high production values, making them sturdier and more attractive than most newspapers. In general, magazines have a longer production timeline than newspapers, so they tend to be slightly less current than daily or weekly newspapers; but in exchange, magazine articles tend to be longer and more detailed than newspaper stories. (Indeed, some magazines market themselves on the high quality of their editorial content).

One of Canada's largest mainstream magazines is *Maclean's*. *Maclean's*, facing impossible competition from the Internet and 24-hour news, no longer satisfies itself with a news summary, focusing more on analysis, backgrounder, commentary and in-depth original articles and special issues, including issues devoted to ranking the nation's universities and health regions. *Maclean's* has regional offices in major cities, but it can be difficult for minor newsmakers to get their attention. There are also many regional current affairs publications, such as *AlbertaViews* and *l'acualité*, just to name a few.

Because Canada's population is comparatively small and far-flung, many Canadian magazines adopt either a local-interest or special-interest focus. You'll find a Canadian magazine for just about any interest you can name, from gardening (*Canadian Gardener, Spring Gardening*) to politics (*This Magazine, Canadian Dimension*), business (*Venture*) to literature (*Geist*), history (*The Beaver*) to feminism (*Herizons*). Canada also boasts several high-profile women's magazines, such as *Flare, Chatelaine, Homemaker's* and *Canadian Living*. Add to this the numerous US and international magazines that are available and you have thousands of possible publications to choose from.

Further subspecialties of magazines include trade magazines and company magazines. Trade magazines cover industries (such as accounting, entertainment, computers) or professions (such as nursing, law, education) or occasionally combine both. Company magazines tend to be internal to staff or are intended for customers (e.g., in-flight magazines) or members (e.g., automobile association magazines).

There are excellent opportunities for communications through magazines. However, the enormous range of interests and audiences makes magazines difficult to categorize or summarize. To find out what magazines may be of interest to you and your target audience, check a media directory, the periodicals section of your local library, a large newsstand, or go to the Canadian Magazine Publishers Association (www.cmpa.ca).

Newsletters

Before the Internet, there were newsletters. For many individuals and groups, newsletters presented the only available opportunity to be an information publisher. Anyone with a typewriter/computer and a photocopier could—and can—produce a newsletter. As with newspapers and magazines, the quality of newsletters varies widely. Some are professionally produced and sold at high subscription rates to select audiences (investment or wine newsletters); others are produced right at the kitchen table and distributed to a small number of highly focussed readers.

What newsletters provide is access to very targeted audiences, which may include specific occupations, hobbyists, service clubs, companies and their staff, unions, charitable and non-profit organizations, and other similarly limited groups. Unfortunately, unlike other media, newsletters lack a central directory or point of access to their creators. The best advice for the practitioner is to define your audience, then find out from individual audience members what they read, listen to or watch. From these responses you can build up your own list of key newsletters.

Forgotten Media

Television, radio, newspapers and the Internet tend to receive the most attention when it comes to media relations. When we think of media exposure, we tend to think of high-profile, highly rated broadcast shows and the front page of the daily newspaper. Yet a number of specialty media exist, which tend to be overlooked or casually cited in discussion of higher-profile media. These outlets deserve closer attention, however, because they usually provide better access to target markets and are easier to reach, in part because so few practitioners pay attention to them.

Canadian Press/Broadcast News

Canadian Press (CP) is often overlooked when it comes to media relations, despite its prominent position within the world of journalism. CP is a news agency, co-operatively owned by approximately 95 newspapers. Newspapers and other organizations pay a fee to belong to CP and in exchange contribute news in their regions to the agency pool. All member media outlets who subscribe to CP and its radio arm, Broadcast News, receive stories from across the country and from special news bureaus (Ottawa, sports, business) that most couldn't afford to staff themselves. CP is often called a wire service, from the days when news stories were telegraphed from town to town.

The agency in turn has its own reporters and editors, who either follow up on story contributions or initiate their own. It maintains correspondents (stringers) across the country. If a major story breaks in a small community, CP contacts its stringer (often but not always a reporter for the local newspaper) for more details. CP is the only dedicated newswire in Canada (existing as a stand-alone service).

CP retains a high degree of respect among reporters, in part because it was the first to establish national standards of style and conduct (other large news agencies, such as CanWest Global, CBC and CTV, now have their own styles and standards). Stories carried by CP meet high editorial standards, and papers will reprint them without question. Hence, getting a story on CP means there is a chance of nationwide exposure, both in the national media and in local media across the country.

Broadcast News (BN) is the radio arm of CP and also maintains a French-language service. Broadcast News is of increasing importance in radio as fewer and fewer private stations (outside of all-news radio) maintain a large news staff—or have a news staff at all. Many rely heavily on BN, and it is to radio what CP is to print. As will be discussed in more detail in Chapter 16, there is an absolute decline in the number of working reporters today, and the newsrooms are shrinking. Therefore, all media are relying more on CP/BN, and they should be on everyone's media list.

Local cable television

Cable television is monopolistic. In exchange for the monopoly, cable companies are required to provide community services, including a dedicated channel on which almost anyone can broadcast with the consent of the cable company (access is limited to community groups that normally wouldn't have access to mainstream media). It's not wide open; community groups wanting to put shows on cable TV have to adhere to the same limitations that mainstream television does, particularly laws on defamation and a reasonable degree of good taste and common sense.

In the past, potential users were pointed to a studio and wished good luck. Today, most community channels are polished and professional.[8] Adopting the logic of "why try to compete with other broadcasters," they offer a variety of programming outside the mainstream, a focus that may present unique opportunities for communicators, particularly if you are trying to reach a younger audience. Indeed, Canadian comedian Tom Green began his career with his own cable program in Ottawa. If you have an idea for a show, contact the programming director at the cable company; or if you want to appear on an already-existing show, contact its producer. These people are often looking for ideas, particularly ideas that the mainstream media may have overlooked.

To work community cable for maximum effect, though, it may be helpful to undertake other promotion (e.g., buying an ad in the local TV guide, sending out a flyer or newsletter to your intended audience) at the same time, to ensure you reach as much of your target audience as possible.

Educational television

Most provinces have an educational television station: TV Ontario, Saskatchewan Communications Network and BC's Knowledge Network, for example. Educational channels may offer news programs, talk shows, specialized series (e.g., the new technology) or documentaries, which may be produced in-house, purchased from other sources or developed in partnership with government or educational institutions. As with local cable, the ratings for these channels are generally low; but in concert with other communications support, such channels offer another, often low-cost, way to reach specialized audiences.

Specialty newspapers

A look under Newspapers in the Yellow Pages provides a quick local summary of all the newspapers in any community. This list will include ethnic newspapers, which generally publish in languages other than English, and newspapers that focus on special interests, such as ethnic groups, religion, seniors, entertainment, sports, business, aboriginal issues, computers, tourism and more. These newspapers are typically free (although more established papers, such as the *Western Catholic Reporter* and *Western Producer,* are popular enough to charge subscriptions) and are distributed directly to the reader or available on a news drop (e.g., entertainment guides to popular restaurants and night clubs).

The quality of specialty newspapers varies widely, from completely professional to barely legible. If you think you might want to work with a specialty periodical, familiarize yourself with the paper, its tone and content before putting it on your mailing list or approaching it directly. Check out what your target market thinks of these newspapers as well, particularly if they're in a language you don't understand.

Media Options in a Mid-sized Market: An Example

To get a sense of the variety of news media, consider a medium-sized market like Edmonton Alberta's Capital City region, (population 1,000,000). This summary has been developed from the sources mentioned previously. In addition to the size and scope of the summary, consider also how each media outlet has a clearly defined audience. Radio stations in particular typify themselves by the audience they try to reach. This example is a summary of newsrooms only and does not include columnists, talk-show hosts or special programming; it simply summarizes who in Edmonton may receive a news release.

Edmonton has been used for illustrative purposes, to give an indication of the range and diversity of news media. To investigate the media makeup of your own city, refer to a media directory or look in the Yellow Pages under Newspapers. There are also many media pages on the Internet, but they are not uniformly up to date; they may provide a general idea of your local media market, but you will have to do further research to confirm current details.

Newsrooms in Edmonton

Television

CFRN (CTV affiliate): All northern Alberta, mainstream adult; number one overall

CITV/Global: All northern Alberta, younger audience (25–40); number two overall

CBC: All northern Alberta, mainstream, very low ratings (news)

Citytv/Chum Ltd.: Edmonton and area, very young audience (teens to 25)

CBXFT-TV (CBC French): French-language station, low ratings; popular among French immersion students as well as small francophone population

ACCESS/Chum Ltd.: education station

Newspapers

Dailies

Edmonton Journal (CanWest): Middle class, number one in circulation (943,320 weekly circulation); editorial left of centre

Edmonton Sun: Blue/pink collar, heavily skewed toward males (525,205 weekly circulation); editorial right of centre

Globe and Mail: Business; editorial conservative*

National Post: Business; editorial strongly conservative*

* both national newspapers are viewed in Edmonton as very Ontario/ Toronto focussed and not as national as they claim to be

Community Weeklies

Edmonton Examiner: Direct delivery to 180,000 residences (includes exurbs,[9] excludes high-rises, downtown); six to eight separate versions (northeast, southwest, etc.).

Various independent community weeklies in Mill Woods, Beverly (*Page* and *Beacon*), Riverdale

Various independent weeklies in surrounding communities (Sherwood Park, St. Albert)

Specialty Weeklies/Newsletters/Magazines

Seniors: Four to six different publications, conflicting and unverifiable distribution

Ethnic/other language: French (two), Chinese (three), Aboriginal (six), Italian (two), Ukrainian, Vietnamese, Korean

Religious/cultural: Jewish (two), *Western Catholic Reporter*

Entertainment: *See, Vue*

Business: Primarily newsletters

Farm: *Western Producer*

Edmonton Woman

University, *Gateway* (bi-weekly, 10 months of the year)

Wire Services

Canadian Press

Radio Stations

CBC Radio One: Drive Home show (information)

CBC Radio One: English news

CBC Radio One: Morning show (information)

CBC Radio One: Noon show (information)

CBC Radio Two

CBC Radio Three

CBC French radio/Radio Canada

CFBR-FM The Bear: Album-oriented rock, targeted to 18–49, primarily males

CFCW-AM: Country, 25–54, number one overall

CFMG-FM EZ Rock: Adult contemporary, 25–54

CFRN-AM The Team: Sports

CFWE-FM: Aboriginal/Country, all

CHBN The Bounce: Contemporary/dance

CHED-AM: All news and talk, all

CHFA-AM (CBC French): Adulte contemporain, tous

CHNR: Student

CHQT-AM: Oldies/gold

CIRK-FM K-Rock: Adult rock, 25–49

CISN-AM: Country, 25–54

CJCA-AM The Light: Gospel, 25–49

CJYR-FM Shine: Religious

CJSR-FM: Alternative (University of Alberta)

CKRA-FM Big Earl

CHMC-FM Magic 99

CHDI-FM Sonic: Modern rock, 18–35

CKER-FM: Ethnic/multilingual (Italian, Spanish, Chinese, Polish, German, Ukrainian, East Indian, Greek, Arabic, Croatian, Dutch, Portuguese), all

CKNG-Joe FM: Contemporary hits, 18–34

CKRA-FM: Adult contemporary, 25–44

CKUA-AM/FM (former Alberta government): Eclectic/college, 25+

Summary: What Are the Media?

One of the major challenges facing the communicator trying to practise media relations is simply being heard through all the clamour. Advertisers face the same challenge. At one time, appearing on CBC-TV would reach the entire English-speaking nation; today it's hard to find someone who hasn't been on television in one form or another. Nevertheless, it is possible for the nation to be engaged in one issue, as 9/11 and Terry Fox proved.

Most of the time, however, media relations is practised in segmented and focussed approaches, each designed to best meet the communicator's target audience, whether it be seniors in Scarborough or the province of Nova Scotia.

Each medium provides various means of communications. Television and radio, often criticized for their brevity, nevertheless offer opportunities for extensive dialogue on magazine and information shows and often provide lengthy documentaries on significant social issues. And as we saw in the previous chapter, newspapers are perceived to present more detail yet are prone to providing the same hasty or incorrect information that broadcast news can. (Remember, reporters say 19 per cent of their own stories are deficient because of poor editing and headline writing).

To sort through the maze of media, the practitioner is best advised to watch the media—all of them, local and national—and analyze their particular strengths, weaknesses, foibles and preferences. National advertising and public relations firms keep careful files on major national reporters, columnists and shows. Media outlets themselves send out news releases and promotion surrounding new anchors and columnists—news itself can be news. You must, of course, assemble lists and study media books, but the best practice is still to follow the media as closely as reporters themselves do.

Basics of Media: How They Work

5

The popular media depiction of reporters seems to be derived from movies like *The Front Page* (colourful, hard-drinking rogues who will cut any corner to get a story) or *All the President's Men* (noble seekers of truth uncovering massive conspiracies and cover-ups). Both images make for good entertainment, both have residual elements of truth in them, but the real picture is a little more professional.

This chapter provides an overall description of how reporters work in Canada, including Quebec. There is a general belief that English-speaking journalism is more factual and French-language journalism more opinionated in their respective approaches to covering news. However, a 1999 study of journalists across the country found that "journalists from both language groups hold very similar conceptions about the relative importance of various journalistic functions."[1]

Who Are the Reporters in Canada?

Most reporters are well trained in their field. One study showed that the average print reporter has 3.5 years of post-secondary education, the average broadcast reporter 2.9 years.[2] The average age is 32.2 and the field, at the reporter level, is predominantly female (64 per cent of the journalism students in the 1984/85 academic year were female).[3] News directors, however, tend to be male (79.1 per cent).[4]

Politically, their views reflect the views of the audiences they report to, unlike US news directors, who are more liberal than their audiences.[5]

However, their expertise tends to be in journalism, not in specialties such as commerce, science or the arts. Although there are certainly exceptions (journalists who come to media from a different academic discipline), most come from one of the more than one hundred schools of journalism and communications across Canada. As such, they tend not to be experts in anything except news. This is an important point to bear in mind: reporters, generally, are expert at news, not at the field they happen to be covering. It is not uncommon for broadcast reporters in particular to cover city hall, business, sports and crime in a single day, moving from one to another, trying to juggle deadlines, interviews, writing and editing on the run, to meet a six o'clock deadline.

For example, in Regina on Thursday, September 16, 1999, city reporters were working on three major stories during the day. One was the trial of a physician on assault charges, the second was voting day for the provincial election and the third was the follow-up to a riot at a young offender facility. While the daily paper, the *Leader-Post,* had the luxury of assigning different reporters to each story, other media had to juggle frantically: get interviews with the head of the RCMP riot squad and the administrator of the young offender facility to finish that story, while following up on the court appearances of the youth involved; try to get coverage and response from the three party leaders as they voted, plus get man-in-the-street response while trying to determine how busy the polls were; and try to cover a trial where the lawyers may or may not speak to them during the breaks, which can be unpredictable, if the session does not go in camera or runs longer than expected. All three stories were known in advance and their coverage could be planned. However, a major breaking story (fire, crime) could further complicate a day like this.

If reporters appear rushed, with very little time for reflection, it's because they often are. On top of their effort to keep multiple balls in the air (after getting all the information down, they still have to go back and write it; broadcast reporters have to edit sound and video tape into their story as well), reporters have to work within tight deadlines. The deadline is just that: if they can't get the story in on time, they will be fired; rather than take that risk, reporters tend to go with what they've got when facing a tight deadline. Broadcast reporters can't move the clock back to allow a little more checking or polishing of copy; newspaper reporters' deadlines are timed around a daily press run and delivery system that has to get the paper delivered to the doorstep by 7 a.m. "Stop the presses!" is a cliché from old movies (9/11 being a notable exception). If a print reporter can't meet a deadline, he or she will have to find another line of work.

Reporters will also have to find another line of work if, in the midst of this frenzy, they make mistakes—and in such a work environment, it's surprising that more errors don't happen. Generally speaking, day-to-day reporters are rushed, inexpert, trying to get to the heart of the matter as quickly as possible and working under career-ending deadline pressure. (Reporters working on features and documentaries or writing for magazines have longer deadlines and therefore more time to spend researching a story). Don't be surprised if they appear a bit brusque. Of course, many people work under stress, and a reasonable amount of civility and courtesy should be shown on both sides. However, reporting is a high-stress occupation, and media practitioners may have to remember to keep their composure while all about them are losing theirs.

How Do They Get Their Stories?

Print and broadcast media have their own rhythms, which affect how they gather news, when they do so and how much finally appears.

What determines the size of a newspaper and the amount of news it carries is the number of ads it contains that day. Advertising is heaviest from Labour Day to Christmas, and so are newspapers. It is thus relatively easier to get stories into the dailies then, since there is so much space to fill. Newspapers are smallest in January and February, and there is more competition to get in a story. With some variation for holiday hours, radio and television newscasts are more fixed. Competition among reporters within each media outlet, however, is still considerable, particularly to get a front-page story or lead item on the news.

The rhythm of newsgathering

Timing is important to all media. Most daily newspapers are now delivered in the morning, which means most news must be "put to bed" no later than 11 p.m. on an average weekday. Although they may have breakfast shows and sometimes noon shows, television stations target the evening (generally 6 p.m.) newscast for their major efforts. As a result, key producers and editors come in at 8 a.m. They scan the dailies, check overnight stories on Canadian Press and the commercial newswires (Canada NewsWire and Marketwire both send news releases around the clock to subscribing media outlets). They then assign stories and deadlines to reporters. At most television stations, reporters are expected to turn in an average of two stories a day.

Most radio stations start broadcasting live at 5 a.m. Early news broadcasts tend to repeat the major stories from the day before, with new stories or story updates entering the stream as the morning advances. Radio reporters begin their day early and immediately start filing stories for broadcast. The reporter has likely already worked up a few stories, mainly by following up from yesterday's stories, plus whatever has been in the papers and on the wires that morning. With the exception of CBC and all-news radio, most stations have small news staffs, most of whom spend the day on the phone, filing stories every hour or so.

For people who are frequently in the news or who work a great deal with the media, this schedule means their day could begin as early as 5 a.m., when the radio reporters get going, and end as late as 11 p.m., when the last chance for rewrite happens at the newspapers. In the event of a crisis, 24-hour availability to media may be necessary and may entail some scheduling to ensure someone is available to talk, in the era of round-the-clock news television.

Assigning stories

Television news outlets typically have a morning story meeting, in which key editors and reporters will meet and try, as much as possible, to determine what news to cover for the rest of the day. Daily newspapers have a similar meeting at the beginning of the shift (usually two shifts a day at medium-size newspapers). Radio stations work throughout the day. The schedule of each media type can be disrupted anytime by breaking news. In the mix for story selection will be ongoing coverage of stories that reporters have been working on for some time (e.g., public hearings, elections), plus the stories that beat reporters are expected to generate. (The basic news beats, according to *The Canadian Reporter,* are police, courts, government [municipal, provincial, federal], sports, arts/entertainment and business/economy).[6] In a larger newspaper, major beats may have their own allotment of pages to fill; in a smaller one, it may be more negotiable depending on what is in the news that day.

After scanning the stories in progress and soliciting ideas from the beat reporters (and sometimes from general reporters who have come across interesting items), the assignment editor (in television) or city editor (in newspapers) hands out story leads to reporters. The leads often come from news releases: anywhere from 10 to 50 per cent of a media outlet's story ideas come from the news releases that swamp them every day.[7] News stories from Canadian Press and international press agencies may also provide story leads. For example, a disaster at a water works in Milwaukee carried on Associated Press (an American news agency) may be the cue to check out safety standards at the local water works. For broadcast media, the daily newspapers, both local and national, also provide a major source for story ideas or follow-ups. Finally, leads may come from the commercial news release services (Marketwire, Canada NewsWire). On top of these are local news releases sent directly to the media by mail, fax or e-mail.

Checking out the story

The reporter may be handed a detailed technical report, given a news release or simply told to check out an assignment. From that point, the reporter may do some initial research, reviewing either his or her personal news files or the outlet's own resources. (Larger media outlets have librarians to catalogue and file all news stories the outlet has run and to monitor news from other media). Most interview subjects assume that reporters get an idea, research it, then seek sources for a carefully prepared and well-thought-out comment. In fact, reporters get the idea or assignment, then start calling around to learn more about it.

Reporters make dozens of calls in a day, running down leads, finding information and trying to verify the information they find. Therefore, when you or your client's representative speak to a reporter, it may be as part of the reporter's search for information, for a comment on the story or for both purposes at once. This fact means that interview subjects must be prepared both to brief the reporter on the issue at hand and to make comment on it. (The interview process is significant enough to merit its own chapters, since the interview forms the key to the reporter–subject relationship. See chapters 11 and 12).

With the advent of the Internet, it is now possible for reporters, even on small-town weeklies, to be better prepared for interviews and do more in-depth research. However, it is important to remember where a reporter begins to research a story: from old stories on file. Reporters and media outlets both keep files, and when reporters start to research an issue, the first place they look is the previous stories on the issue, either by themselves or by other reporters. This makes it important, then, to ensure reporters' stories are accurate and to ask the reporter/editor to correct the file when errors of fact are found in a printed or broadcast story, so that the mistake won't crop up again and taint future coverage.

The advent of the Internet has also had another advantage. Reporters and communicators alike can call up the *Globe and Mail* or the CBC archive and access old stories. Special websites have been set up for media and other interested parties that want to research news stories on the Internet in a more organized fashion than generic search engines allow.[8]

Once reporters get or develop a story idea, their next goal is to make it interesting—to find the angle or hook for the reader. If, after checking it out, the lead is in fact newsworthy (many stories die because they're boring or less than what they seemed on the surface), the reporter begins to put together the story.

What Makes a Good Story?

Reporters—and readers—want a good story. The story should be interesting and relevant to the audience, and it must be written clearly enough that it can be quickly and easily understood. (The need for clear, direct writing applies to broadcast reporters, who write up their stories before reading them on camera or on mic, as much as to print journalists). What makes a story interesting is often a combination of the interests of the audience, the interests and abilities of the reporter, and a long history of journalistic tradition.

The question "What is news?" is a primary philosophical issue in media relations. Many people are indifferent to sports, for example, yet it constitutes a major part of mainstream news. Every television and radio station devotes extensive time to weather, even though it is usually straightforward and it all comes from the same place (Environment Canada, which will provide a free, recorded forecast to anyone who calls or logs on). Nevertheless, without getting into that debate, we can identify a number of elements that characterize a good news story.[9]

Drama and emotion

News is about people. When the driest statistical summary from Stats Can is released, reporters will look for people who either exemplify the statistics or are affected by them. This is backed up by a survey of 72 media professionals undertaken by Angus Reid in 1993. To the question of newsworthiness—that is, what makes something "news"—the greatest percentage of respondents (73 per cent) found it in a subject that "affects people."[10]

Odd or unusual

Second on the Angus Reid survey of newsworthiness, at 37 per cent, was the "unusual/unexpected." This is the classic category of "man bites dog" journalism. That a plane landed safely is routine and expected; a plane crash is news. Third in the poll, at 33 per cent, was "important," a concept that is difficult to describe. What is important to one person may not be to another.

Local angle

Local news ranked next in the survey, at 17 per cent, which reflects the media's concern with its own audience and the issues that affect the audience directly. This angle, combined with an issue that affects people, makes front-page news. A plant closure that lays off thousands in Wichita, Kansas, for example, isn't newsworthy in St. John's; but if it happens in St. John's, it's front page.

Topical, timely

When you're looking to get your story in the news, you must consider topicality and timeliness. Examples abound at every holiday season: Thanksgiving news comes complete with instructions on how to cook your turkey safely; Christmas comes with safety warnings regarding the dangers of Christmas tree fires. But local events, whether annual or irregular, can also lead to topical hooks. For example, a reporter might prepare a sidebar on fire insurance for rural homes to run alongside a story about a major forest fire; might interview a local cowboy poet during the Calgary Stampede; or might write a profile of a well-known local personality who has multiple sclerosis the weekend before the Super Cities Walk for MS.

Conflict

Disagreement is generally more newsworthy than agreement. This is why politics and sports make easy news: it is easy to find disagreement. As a practitioner, you need to give some thought to whether you want to expose yourself or your client to this phenomenon. Because the reporter wants a balanced story (see below), he or she will often look for someone to disagree with the point of view you express, or at least to offer a different perspective.

Is conflict in the best interest of you or your client? If you are lobbying government for regulatory change and are in the midst of negotiations which may get what you are looking for, you probably don't want to be in the news in a position of conflict with the regulatory authority. On the other hand, if you're in business and one of your competitors is getting media time with a new product or service, you will likely want to respond strongly that yours is better and cheaper and has been on the market longer (e.g., Mac versus PC advertising).

Relevance to audience

Although stories sometimes run because of their sheer oddity, more times than not they run because editors know what their audience is interested in. A human-rights ruling extending retirement age, for example, will be of more interest to seniors' media than to YTV or MuchMusic. As we discussed in Chapter 3, many media outlets have finely targeted audiences. Being sensitive to the market they are trying to reach, and demonstrating that your story idea is relevant to that audience, will increase your chances of getting coverage.

Universal appeal

Stories that affect, or have the potential to affect, everyone are also newsworthy. A story about a child with a rare disease is interesting because it is unusual. But it is also effective because all parents worry about the health of their children and are interested in children's health generally. Reporters like stories that their audience can relate to, no matter how unusual the topic may be. Universality is closely related to relevance to the audience.

The issue of what is newsworthy is more often intuitive and experiential than rational and analytical. As Walter Lippman commented some 80 years ago,

> Every newspaper when it reaches the reader is the result of a whole series of selections as to what items shall be printed, in what position they shall be printed, how much space they shall occupy, what emphasis they shall have. There are no objective standards here.[11]

You will be much better equipped to catch media interest in your issue if you share the media's sense of what is newsworthy. One way to develop this sense is to follow the news closely (i.e., read the local newspapers, watch TV news, listen to radio news); in time you will acquire the same intuitive sense of newsworthiness that media have.

How Do They Present the Story?

Once reporters have an interesting story, they are expected to work within technical guidelines to write it. As we discussed earlier, the story must be clearly written. It should also be verifiable, accurate and complete. The story should fairly represent what people said and be balanced, objective, without taking sides against any party.

Of course, the ability of a reporter (or indeed anyone) to actually be objective is the subject of intense debate. Nevertheless, objectivity is a value shared by most reporters: they are dispassionate observers who relate the issue without taking sides. This trait is most pronounced in hard news; other elements of media have greater leeway to show bias (e.g., talk-show hosts, documentaries and opinion pieces such as editorials and columns).

The Canadian Reporter outlines the key elements a reporter should consider in writing a story.[12] Some are straightforward, such as accuracy, simplicity and completeness. Others require a bit of explanation.

Synthesis

The reporter must take a great deal of information and opinion, under a hard deadline, and synthesize, or blend, it into a coherent story that is fair and interesting.

Abstraction

This quality refers to the need to keep descriptions simple. Two basic rules of good writing are "show, don't tell" and "write concretely." Abstract issues such as government budgets are often depicted through the impact they have on typical Canadians. As much as possible, the reporter should avoid abstractions such as opinion and judgement; he or she should present as many facts and details as possible, then let readers form their own conclusions.

Evidential rules

A good reporter must be able to confirm that what the source said is factually accurate. In general, reporters want third-party verification of what a subject says; the good communicator will supply that verification if possible, or refer the reporter to that verification.

Judgement

This quality refers more to the decision-making of the craft than to moral judgement. Similar to synthesis, judgement recognizes that the reporter must select the most relevant pieces of the gathered information and opinion, and select a theme that will organize and dominate the story.

Within these specific technical parameters, a story should be fair and balanced. This requirement can be difficult to meet and requires some study and application. For example, in 1999 the *Calgary Herald* introduced the FAB formula to its editorial policy: stories must be Fair, Accurate and Balanced.[13] Fairness, which takes up three pages of the *Canadian Press Stylebook*,[14] includes accuracy, impartiality, sensitivity and sticking to the facts. Accuracy simply means that the information contained in a story is factual and verifiable; basing a story on inaccurate information is cause for a reporter to be fired. Balance implies that all sides are given a chance to state their point of view in a story; it does not mean that if one side receives 20 seconds of coverage, the other side must also receive the same amount of time. For communicators, the FAB formula means that if you criticize someone, the reporter will call that person to hear his or her version of the facts.[15]

With all this in mind, the reporter can now write the story. The typical newspaper story starts with the most important fact, then proceeds to the next most important, then the next, and so forth. The story does not end with a conclusion; it wraps up with the least important item. This unique writing style reflects the fact that many reporters are working on stories, and in the newspaper world, the stories literally have to fit the space allocated to them. Throughout the day, editors are monitoring the stories coming in, trying to determine which goes where—if it runs at all. To make room for worthy but lengthy stories, particularly in a crush at deadline, editors will simply trim the story from the bottom; this formula ensures the editor trims the least important parts of the story. (Magazines, which have longer lead times, have the luxury of a different editorial process that allows cuts and alterations to be made throughout the text). While there are certainly different styles of newspaper writing (feature stories, editorials and regular columns, for example), this structure is still the standard for basic newswriting.

Key to the newspaper story is the lede, or first sentence. Writing a strong lede is a much-valued art in journalism: it encapsulates the story, sets the theme and draws the reader in. A story that lacks a good lede simply will not be read. Given that most newspapers contain about the same number of words as a novel, most readers skim the news, looking at interesting headlines and being drawn into the story if something catches their attention. The lede is thus essential to grabbing and holding the reader. (We will discuss how to write good ledes in much more detail in the section dealing with writing a news release; see Chapter 8).

Once written, a story may be scrutinized by as many as three editors: a section editor, such as the City Editor, a managing editor and a copy editor, who, in the rush to get a story into print, makes the final check for grammar, spelling and internal consistency. (At many smaller dailies and community newspapers, only one editor will review a story). A major news story may be reviewed by even more editors, including a lawyer if there is concern about defamation. A similar process occurs in television and radio. At large stations, such as CBC and Global TV, several editors will review a story, while only a single editor may approve an item on local radio and small TV stations.

The editor may challenge the story's facts, angle, conclusion or any other larger part of it; the copy editor is concerned with style, use of language and consistency. It is not uncommon for the editors to ask for a rewrite or simply do it themselves, which can cause some tension between reporter and editor (as we noted in Chapter 1, many reporters believe errors in their stories are the result of poor editing and inappropriate headlines). Once the story is through the editorial process, it is laid out on computer. Further changes may be made to the story as the layout technician tries to make it fit the allotted space. In layout, the story may receive a position of prominence or be buried, depending on what else is happening in the news and how much room is available on the page.

The final process is to add the headline, subheads, photos/artwork and captions. This step comes last because only at this point is the final physical configuration of a story known (e.g., one column with a two-line headline, four columns under one headline). The reporter sees nothing of his or her story after the final rewrite, although this rewrite may be at the last moment before deadline, depending on the importance of the story. (In general, feature stories, columns and recurring items are the first to be laid out; breaking news and sports pages tend to be last).

Reporting for Broadcast

In broadcast, the same journalistic structures are used, but the story is adapted to the ability to insert taped narrative and images. Normally, the reporter writes the story, then tapes his or her narration, inserting audio/video footage as appropriate. Given the difficulty of making changes, the broadcast reporter will discuss the shape of the story with an editor or producer in more detail than will the newspaper reporter, for whom change is easier. Once the story is complete, it will be scheduled into the broadcast; depending on the nature of the story and the other news of the day, it may be changed from the time the reporter finishes recording it. It may even be scrapped and the reporter will go to air live, in the event of late developments or breaking news.

The structure of the story prepared for television, however, tends to be distinct from that of a newspaper story. A study of the content of US network television news indicates a unique structure in the TV news story.[16] First, the television report begins outside the story, with a lead-in from the anchor desk. Writing this lead-in is the job of a writer or producer who, in assembling all the stories for broadcast, tries to sort them by theme, usually starting with predominant local stories, then broadening to regional, national and international news. The television reporter does not need to worry about the lede; it will be provided by the anchor. The reporter's story often begins with background to the story ("It all began when a group of housewives decided to build their own bomb shelter"), then turns to the supporting video clip ("Ruth Price was there").

A good broadcast story will contain at least two recorded interviews, and the reporter will lead into both, often acting as a mediator to explain the story; the TV reporter has a much more active, engaged role than the more distant, nearly anonymous newspaper reporter. Television reporters can use visuals to explain complex matters, as can newspaper reporters, but television reporters are more sensitive to the need for visuals; newspaper reporters often rely on a photographer to provide them.

A full story ends with a standup, so called because the reporter is filmed standing up, normally outside, delivering his or her conclusion. Unlike newspaper reporters, TV reporters conclude a report by either wrapping up the story ("an unfortunate outcome for the people involved") or leading into the next phase of the issue ("the hearing continues tomorrow"). Of course, this summary describes a major, 60–to 90–second television story. Many reports are simply interviews done with subjects, with explanatory narrative supplied by the anchor. A television reporter may work on several stories in a day, supplying information and video for the desk to sort out.

Fully 70 per cent of what appears on the screen in a television news story (apart from pictures of the reporter) is close-ups of people, usually the people providing the interviews.[17] This fact relates to the survey that showed that editors and reporters want to know about stories that affect people; people are the primary object of the television lens, in close-up. If you are looking for media coverage, a key issue for you to consider is how your story affects people, particularly the people who make up the audience of the media outlets you are soliciting for coverage. Visuals help; good, natural spokespeople who can speak to the issue clearly and passionately help even more. Whenever possible, communicators should handle interviews standing up, outside with the reporter, to appear on the same level of credibility with the reporter.

Radio reporters file stories somewhat differently. Except for CBC radio reporters, who are given more time to work on a story, most radio reporters may have half a dozen stories to file in a day to meet hourly broadcasts. Thus, radio reports tend to be quicker and simpler. Like television reporters, the lede to the story is supplied by an announcer, and the typical story (which is about 30 seconds long) focusses on explaining the issues and presenting a comment from an interview. (Of course, on-air hosts and talk-show contributors are allowed the luxury of exploring issues in greater depth. All media allow longer consideration of feature stories, and opportunities exist for extended, in-depth discussion on talk shows and documentaries). And just as television reporters look for great visuals, radio reporters search for great audio (e.g., leading into a labour dispute story with chants of "Strike! Strike! Strike!" before beginning the narrative).

This chapter has provided a quick overview of a typical media day. For more details of life at a daily newspaper, please see Chapter Seven, "A Day in the Life of a Newspaper," in *The Canadian Reporter*; for insight into the mechanics of getting a television broadcast on air, please see Chapter Five, "Behind the Scenes: Nuts and Bolts," in *How to Watch TV News* (see the bibliography for more details).

What the journalistic principles reviewed in this chapter mean for you as a communicator is that you can expect to receive positive media coverage as long as you understand it within the scope of newswriting. Positive does not mean supportive; it means that your story will be told accurately as long as you have the facts (preferably verified through a third party) to back it up. You can expect other views to be introduced, according to the concept of balance, and those views may be critical. If this kind of presentation is not to your liking, you should be looking at other means of communications. However, if your side of the story is accurately portrayed, if you tell your story well (and this is more your job than the reporter's) and if you have external verification for what you're doing, it shouldn't really matter what the opposition has to say.

As for you, who may be having a bad day trying to juggle a number of uncontrollable balls when the media call, please remember that your stress is matched by that of the reporter, who is experiencing a similar number of pressures. A small step toward civility, courtesy and human consideration on both sides can go a long way toward making the day, and the job, a little easier.

THE PRACTICE OF MEDIA RELATIONS

TWO

Getting Started: A Media Plan

6

Now that we have a basic understanding of how the media work, let's shift our focus from media to media relations.

Proactive and Reactive Media Relations

Practitioners tend to speak of two kinds of media relations: reactive and proactive. "Reactive" means waiting until the media call you, while "proactive" implies that you are more assertive and actively seek out media opportunities.[1] For example, a software developer trying hard to get her new software covered in the trade press is practising proactive media relations. If she's minding her own business when the local newspaper calls saying it's doing a feature on new startup businesses in the community, she is practising reactive media relations. In general, most practitioners prefer to work proactively, but in fact, both forms have their relative strengths and weaknesses.

Seeking out media attention is generally good for an organization; as we discussed earlier, you should practise media relations regularly to help build up skills and experience in it. Too often, however, the proactive approach means flooding the media with unnecessary news releases and non-newsworthy news conferences. On the other hand, a passive approach to reactive media relations often means that good opportunities to communicate are passed by. In its most literal sense, reactive media relations—having the media call you instead of you calling them—can be very successful and certainly worth your consideration if properly planned and managed.

A sample case

Let's look at proactive and reactive media relations in a real-life situation. I served as communications consultant at the Edmonton Board of Health from 1988 to 1993. The Board's business was the protection and promotion of public health through its health inspectors, public health nurses, nutritionists, dental and speech staff, and homecare workers. For more than a century, public health has worked with media, using them to advise the public of threats from communicable diseases ranging from the flu to hantavirus to AIDS to SARS.

I set up both a formal communications plan and a media plan. I looked at the organization's strategic goals and objectives and developed communications goals that supported the organization's goals. I studied the resources I currently had available as well as the history of the organization, which showed that, from the turn of the century, the media had been a good means of delivering health messages to the public. I researched media coverage, developed media policy and procedures, and got approval from the board to implement them, then designated media spokespeople, provided media training to them, sent out a list of our spokespeople to the media and looked for opportunities to get stories in the media. Over a year, I monitored print coverage of the board, analyzed it to see which of our issues the media were most interested in and examined whether the coverage was in fact helpful to the organization in meeting its strategic goals, particularly in the area of health education and promotion.

Over the next two years, media coverage of the board and its issues increased ten-fold, and almost all the coverage counted as positive (that is, fair and accurate). We monitored coverage through news clippings in the two dailies, the *Edmonton Sun* and *Edmonton Journal,* before and after the media program was established; our marker was simply any mention of the name "Board of Health." Before we undertook the media program, the papers ran an average of 35 stories a year on the board; within a year this number was up to 130, peaked two years later at 350, and settled into an average of 200 stories. Given the five (at the time) television stations and the fifteen or so radio stations, we estimated that annual coverage of the board in the Edmonton area was approximately twenty times the newspaper coverage. This increase in itself was excellent, but further analysis showed that news releases and news conferences (of which only one or two were held a year) accounted for only about fifteen per cent of these stories; the rest came through reactive media relations.[2]

The reactive media came simply because the board approved policies on how media relations would be handled. All management and approximately a third of staff were given media training, then contact names of experts in different disciplines (e.g., John O'Laney for information on landfills, Dr. Karen Grimsrud for information on AIDS) were sent to the media; business and after-hours phone numbers were also supplied. As the media realized they had good contacts in these and other select areas, they called the contacts directly, without going through the communications consultant. (Indeed, many Edmonton reporters weren't even aware that the board had a communications person, since they didn't need to work through me).

Over time, as reporters realized they could get reliable, accurate information, a solid relationship developed between the board and media, which in turn built on itself (reporters in a newsroom will share information with their colleagues on who is and is not a good source). As communications consultant, I would often find out about news coverage of the board by reading the morning papers. Because this aspect of communications largely took care of itself, I was able to get more involved in contentious media issues, such as labour negotiations and budget, and other communications activities, such as publications and advertising.

That being said, there nevertheless is a clear role in media relations for the proactive approach (chapters Eight and Nine go into considerable detail about a range of means for communicators to approach the media). In practice, most practitioners employ a combination of proactive and reactive media relations, having a plan in place to seek and get media coverage, while simultaneously ensuring that all media calls are answered promptly and properly, regardless of whether they are the type of calls their plan puts forward.

In either choice, planning is key to making a reactive, proactive or mixed media relations program successful.

Centralized versus decentralized media relations

A centralized media relations program has all media calls referred to one person, usually in the communications branch; a decentralized system lets the media approach whoever they wish. There are strengths and weaknesses in both.

The centralized system is clean and efficient, and lends itself to those types of organizations that are command and control in their corporate culture, such as the police/emergency departments or the military or many major corporations. It also lends itself to disaster situations, where the site may be closed to media and an emergency operations centre (EOC) set up, with a media component. One major disadvantage of centralized is that media prefer to go directly to the source, not through a communications person (45 per cent of Canadian reporters want to speak to a frontline person with no exceptions instead of a media relations person).[3] Furthermore, particularly during peak times, the centralized system can become a bottleneck, with calls from media either not returned or returned too late.

The decentralized system is more difficult to implement, but as the Board of Health example cited above shows, it can result in significant improvements in coverage. It meets the media's desire to talk directly to the frontline person, but requires co-operation from the organization and extensive training.

Like the proactive/reactive debate, often what results is a mixed system, in which large corporations may have some people who talk to investment/business media, others doing day to day work, and others specializing in crisis media. I do have a bias toward decentralized, since I've seen its effectiveness, but I've also worked in organizations where I was the one contact, because the organization was simply not ready at the frontline level to deal with media.

Before we get into the planning process, here is a final thought on the role of communications within any given bureaucracy (which includes the smaller but no less political bureaucracies of voluntary and community organizations).

One of reporters' major complaints against communicators is that they act as a barrier to gaining access to the organization. A survey of Ontario news editors by Brian Biggar showed that 71 per cent of editors agreed with the statement "Public relations practitioners often act as obstructionists, keeping reporters from the people they really should be seeing."[4] What reporters find difficult to understand—and what practitioners need to recognize—is that few organizations are good at dealing with anything other than their specific function. A mining company is designed to mine, a police department to police, a gardening society to garden and so on; within the context they were designed for, such bodies do their work well. However, anything outside that function may be difficult for the organization to respond to, and few organizations are designed to deal with media. As a result, an organization can come across as unresponsive, or even obstructive, when in fact it simply doesn't know how to deal with the media.

Let's go back to the Edmonton Board of Health as an example. Until the media plan was established, the organization tended to respond to media in an ad hoc manner. It wasn't that the Board was unresponsive; it simply didn't have the tools or expertise to deal with media. For example, shortly after I started, I saw a secretary throwing a phone message from a reporter into the wastebasket, along with the comment, "That's what you get for being rude." It took some time to get staff—particularly the receptionists—to realize that all reporters' calls were a priority and were to be referred to the appropriate spokesperson or to me. (It was also a revelation to me how important it was to ensure that the "answer all media calls" message went to the receptionists and support staff who were our first contact with the outside world).

To the Board of Health, the benefits of communication through the media were public health education and promotion: the public received information through the media that could help improve or preserve their health.

Practically, however, the board was looking for some demonstration that the attention being paid to the media was in fact useful. Once we started keeping statistics on media coverage and could show that the public was becoming better informed, the board began to see the benefits of a media relations program. However, this recognition took a couple of years.

For you as a practitioner, a key challenge is determining what your organization or client needs in terms of communications support, and then finding a way to meet those needs. The role of the media relations plan is to define the benefit to the organization and deliver measurable results. Planning is essential to your success.

Planning for a Media Event

As with all types of formal communications, to carry off a media event you must establish a plan. Different planning models exist for different purposes. Before looking at a comprehensive model for setting up a long-term media relations program, let's work through an exercise designed to help plan a one-time media event, be it a news conference, media stunt or simple news release.

The following model provides a simple example of planning for proactive media coverage. It is an eight-step process and can be accomplished quickly. Based on this model, your event plan will outline what you hope to achieve through your media efforts, how you will deal with the media and how you will know whether you've been successful.

1. Set a goal

Your goal is not to get media coverage; that is only a means to an end. What do you hope to achieve from media coverage? What will media coverage bring you? Will it get you more customers, increase awareness, bring in more contributions, clarify a misunderstanding, set the context for a public inquiry or simply exist for the record? Your reason for seeking coverage should be as measurable as possible, and the success of the enterprise must be related to the type and amount of media coverage you get.

For example, let's say you are looking to recruit volunteer drivers for a New Year's campaign to reduce the incidence of drunk driving. If you make media relations your total communications plan, at the end of the event you should be able to say you recruited X number of drivers thanks to media; better than that, you should be able to point to a reduction in drunk-driving charges and accidents. (You may not always be able to point to a direct cause-and-effect relationship between holding a media event and changing behaviour such as reducing the incidence of drunk driving. Such a campaign, in addition to news coverage for awareness, requires legislation to enforce the behaviour change, the co-operation of police to enforce the law aggressively and the willingness of courts to apply strong deterrent sentences). Notwithstanding these limits, an analysis of media coverage will give you an idea of what worked—and what didn't—and where you may want to go the next time.[5]

If, on the other hand, you are trying to boost sales by contributing to a community organization, you may get media attention, but if you don't see your sales increase, you have not met your goal (and maybe you need to rethink your sales and community relations programs).

You should always have a reason for dealing with the media, and in the case of planning a special media event, you should also have a purpose. If you don't have a reason to look for media coverage, don't expect reporters to give you one. Whether you get media attention is always a bit of a gamble, but you should be able to explain to your client, the media and yourself why you are seeking coverage.

2. Determine your key message

You should go into any media event knowing what to say and what your key message is. Ask yourself explicitly, What message do I want to communicate? You should be able to compress it to a few strong, simple words, e.g., "Don't drink and drive this holiday weekend," "Support our local poets," "Art is for everyone," "Give flowers for Christmas." Generally speaking, your message should relate to your goal; if you have difficulty expressing what your message is, you may need to reconsider how clear your goal is. Depending on what type of media coverage you hope to receive (e.g., extended feature or talk show coverage versus a quick, hard news item), you probably need only one message. Considering how brief a 30-second broadcast spot is, and knowing you will get only about eight seconds of that spot, you must have a message that fits a tight time frame. If your message is complex or needs amplification that media can't provide, you may need to consider other communications strategies.

3. Determine your key audience

Bearing in mind the media are a means to reaching an end—that is, your target audience—you must clearly define who you are trying to reach with your media coverage. The more narrowly defined your audience is, the more likely you are to reach it. You can define your audience by age, geographic area, income, buying habits, lifestyle and so forth, but you need to know clearly who you are trying to talk to.

4. Choose your media

Once you know *who* you're trying to reach, you must decide which media are best suited to reaching that audience. As Chapter 3 shows, you can choose among several different types of media, each aimed at different audiences; within these media are various opportunities for coverage. Choose the media most likely to reach your audience. It is perfectly reasonable to direct your efforts at the media outlets that will most likely be interested. For example, if you are targeting seniors, the media focussed on teens and young adults will be glad not to be bothered with your media request. Bear in mind, however, that once you have approached any media outlet with a story and the news breaks, you are in the public domain and other media may be interested in picking up the thread. It is your obligation to deal with their interest, even if they are not your preferred media.

5. Approach the media

We will discuss specific approaches to getting media attention in greater depth in chapters 8, 9 and 10. Basic approaches include news releases, news conferences, media stunts, tours, talk shows, sponsorships and public service announcements; these broad strokes can be considerably refined as you develop your skills and strategies. The point to bear in mind is that you are pitching your story to the media and therefore must demonstrate some benefit to them or their audience.

6. Do the interview and supply the information

This step forms the crux of the relationship with the media, and subsequent chapters are devoted to handling the media interview. No matter how well you have planned, no matter how much preparation and practice you have undertaken, if you cannot convince the reporter that what you are saying is newsworthy, it will not appear in the media.

7. Monitor and evaluate coverage

After the event is over, look at the coverage you received (if any) and analyze it. Did you reach the media you wanted to reach? Did your message get out? Was the coverage fair and accurate? Newspapers and magazines are easy enough to clip; many larger radio and television stations now post their stories on their websites, either in text or in video or audio (you may need special software to be able to access audio and video). Private companies (see Media Monitoring in the Yellow Pages) can provide news clippings and broadcast tapes if the story coverage is larger than your local area.

What are you looking for? Usually the big issue is whether the media got the key message and transmitted it clearly. Did they get the facts right, or is there a need for more clarification with some media? Are some reporters or outlets more interested in this item than others, and may there be more opportunities in the future, perhaps feature stories or editorials? How much interest was there: was your message front page/top of the news hour, or was it buried? What was the media tone: did they take the issue seriously, or was it more skeptical or light-hearted? A final question: based on the coverage, if you were to do the same thing again, what would you need to do differently to get your message out?

8. Evaluate your strategy

Did you achieve your goal? At this point, look back to what you intended to achieve at the beginning of this exercise, both for its own sake and to learn for future events. If you achieved your goal, try to determine whether it was directly related to media coverage or if another element in your communications plan was responsible for your success. If you didn't, try to determine why: was media a factor, or should you choose a different communications method the next time?

Long-term Planning

To establish a more formal, ongoing media relations plan, you require a different model, one that puts more emphasis on research and training, and on long-term results. Such a model forms the spine of the next several chapters. We will look at developing media policies and procedures, approaching media, undertaking media training, writing news releases, organizing media events and, most importantly, handling the media interview.

While it is certainly possible to practise media relations without a plan, planning forces both the practitioner and the client to think through the purposes for establishing a media relations program, and helps develop detailed options for managing media relations. The model presented in this book allows for further discussion of media relations; other practitioners may have different models, but most practitioners can point to some kind of plan behind their media relations.

Here is the nine-step planning process:

1. Conduct situation analysis and analyze business plan.

2. Set goals and get approval to develop a media program.

3. Research media coverage of you, your organization and your issue.

4. Develop media policies and procedures.

5. Get media training.

6. Approach the media.

7. Do the interview.

8. Evaluate coverage.

9. Revise and update the plan.

We will expand on each of these steps in subsequent chapters.

The First Steps: Research, Goals and Training

Media relations can sometimes be as simple as providing factual information to a reporter, in which the practitioner needs nothing more complicated than common sense.

This chapter, however, assumes you are making a more thoughtful, strategic and planned approach to media relations and preparing a business plan that outlines in some detail the reasons you are pursuing media relations (you may want to refer back to the first chapter on why you should or would want to practise media relations). Most of the elements discussed in this chapter are normal parts of any business or strategic planning: define the purpose of developing a media relations plan, research media coverage of your organization or issue, set goals and objectives, develop policy and procedures, provide training, implement, evaluate and revise. Later chapters will look at various options in reaching the media and dealing with them, but first you need to think through clearly why you are going down this road and what you hope to achieve from the journey.

The Situational Analysis

Before getting started with your media relations plan, you need to be able to answer one question: why are you proposing to use news media? To answer this question, you must conduct a situational analysis of your organization and its media needs.

In the private sector, the starting point for the analysis is the company's strategic plan, which every company should have (even small companies usually require a business plan to obtain bank or other financing). The strategic plan sets out overall goals and objectives and names targets for growth (e.g., increase sales by 10 per cent in the third quarter, capture 30 per cent of market share by the end of second year). Start your analysis of the organization's strategic plan with a broad question: how can communications help the company achieve its business goals? It may be that other communications activities, such as advertising, would be more effective (refer to the list, Alternatives to

Media, p. 11-14, for other means of communications). But if, after doing this exercise, it appears your best option is to use the news to help the company achieve its goals, then you can proceed to setting your media relations plan. Your communications goals will relate directly to the goals of the business plan (e.g., "Obtain wide media coverage of our product so that sales increase by 10 per cent in the third quarter.")

Non-profit organizations, volunteer groups and small businesses may not have formal strategic plans. However, they usually have a mission or vision statement and volunteer boards that carry corporate memory of the organization, its history and its communications needs. No matter how small the group, it should at the very least have a defined purpose for engaging with the media. A local 4-H club, for example, may send a summary of its monthly activities to the local newspaper because it wants to recruit more members and wants public recognition of the work of current members.

Whether or not your organization has a strategic plan, it is always helpful for a practitioner to conduct a situational analysis, to determine not only how but why media will help the organization achieve its goals. Another way of looking at the situation analysis is this: what problem would an effective media relations program solve?

One type of situation analysis is SWOT analysis (Strengths, Weaknesses, Opportunities, and Threats), which will look something like this:

Strengths: What are the strengths of our organization?

Weaknesses: What are our weaknesses?

Opportunities: What opportunities in the current environment can we exploit to build the business or help the organization achieve its goals?

Threats: What threats do we face, from rival companies/organizations or to changes in the economy or legislation?

Another type of situation analysis is the environmental scan, in which the business, social, economic, political or media spheres are analyzed to determine their potential impact on the organization. A survey for a member organization, such as a bar association or an advocacy group, might start with SWOT analysis, but then expand to survey members about their media expectations and tolerance, and to survey the public about their knowledge and attitudes toward the organization and its issues. Such an analysis would look at political issues that may affect the organization (such as proposed new legislation or regulation) and examine any legal restrictions on their ability to communicate. It could also include surveying other, similar organizations in other provinces, to find out what their media plans are like.

A situational analysis need not be complex. A situation analysis may be as brief as a few key paragraphs or may be a stand-alone document, contracted out to be performed by dedicated personnel. For example, *Situational Analysis: Fetal Alcohol Syndrome/Fetal Alcohol Effects and the Effects of Other Substance Use During Pregnancy* is a publication by Health Canada that summarizes the literature and research on the issue, programs by the provinces and a survey of those involved in FAS, asking for their thoughts on future directions to help the federal government develop programs and policies on the issue.[1] The third step (researching media coverage) allows for more in-depth research.

The situational analysis states the organization's situation clearly and identifies the problem to be researched. Here, for example, is Jell-O's situational analysis from its 100th-anniversary celebration:

> Sales of this famous dessert were flat. Brand research showed Jell-O, on the eve of its 100th anniversary celebration, was not top-of-mind with consumers who were moving to "newer" desserts. Research in company archives provided extensive historical information and graphics about the use and promotion of Jell-O through the years.[2]

Using a variety of promotional tools—advertising, a cookbook, a new flavour (champagne-flavoured Jell-O) and a gala event with spokesman Bill Cosby— Jell-O achieved its goal: a five-per cent increase in sales.

In all, the situational analysis will help define your purpose for media relations, which will serve as the basis for your media program.

Basic Planning

The next step is to get approval from your organization or client to undertake a media relations plan. Do this before you establish your communications goals. If in fact the organization is averse to the idea, or has other preferred means of communications, it's best to find this out before you undertake a great deal of effort. When it comes time to propose a media relations program, you must determine and present the reasons the organization should adopt a media plan (as discussed in Chapter 1) and what benefit the organization will achieve from it (looking back to your situational analysis).

Media is generally one component of a more comprehensive communications plan. Therefore, to help the media-planning exercise, be sure to refer back to the overall communications plan, if your organization or client has one. Your media plan should complement and support the overall communications plan: the goals, messages and audiences of the media relations plan must be consistent with those of the overall plan.

Setting goals or expectations for the media plan is part of the approval process. As with the event plan (see Chapter 6), your goal is not to get a certain amount of media coverage but rather to define what the organization hopes to achieve through its media relations. Remember, goals are broad statements of purpose (e.g., to ensure the public has accurate information about the organization). Objectives are more concrete and measurable (e.g., to increase the number of people attending an annual concert, to reduce the number of inappropriate calls to a call centre) and represent the specific steps you will take to achieve a certain goal. Objectives flow out of goals, while goals normally derive from an overall mission or vision.

So, for an organization such as a school district, the goal may be to use media relations as one means of promoting its evening and weekend programs. For a large corporation, the goal may be more focussed, such as helping the investor relations division to communicate with the investment community primarily through business media. For a non-profit organization, the goal may be to build community support around a particular issue or cause. Goals may also include concepts such as accountability (reporting an organization's activity to the general public or key audiences through the media). The goal for an organization that has gone through controversy, such as the Red Cross, may be to restore its credibility, as well as to define its new role and services. Goals organized around concepts are particularly applicable to government and government-funded agencies such as schools, health regions and universities. But the point of establishing goals remains the same: to define *why* you are dealing with the media and *what* you hope to gain from the experience.

As with the event plan, the two other components of communications planning are defining your audience and selecting key messages. The more narrowly defined your audience, the more likely you are to reach it; however, governments and national organizations may, of necessity, have a Canada-wide audience. As for messages, the fewer, the better. Such messages tend to be broad ("We provide health information to the public" or "Use our services"). As you work through objectives and events, your messages can become more focussed.

Communications planning is a subject worthy of its own attention, and you can pursue it in greater detail elsewhere.[3] For the sake of our discussion, I recommend you keep four points in mind:

- Keep your goals brief and clear
- Define achievable, reasonable objectives
- Define your audience as narrowly as possible
- Keep your message as brief and clear as possible

You will fill in specific details as you plan individual events, based on your purposeful, focussed media relations plan.

Once an organization opens itself to the media, it may invite media involvement in areas other than those specified in the plan. Be willing to be flexible when dealing with the media; don't be so tied to your plan that you deal with the media only when it suits you. If you want to develop solid, constructive relations with the media, you have to deal with them on many different types of issues, including some you didn't plan for when you started. Thus, when it comes to media planning, be organized enough to know what you're doing and why; and be flexible enough that you can roll with some unpredictable moments.

Research

Once you have received approval and developed a rationale for using media as a means of communications, you must examine how the media is currently covering you. This is called content analysis, a research technique used by social scientists since the 1930s and still used today by researchers to monitor social trends and issues.[4]

Academics may debate whether media act as a mirror, reflecting what society feels is important, or as a filter, directing what information will be released to society. Content analysis tends to straddle both theories: its first assumption is that media want to reflect what their audience is concerned about; but its second assumption is that media retain the option to direct society's attention to what editors feel are important social issues. Content analysis summarizes and analyzes the content of newspapers, counting what kinds of stories appear at what times and how they are treated. Among other things, it assumes there is limited space in a newspaper; when editors decide what to include and what to leave out, they help define and shape social issues and values. That is, these decisions are not wholly reflective but rather show a degree of personal and traditional preference.

For the practitioner, content analysis is fairly straightforward and can be tailored to individual or organizational needs. You can begin by simply looking at media coverage of your organization or issue over a period of time (I suggest at least six months), starting with newspaper coverage. You can find back issues of daily and weekly newspaper at your public library; provincial legislature libraries collect copies of all newspapers. Then you count the number of times your organization or issue appears, how much space you receive, what angle the media take, where you appear in the paper, whether the paper makes editorial opinion about you, the ratio of feature stories to hard news and so forth.

With this information in hand, you should have a picture of how the media cover you and a sense of what direction your media plan should take. The questions you need to ask to help inform and guide the development of a media plan are as follows:

1. Are the stories well informed, or are there gaps that the media plan has to fill?

2. How high you are on the media's priority list (judged by the prominence and frequency of their coverage)? Will the media plan need to focus on getting media attention in the first place, or is it an issue of having your message accurately represented in the existing coverage?

3. Are there some media outlets that provide better coverage of your issue that you want to develop a closer relationship with? Are there some outlets that are hostile or indifferent, that you will need to approach differently when you seek coverage?

4. Is the media's coverage of your issue fair and balanced, or does it tend to come down on one side of the issue? (Notwithstanding their goal of objectivity and balance, media coverage can be biased). If so, what side are they coming down on with your issue? Is that what you want to have presented?

Thanks to the Internet, you can undertake the same process with radio and television stories, since major stations not only post but archive their daily news stories; stories can be easily searched by name or issue. (Researchers can use the same databases reporters use; see Chapter 5 for some websites on which you can begin a search). New technologies and software programs are always in development. One good place to check the latest and easiest software to search for news stories is with the library of your local university or college, which keeps abreast of this kind of technology.

Content analysis is part of the overall research you may want to conduct as part of the initial preparation of a media relations plan. You should also research your target audience for their demographic characteristics (age, income, education, location, etc.), for their knowledge and awareness of your organization and issues, and for their news media preferences.

For basic demographics, you can either conduct your own research or look at available data. Statistics Canada collects and analyzes mountains of data, which is available (sometimes for a price, sometimes at no cost, depending on the information being sought) in hard copy, disk or on the Internet (www.statscan.ca). Public libraries will also have Stats Can reports and data at no cost, usually through the reference desk. You can also undertake your own research, through public-opinion polling. Such polling can range anywhere from a few hundred dollars to buy a question in regular (omnibus) polls that most private research companies conduct, to more comprehensive and dedicated polling that can run into six figures. Such polls are usually done by telephone; you can also conduct written surveys with clients or other key groups that you can reach by mail.

Focus groups are a common research tool these days, in which small groups (six to ten) of the target audience are brought together for a focussed (hence the name) but non-directed discussion of your organization and your issue. Focus groups are valuable for bringing forward emotional responses; surveys provide statistically supportive data (e.g., 25 per cent of our target market has never heard of our product, and they are primarily from rural areas). Companies can charge $2,000 to $5,000 per group, depending on how complex the information being sought is and how difficult it is to get the group together. When resources permit, focus groups should be held first to get some insight into the target market, followed by polling to verify if those responses are common within the target market (one of the drawbacks of focus groups is that group dynamics sometimes provide misleading information).

For your target audience's news and media preferences, you can again conduct your own research or you can check the marketing demographics of the media themselves (refer to Chapter 4 for a discussion of how media target their preferred audiences). If you want to go into more detail, consult a media directory (such as the Matthews Media Directories) or contact a media monitoring agency. Advertisers use media monitors to determine when and where to place their ads.

There are four basic monitors:

- NADBank (Newspaper Audience Databank), which provides summaries of newspaper readership, demographics, shopping behaviour and household income;
- PMB (Print Measurement Bureau), which analyzes magazine readership;
- BBM (Bureau of Broadcast Measurement), which summarizes listenership to radio stations, broken down into 15-minute segments;

· NBI (Nielsen Broadcasting Index), which provides viewership data for television.[5]

These are commercial services of mainstream media. Data on new and alternate media are harder to come by. Some mainstream media, such as BBM and NBI, release their data through the media after every survey. A good advertising or marketing agency should be able to provide you with a summary of your audience's key media preferences, for a fee.

In addition to hard data, you can also find research on psychosocial aspects of your target audience. For example, Canadian studies have shown that seniors consider themselves to be 10 years younger than their chronological age and want to be perceived as such. Such a fact is important for marketers to know. Here's another example. A cover story in *BusinessWeek* examines the sometimes surprising spending habits and attitudes of the baby-boomer generation. The boomer generation is a significant player in the market place, more willing to try new things than their twenty-something counterparts and with stable careers and money to spend, they are not a segment to ignore.[6]

Information like this leads down many paths. For example, knowing that boomers are willing to try new things may affect how you present material to them.

You can get this kind of information either through the library or from a search on the Internet; or, if you have the resources, you can commission psychosocial research through a firm like Ipsos Reid.

Once you've done this and whatever other research you feel will be helpful, summarize it and include it in your media plan. This information will help colleagues and superiors better understand how the media are dealing with the organization's issues. Then go back to your initial goals, audiences and messages. Check them against your research and revise as necessary. For example, your goal may be to ensure your target audience has accurate information about your issue presented through the media. However, your media research may indicate that media are providing inaccurate information. In such a case, you must check where else your targets get their information and try to provide more accurate information through that channel. This realization might also mean abandoning, or at least reducing, your reliance on media as a communications method, which is why you must work through the media plan in concert with an overall communications plan.

Once you have finished this stage and have a clear understanding of what you're trying to do and why you're trying to do it, you need to establish some basic ground rules for dealing with the media, otherwise known as policies and procedures.

Policies and Procedures

A policy states what you intend to do and why; procedures outline how you conduct your policy. Policy can be brief or complex, depending on the organization and its issues and values. The media policy of the Edmonton Board of Health was succinct:

> EBH shall continue its policy of co-operation and accessibility to the media in Edmonton, consistent with EBH policy on client confidentiality, labour/staff relationships, budget and legal issues.[7]

The general intent of this policy was co-operation and accessibility. The "why" was tacit: as a public body, funded to perform a public service, the board did not need to state that the organization was accountable for its actions. Exceptions to the overall policy were noted. In some areas the board was under legal restriction; in others (such as budget and labour) it chose to hold items more closely. Later, a clarification was added: "Incidents of communicable disease outbreaks or environmental health issues should not be commented on until the investigation is complete. At that time, staff may talk to media about the incident."

There is nothing magic about policy. Continuing with our example, some public health agencies in Canada do comment on investigations in progress. The point is that thought has been given to how this specific organization deals with the media, so that everyone in the organization has standard guidelines to follow and refer to.

Policy can certainly be more complex. For example, the federal government's overall communications policy is 56 pages long (English and French) and outlines philosophy, defines the communication function, outlines the various roles of ministers and the Privy Council Office, speaks to the use of both official languages and outlines advertising, polling and other communications issues.[8] The media portion (Sec 4.7.2 Media Inquiries) of the federal policy reads as follows:

> Enquiries from the media should normally be directed to the designated spokesperson for the particular subject. Designated spokespersons are restricted to discussing matters of fact or already approved government policy in an open, on-the-record basis. Off-the-record background briefings or interviews are only permitted in exceptional circumstances and are subject to prior ministerial approval. All speculation and questions on proposed policy should be directed to the minister.[9]

Note that this policy applies to the civil service, not the political level. MPs and ministers can speculate, argue, opinionate, go off the record, leak or do whatever they feel, within the bounds of party discipline. Nevertheless, the federal civil service (and its provincial and municipal counterparts) has guidelines that stake out clear limits in dealing with the media.

Along with policy often come procedures, which provide the detail for how policy will be delivered. In media relations, procedures may include who the designated spokesperson is and what areas that person is authorized to speak on. The federal policy above leaves that decision unstated: individual departments develop their own procedures according to their needs and issues to determine who will be spokespersons. The same would be true in the private sector. A large chemical company, for example, may have one spokesperson for emergencies who is well versed in chemical risk and management, while a different spokesperson addresses investor issues with the business media. There is no rule for numbers of spokespersons; they can range from a single, central source to 10 pages of highly specialized, widely scattered experts. Universities have been a long-standing source for reporters and were very quick to capitalize on the Internet by putting their contacts, along with their areas of expertise and phone numbers, on their websites (e.g., Professor P. Parker, northern rural economics; Professor I. Jones, sub-Saharan agriculture). Most universities have a media room on their websites to make it easier for reporters to reach their contacts.

Another common procedures issue is approval. Some organizations want all media contacts to be approved by the CEO before they happen. Others distinguish between routine media contacts that do not require executive sign-off (e.g., how many pounds of potatoes PEI produces in a year) and more contentious, higher-profile issues that the executive wants to be a part of (e.g., whether PEI should retaliate against a US embargo on potatoes).

An important procedural consideration is ensuring all media calls are answered. Particularly in large or volunteer-run organizations, this can be an issue. People who answer the telephone must know what to do when the media call: not only whom the call can be transferred to, but where to send the call in the event that the designated spokesperson is not available. Media calls must not be parked in voice mail. You may need to explain explicitly to any staff that take media calls that they are to ensure these calls are returned. When recording voice mail greetings, designated spokespeople must leave a number where they can be reached or have an option (e.g., "Press zero for immediate assistance") to ensure that media calls are taken by someone who understands their importance.

A possible procedure to develop is recording media contacts and monitoring media. At some point, your media coverage will need to be evaluated. To do so, you must either monitor and collect all media coverage or develop a media contact report system (a form on which the reporter's name, outlet, issue and result of contact is recorded). Media contact reports are more usual in large organizations, which have the resources to develop, file and organize a set of contact reports; smaller organizations may simply need to collect clippings.[10]

When an organization starts developing procedures for dealing with media, it automatically gets into the issue of whether its media relations will be handled centrally or in a decentralized manner.

Centralized versus decentralized

The two major styles of media relations are either to centralize it through one office or person, or to decentralize it among a variety of specialists. Both styles have their advantages and disadvantages. Practitioners often meld the two styles, adapting as appropriate to the organization or circumstance. For example, during a series of illegal health-care strikes in Edmonton in 1997, the typically centralized media operations of the Capital Health Authority became decentralized, with media spokespersons at the bargaining table, in the front lines of hospitals and at Labour Relations Board hearings. The communicators kept in touch with each other primarily by cell phone as events developed on the various fronts.

The advantage of a centralized function is that it allows for co-ordination. Traditional bureaucracies are comfortable with this kind of command and control. Having centralized communications also provides media with a single access point from which they can expect to get an answer. Members of the media are often not aware of who to call for comment in a large organization, and a good deal of a reporter's time is spent making multiple phone calls to find someone who can comment on their story. A single point of contact gives them initial access to a source, someone who can, it is to be expected, steer them in the right direction.

The disadvantage, particularly during peak periods, is that media offices can become overstrained. In this case, they end up acting as a bottleneck instead of an access point for media, thus buttressing media perception that public relations people act as obstructionists rather than facilitators.[11] Another disadvantage, from the communicator's point of view, is that a good deal of time can be wasted on routine issues that are better handled at the source. For example, a call on how many pounds of potatoes PEI produces in a year might go to the research office to be dealt with directly instead of a media officer taking the message, contacting the research office and calling the reporter back.

The decentralized system puts the reporter in direct contact with the source. (Of course, we presume that the media know who the best source is, but that knowledge can be developed through regular communications with the media). In order to establish such a system, it is particularly important that clear policies and procedures be in place and that all contacts receive media training. However, with these precautions in place, decentralized media relations can be highly effective in enabling an organization and its staff to be a reliable source for media.

The disadvantage to a decentralized system is that occasionally the media office will be out of the loop, although this is more a matter of comfort than risk: a well-trained staffer will advise the media office when the organization has been contacted by the media. A more important drawback to a decentralized system is that it takes time to set up, and the practitioner must ensure the system is maintained as staff and issues change. Having worked in both situations, I am biased in favour of a decentralized system, keeping the media office as back-up in case of major issues or staff absences. The major reason is that media prefer to speak to frontline staff, and will often refuse to speak to anyone else. Forty-five per cent of Canadian reporters want to speak to a frontline person instead of a media relations person.[12]

The key issue to both systems is that the media be able to access them. An Angus Reid survey asked media what constituted poor media relations. The biggest response by far was lack of accessibility (69 per cent of respondents), which included evasiveness/stonewalling (38 per cent); inaccessible/unavailable contacts (10 per cent); unreturned phone calls (6 per cent); and slow responses (3 per cent).[13]

The next step in developing the media plan is getting media training for spokespeople, which will include training on the organization's policies and procedures for dealing with media and the purpose of the media plan.

Media Training

Media training is highly recommended for any media spokesperson, whether a novice or a veteran. In-house communicators can provide media training, if they have media experience, or training can be provided by outside consultants. (A number of media and advertising agencies offer media training, as do some community colleges and university workshops).

The typical media-training package will be a one- or two-day seminar that includes media theory and practice (such as this book contains). It should also include an examination of the organization's media policies and procedures and should provide some background on how the media currently perceives the organization or its issues. (You will have obtained this information through your research in developing the media plan). Good training will include mock interviews (on camera) with selected spokespersons, conducted by the trainer, which will then be played back to the spokespersons and critiqued for improvement (this can be done in a group or individually). The interview topic, which should be discussed beforehand, should be the area the spokespeople will be commenting on or the major issues facing the organization.

Mock interviews should be handled with care. Interview subjects are highly stressed, sometimes even traumatized; most reporters are not sensitive to this fact. Reporters, who conduct dozens of interviews or discussions in a day, are inured to the experience and often overlook the fact that few people outside politicians have the same comfort level with an interview they do. For most people, a media interview is on a level with a job interview, public speaking or defending a thesis—that is, among the most fearful undertakings imaginable. A good media trainer will recognize the subject's stress, provide a real-life media experience but not attack or degrade the subject to the point that he or she doesn't want to do media or is intimidated or humiliated by it. The purpose of media training is to give spokespeople the skills and attitudes that will make them good representatives for the organization and for the media. You want to build them up, not tear them down.

If you offer the training in-house, you must have a media background or extensive dealings with media; otherwise, hire a trainer. There are companies that provide media training (look in the Yellow Pages under Public Relations or Advertising). There are also community agencies that provide low-cost or no-cost assistance to like-minded advocacy groups, particularly those dealing with environmental and health issues.

I do not recommend hiring working reporters as media trainers, although some companies have them as part of a team working with communications professionals. Generally speaking, reporters are very good at what media want from spokespersons, and they understand how the news works. Fundamentally, though, the media want people who will fit their agenda, which is not necessarily yours. For example, we have seen that conflict makes good media, and reporters encourage direct, sometimes confrontational, language. Your agenda may not include that. In the best of all possible worlds, you should deal with the media to further your issue and your agenda, not simply to provide a quick sound bite that will make for easy journalism.

If you hire an outside media trainer, you should follow some basic guidelines.[14] First, do a reference check, particularly on the persons who will be performing the hands-on training. Find out their experience in media and their preferred training style—particularly how they handle the interview subject. Ask whether they can mock up different interview situations, such as the scrum, feature, live television, open mic and so on. Teaching or publishing experience helps, as does specific experience in media relations with your business or issue.

Some media trainers specialize in particular areas, such government and political issues, health and the environment. Your trainer should know your business and the issues you deal with; if not, he or she should do the necessary research. However, that research will cost time and money, and likely won't result in a good "feel" for your organization. You need to weigh your options carefully.

Determine whether the trainer's style fits your needs, issues and organizational culture. For example, if you are preparing for highly politicized public hearings on which your business depends and which you know will be high profile and contentious, you will want a politically savvy, tough-minded trainer who can offer support in other areas such as testifying and lobbying. On the other hand, if you are a non-profit group with a less confrontational style and more basic media needs, you will want someone lower-key who understands your values and concerns.

Check out the handouts the trainer intends to give participants. You should be allowed to see them but don't expect the trainer to give them to you: these materials are part of their business and the service they charge for. Handouts can range from copies of overheads to manuals; quantity doesn't matter much as quality.

Finally, check out the fee structure and what it covers. You can lower your costs considerably by sharing your research and the policies and procedures you have developed, but do expect the trainer to charge for preparation time. Also expect the trainer to ask some basic questions: what are your media needs and issues, will this be generic training or focussed on a particular issue? Give extra points to companies who ask for personality profiles of the interview subjects and who ask for briefing before they conduct training.

Costs depend on services purchased and the amount of time a company invests in providing the service. Fees can range from as little as nothing (from a company willing to do *pro bono* work) to $150 (a typical one-day university or college workshop) to $500 a day (generic training for non-profits) to $5,000 a day (high-profile, customized workshops). You can also expect to pay much more if you have a very ugly and very high-profile issue that requires extensive media consultation. For example, when Mulroney received his settlement from the federal government in the Airbus case, it included $587,721 in fees to his public-relations consultant. Judge Gold's decision on the value of this consultation was stated as follows:

> I have no doubt that if the claimant [Mulroney] had not received the [PR] services rendered ... he would have been at great disadvantage in the prosecution of his suit and unable to meet the defendant's case on many of the issues.[15]

Here's hoping you won't have to deal with the same type of issue Mulroney did. But if you are going to be dealing with media in any fashion, you must be prepared and you may need to seek professional advice.

Approaching the Media: Media Drivers and the News Release

8

After so much preparation, it is now time to look at actually approaching the media. We'll begin with a brief discussion of key media—the media that tend to drive all other media coverage—then make a closer examination of all the different ways there are to practise media relations.

Media Drivers

Overall media coverage tends to be heavily influenced by two key media. If you can get coverage from these two outlets, which I call media drivers, a story running in them will very likely generate other media to replicate or follow that story in their own medium.

The first media driver is Canadian Press (CP). As we have already discussed, CP is a co-operative news agency, to which members contribute news and which generates its own news. CP has a high degree of credibility among other media, and stories running with the CP byline will be automatically picked up and broadcast by other media, particularly subscriber media. Since most media outlets carry a good deal of wire copy in their pages and on their broadcasts, having CP carry your story ensures wide distribution.

The second media driver is the local daily newspaper (weeklies in communities that don't have dailies). As we discussed in Chapter 5, one of the major sources of news stories for broadcast media is the daily newspaper. At understaffed commercial radio stations, editors will often take a story from the daily, rewrite it for broadcast and air it, largely unchanged from the way it appeared in the paper (this practice is called "rip and read" journalism). In television, and to a lesser degree radio, reporters will be assigned to follow up on the story, which usually means more interviews and a search for new angles in the story. A good deal of morning radio coverage is driven off the front page of the morning daily news coverage, and often the six o'clock local television news follows the lead of the morning newspaper.

The importance of the daily newspaper, in particular, seems to have been lost with the attention given to television news and, to a lesser extent, the Internet. Television and the Internet are often described as "new" media replacing older media such as newspapers.[1] However, research indicates that newspapers, not television, are the public's main source of routine news. In one American survey (1994), adults indicated that 70 per cent read a newspaper regularly, while only 35 per cent viewed a television newscast regularly (29 per cent watch sometimes).[2] This trend is even more tilted towards newspapers than an earlier study, which concluded that an "equal proportion of the population [is] reading newspapers and watching television news on a typical evening."[3] The future of mainstream media like newspapers versus new media will be discussed in Chapter 16.

In any case, when a story appears on CP or in the local daily, it is likely to be widely disseminated. If that is the goal of your media relations efforts, then you should concentrate on getting into those media. Don't try to schmooze or cajole them into covering you: your story must have legitimate news value. If it doesn't, don't bother them with it; editors get irritated and react against attempts to pass off PR as newsworthy when it is not (see Chapter 5).

The News Release

The oldest (first used in 1907) and most reliable way to reach the media is through the news release;[4] it is also, strangely, the most reviled—but more about that later. The news release is sometimes called a "media release" but never a "press release;" "press" refers to print media, and broadcast media have been known to discard "press releases" as an indication the sender is clueless about media relations. The news release is generally the most reliable type of media outreach since it forms the source of many, if not most, news stories.

Biggar summarizes extensive research indicating how often the media rely on news releases for their stories:

> The frequent use journalists make of PR materials and sources is well documented. In 1927, for example, a writer for the American Mercury reported that of 64 local news items in one edition of a New York daily newspaper, "42 were rewritten or pasted up from material sent in by press agents." ... In 1962, Scott Cutlip reported that some 35 per cent of the content of American newspapers comes from PR sources .... Seven years later, a content analysis of newspapers in six Canadian cities, coupled with interviews of news reporters and university information officers (i.e., university public relations officers), found that "newsmen acknowledged that information officers provided substantial quantities of useful information that the newspaper could not or would not

gather on its own." ... Another study of the influence of public relations on news coverage estimated that about 40 per cent of news on the environment came from public relations practitioners. Moreover, about 20 per cent of the stories consisted simply of rewritten press releases .... A 1979 study of six major Canadian daily newspapers found that 14 per cent of all editorial items had public relations input .... In a study conducted in 1984, another researcher found that about half of the information provided by PR officers at six state government agencies in Louisiana was used in news stories subsequently published by eight daily newspapers in that state .... These examples underscore how the two sides have come to depend on one another. They also, perhaps, give credence to the complaints of writers like Nelson, who argues that the media complacently accept and report PR-generated news stories, to the detriment of the public interest.[5]

New technology notwithstanding, the major point of contact between the practitioner of media relations and the media themselves is the news release, and so this section will address the preparation of the news release in some detail.

The news release is one of the most reviled forms of reaching the media, from the media's point of view, since they are swamped by them and see more bad or inappropriate ones than useful ones. The average editor/producer sees about 335 news releases a week, or 67 a day.[6] This is in addition to the stream of news releases they get from Canada Newswire and Marketwire, as well as a large daily volume of Canadian Press wire copy. For example, the Angus Reid survey of news editors showed, of the deluge of news releases that comes across their desk, only 13 per cent are considered useful.[7] As low as this figure seems, it is actually higher than the findings of other studies, which report a use rate of only three to eight per cent of news releases.[8]

The reasons that so many news releases are rejected deserve some attention. The Angus Reid survey showed that 18 per cent of news releases were rejected for being too long, 11 per cent for being too numerous (that is, too many, too frequent releases from a single source), 11 per cent because contacts (given in the news release) were unavailable and 10 per cent because they were poorly written. On the other hand, a US study of news releases used by select Oklahoma newspapers in 1986 showed that those that were successful related to coming events, timely topics, consumer information and research articles.[9] Unsuccessful releases fell into the categories of past events, features and "brag" stories, and puffing up the institution instead of providing usable information or news.

This information leads to a point both the practitioner and the client must understand if the news release is to be used: the information must be newsworthy, not glorified advertising. As one practitioner put it,

> Never think of publicity as advertising. A straight sales angle will instantly doom your attempt as far as the media are concerned. Instead, strive for journalistic merit, endowing your promotional activity with the timeliness of a news event or the warmth and human interest of a feature story.[10]

Research indicates media are receptive to news releases that embody reader service and have high impact or that are timely, targeted and on the wire services.[11]

Once you have determined a topic and an approach that is newsworthy, you need to write the release in a manner that a news editor will accept. Noting that one of the reasons editors reject news releases is because they are too long, keep your news release to a single double-spaced page. You can add additional pages as background material, but the news should be brief and immediately apparent to the news editor. The release should also be written in news style, and special attention should be placed on the lead sentence, since most editors only glance at the news release and do not read it thoroughly.

One final thought about a news release: if used, it will rarely be used verbatim. The real purpose of a news release is to get the media's attention and prompt a reporter to call you or the contact for more information. In that sense, a news release is more like a tipsheet than a story, tipping the media off to a good story. To get that attention, a good news release will focus on the introductory sentence to the release, which will summarize why this story idea is newsworthy. Reporters put a great deal of creative time into the lead sentence, so when it's your turn to do the writing, the lede merits special attention.

The Lede

The lede is the first sentence in the news release or story. It must engage the reader's interest and motivate him or her to read the rest of the story. From a media perspective, there are a number of standard types of ledes. Matching your lead to these templates will help get your news release read.[12]

The summary lede

The summary lede gives a succinct summary of the situation and is the most common type of lede for straightforward, factual news (e.g., "Profits are up 82 per cent at Widget Corp this year," "10,000 protesters will picket the ABC nuclear plant tomorrow," "Researchers have discovered a new strain of the *E. coli* virus)." This type of lede is most common in hard news stories, when the novelty or drama of the event is such that a straightforward sentence can describe the newsworthiness of the story.

The question lede

One way to lead into more complex and contentious issues is through a rhetorical question, followed by an amplifying or explanatory sentence. Here are two examples: "Is Alberta's new health care plan a Trojan Horse for privatization? That's the question Alberta doctors will debate at their annual convention later this week..." and "How far will the new Premier take BC with the massive electoral victory he has achieved?" This type of lead is often used in analytical writing, long after the newsworthiness of the event (such as the case of the BC election) has ceased to be news. However, you must take care the question isn't too arch or arcane for a busy editor to understand immediately.

Teasers

Again, beware of excessive archness or cuteness that will "zing" your news release, with appropriately colourful language directed at you and your organization. Here is a successful teaser: "Everyone in Ourtown is an heir to the ancient estates of Earl Gray of Mayo."

The quotation lede

Leading with a quotation can be difficult and requires some skill. You need a good, attention-grabbing quote that can neatly summarize a complex situation in a few words. In the news release, a quote will often be inserted in italics under a headline (which explains to the editor what the story is about) and before the lead. It might look something like this, for example:

Company hauled before Labour Relations Board
"This is 19th century big-boss capitalism at its worst!" Frodo Fizwick

The International Guild of Woodworkers, Carvers and Elves today launched a formal complaint before the Nunavut Labour Relations Board, charging employer Santa Claus with 67 violations of the Labour Code, including no overtime for Christmas.

Direct-address lede

A direct-address lede in a news story would read something like this: "You may not want to read this while you're eating in a fine restaurant." Since the "you" in a news release is an editor, your version of this technique would have to specify who the "you" is, e.g., "Diners don't want to know what is going on in kitchens while they're eating, says the local health inspector."

Astonisher/shocker lede

This form of lede assumes you do in fact have something astonishing to say. If you don't, don't irritate the media with non-news. Here's an example of shocker lede that works: "The man who successfully challenged Microsoft's dominance in the compressed-data software market began his business in his mother's garage in Ourtown."

Flash-by lede

This kind of lede is used to summarize a number of newsworthy events, e.g., "Saturday's sudden snowstorm caused 200 fender benders, 150 cancelled flights, 2,000 calls for tow trucks and 35 minor injuries, but spared the city any deaths." From a news release perspective, it is not necessary to even write a lede or story for this kind of statistical summary. You can send out an update or fact sheet that might encapsulate the same information as shown at the top of page 107. You could also put this kind of information on a website and update it regularly.

The examples you've just worked through are the typical ledes taught to journalism students. It is equally important for you to understand, and avoid, the pitfalls of bad ledes. Most of these examples are marred by the same problem: poor writing.

Cluttered

"Too long" was cited in the Angus Reid survey as another reason for rejecting a news release, and this criticism applies to the lede as well. The lede should be succinct and interesting. You can handle the five W's and an H (or two H's) in the rest of the release or in an attached backgrounder; don't attempt to put so much information in the lede that it becomes cluttered. Here's an example of a cluttered lede: "The XYZ Food Services Company Inc., famed for its bottomless cup of coffee and twice recipient of the coveted Copper Kettle Award, announced today from its headquarters in Ourtown a new concept in food service that will revolutionize the industry, using thermal technology to keep hot food hot and cold food cold while out on the golf course." Somewhere in that sentence lives a promising lede, such as, "Golfers will be able to get a full meal while out on the links, thanks to ...."

UPDATE: Saturday snowstorm

RELEASE: 11:00 a.m. Sunday

MINOR VEHICLE ACCIDENTS: 200.

MAJOR VEHICLE ACCIDENTS: none.

MINOR INJURIES (NOT REQUIRING OVERNIGHT HOSPITAL STAY): 35.

SERIOUS INJURIES: none.

FATALITIES: none.

CANCELLED FLIGHTS, AIRPORT: 150 (airport opened 7 a.m. this morning,
all flights now on schedule).

TOW CALLS: 2000.

NEXT UPDATE: 2 p.m.; if no new development after that, we will
discontinue updates.

MEDIA CONTACT: Bob Smith

EMERGENCY RESPONSE OFFICE: 555–1212

Cute

As we discussed earlier, unless you are pitching to a medium that encourages cuteness (magazines/columns about new babies, teen magazines about the latest idol, talk shows with an emphasis on fun and humour), don't bother with trying to be cute in the lede. Just spit out the news so the editor doesn't have to search for it.

Vague

Normal business-writing practices don't apply to writing news releases. Be clear and direct about what you're pitching. Typically, a club secretary will write something like "The annual meeting of the uptown Elks will be held tomorrow afternoon, featuring a special speaker in addition to the election of officers." Such a lede is wordy, uninteresting and vague. If the speaker is special, he or she deserves to be highlighted: "Canadian astronaut Roberta Bondar will be the featured speaker at the uptown Elks tomorrow afternoon. Ms. Bondar's topic is 'Soft Landing: Life after Orbit.'"

Hype and cliché

Some words should be expunged from your vocabulary, on the grounds that the media are expunging them from theirs. Business editors are deluged with news releases that use the same language to describe business achievements, no matter what the business does. Surveys of business editors show that they discard incoming messages that contain the following business clichés: best, first, first mover, leading, leading edge, solutions, end-to-end, cutting edge, customer-centric and mission critical.[13] E-mail filters track and kill messages based on subject line; they can also automatically trash messages from PR/advertising/communications firms that consistently overhype stories. Instead, as one study noted, "The editors collectively issued challenges to communicate with clarity about what companies really sell, then provide ongoing data or other proof of any claim to superiority or leadership."[14]

Bureaucratic language and jargon

Don't fall prey to bureaucratese! Always bear in mind that mainstream media write at about the grade 8 level, and few people in the public are as technically versed in an issue as the people who manage it. A news story is written for the layperson, not the expert, and a news release must be written in the same style. Here's an example of a bureaucratically written news release:

> The bargaining agent for the province's acute, long-term, psychiatric and rehabilitation facilities today announced it will be petitioning the government for essential position designation in the event of labour disruption or work stoppage during the upcoming collective agreement negotiations.

There are a number of bureaucratisms in this sentence that would make it a stopper for the media and the public alike. To make this release more intelligible, use the actual name of the agency and adopt more commonly understood language ("essential services" instead of "essential position designation" and "strike" instead of "labour disruption or work stoppage"). Here's the same lede, written with less jargon:

> The provincial hospital association is demanding the provincial government declare emergency and other key health services as essential, in the event of a strike by the provincial nurses' union if contract negotiations break down.

The rewrite is not as technically accurate, particularly in a legal sense, as the first example; however, it is more meaningful to the lay reader. You must be sensitive to maintaining accuracy while simplifying, first so as not to mislead media or the public, and second because news releases are public documents and can be used as legal evidence. The messages in a news release and other media and public statements must be consistent with other messages that may be used in courts, hearings or tribunals. There is room for tailoring the message for different parties so that they can understand it, but the essential content of the message must remain the same.[15]

Passive

Active sentences tell us who is doing what. Passive sentences tell us what has been done (sometimes by whom). Editors find passive sentences boring. Editors want stories about people, and stories written in the active voice emphasize the *who* of a story rather than the outcome. For example, here is a passive lede: "A motion was passed by City Council approving reduced transit fares for seniors." The focus is on the motion, while the agents who caused the action and the people who will be affected by it are referred to only indirectly. Written in the active voice, the sentence translates to "City Council approved reduced transit rates for seniors." While that is better, it still doesn't go as far as it could. A further, thoughtful rewrite creates this sentence: "Seniors will pay lower bus fares thanks to a Council decision last night."

From the communicator's point of view, this last example demonstrates an especially successful strategy for getting media attention: audience benefit. Seniors benefit because of the decision. Simply changing the sentence to the active voice gave Council credit for its decision, leaving a lede too close to a "brag" release, which media hate (and which politicians, unfortunately, love). Putting the focus on seniors makes the release more media friendly and newsworthy. Such a strategy is even more effective if the media you are sending to have seniors in their audience. This point gets back to defining your target audience, writing information of interest and value to them, and targeting your release to media who reach the audience you are trying to find.

"Benefit to audience" is a major selling point of a news release, although you should bear in mind that not all effects are beneficial. If your action has an effect on an audience that is not positive, don't try to spin it that way. If, in our example, City Council had not provided a special fare for seniors, the release from the city might have read thus: "Seniors did not receive a further discount on transit fares, after Council decided last night that the city budget could not afford it." This still puts the effect on audience first and foremost, and gives a reason for the decision; it is much more honest than an attempt to spin a positive benefit out of it, such as this: "Seniors will get a boost to their cardiovascular systems, thanks to a Council decision that encourages them to get more exercise by walking than by taking the bus."

Format

With a good lede, most of the rest of the news release is straightforward. You should address two key questions in a news release (the media will ask you anyway): what are you doing and why are you doing it? Depending on your issue, the answer to either question might be your lede, but the answers to both questions should be in the news release. If the issue relates more to a position that you are taking, the questions could be rephrased: what do you believe and why do you believe it, or what are you advocating and why are you advocating it?

A quotation in support of the lede often, but not always, appears in the second paragraph. In many cases, this quotation is a key message from the communications/media plan. This key support is followed by the next most important fact, then the next most important, and so forth, moving toward the least important elements of the message. An opposing point of view can sometimes be anticipated, and you may want to address this perspective in the news release as well; but this point is discretionary: you also may not want to give the opposition the time of day in your news release. (After all, they can do their own.)

Finally, some essential elements to a news release. Don't overlook any of these points in your zeal to come up with a good lede.

First, put the release on letterhead that says who you are. If you don't have letterhead, type the name of your organization clearly at the top of the page.

Second, date the release when you send it out. While there are occasions when you can ask the media to hold a news story until a certain time (called an embargo), most releases should be sent when you are ready to release the information. The date is typically followed by the notation FOR IMMEDIATE RELEASE (written, as shown here, in all caps).

You can ask for a news embargo on certain stories: for example, budgets, scientific or technical data that the media need a chance to study or events timed to coincide with other events. Under the embargo, the media agree not to release the information you provide them until a specified time, such as after a technical briefing or after a key speech has been delivered. But be careful with embargoes: some media may proceed with the story regardless of your request if they feel the subject is newsworthy. In that case, all bets are off. The Canadian Press policy on broken embargoes is clear:

> CP editors should tell the source of the embargoed material that we will abide by the release time only as long as others do. We will release the material immediately if someone else is found to have broken the embargo. CP will take no account of the size or importance of the newspaper or broadcaster that broke the embargo.[16]

You should have a backup plan in case the media do break the embargo. Chiefly, you should be able to move immediately once the embargo is broken and hold your own news conference so that you get your message out first, as you intended. That may mean rescheduling an event or having a backup spokesperson ready to go; it may mean getting to a key beat reporter or columnist directly with the full story; or it may simply mean holding the fort and telling all media that you won't comment until the event is ready or the spokesperson available. The key is to have a backup plan in case the embargo is breached. For most stories, using the date tag FOR IMMEDIATE RELEASE is the safest way to distribute news releases and other information.

The most critical element of the news release is having a contact name, with title and contact phone numbers, at the top or bottom of the page. Remember that the media will not likely use your release as is; they will call and ask a few questions, even if their contact is only pro forma to confirm the information and the quote.

Again, keep the release to a single page. If you have more information, attach it as a backgrounder. Thus, a typical news release might look like the example on page 112.

In this example, the headline and the final quote are optional. The media contact person's phone number should be that person's number during the day; most media relations practitioners have cell phones since they may be called out of the office for another media issue. The —30— at the end of the story is traditional; it simply indicates the end of the story. On rare occasions you may want to send out a longer release. To indicate there are more pages coming, add "more..." to the bottom of the first page.

When you send out your news release, address it appropriately:

City Editor for daily newspapers (or other appropriate editor if not city news, e.g., sports editor for sports news);

Assignment Editor for television news;

News Director for radio news;

Producer for open-line, talk, news magazine and special-interest TV and radio shows.

You can fax, mail or e-mail the release, depending on how quickly you want to get it out, or you can send it through commercial news release services (such as Canada NewsWire or Marketwire). These services can distribute provincially, nationally and internationally as well. Check with your media first before sending releases by e-mail. Some do, some don't. My colleague Garry Ens of Red River College surveyed Manitoba weeklies to determine if they accepted releases by e-mail; only one of 90 said yes. Conversely, the Automobile Writers Association advised automakers they didn't ever want

FOR IMMEDIATE RELEASE
Special transit fares for seniors

Ourtown seniors will receive a further special discount of 10 per cent for using city transit, Council decided at its meeting last night.

"This is in line with our policy of keeping Ourtown services affordable to all the public, particularily those on fixed incomes," said Mayor Ben Franklin.

The 10 per cent discount reduces the overall senior's fare to 25 per cent of a full fare. For seniors, this means a standard fare falls from 65 cents to 50 cents; the 10 per cent discount also applies to monthly bus passes, holiday fares and ticket packages (see attached summary outlining all regular and senior fares).

The discount takes effect April 1; it is intended to reduce income to transit by approximately $35,000 a year.

"While we will have to adjust our budget for this, we feel it is the best way to allow seniors to use transit and take an active part in the life of the community," said Mayor Franklin.

—30—

For more information, contact:
Bob Jones, Media Relations, Transit
555-1212 (pager 222-2222), e-mail bjones@transit.ca
Attachment; more information on city transit on our website:
www.ourtown.ca/transit

to get paper again; they preferred an e-mail linking to the appropriate web page. Generally, the bigger the media outlet, the more likely it is to have firewalls to keep out viruses, spam and Trojan Horses. Some are even more specific, asking for news releases to be embedded in the text of the e-mail instead of attached as a separate document. One rule holds firm: check it out with the media you're working with first.

If you are dealing with a particular beat reporter, you can send the release to that individual, although a phone call would probably be better. Beat reporters like to touch base with their contacts and appreciate hearing from them when there is news.

In most cases, send out one copy to each media outlet. It is reasonable to call large outlets to confirm whether they received it: large media have their own bureaucracy and you don't want your release to get lost. Do not, however, send multiple copies of the same news release to the same organization (with one important exception). This is called "double planting" and may result in two reporters from the same outlet working on the same story.[17] When they find out, they will not be happy—particularly not with you. From their perspective, it's bad enough they have to compete with reporters from other media; it's even worse to compete with their colleagues. You can, however, pitch the same issue to different editors in the same newspaper, as long as you pitch different stories and tell them what you're doing. For example, if your company is expanding to include a new food product, you can send a release to the business editor about the expansion and the food editor about the different uses for the food product; but make sure you inform both editors of what you're doing. It would embarrass a newspaper if its business columnist expressed doubt about the success of your product while the food editor raved about it.

The one major exception to sending single releases is the CBC. Each CBC program has separate production, and if you work with a major CBC station, you must send separate news releases for each of the following areas:

CBC-TV English News (assignment editor)

CBC-TV French News (assignment editor)

CBC Radio One English News (news director)

CBC Radio One French News (news director)

CBC Radio One Morning Show (producer)

CBC Radio One Noon Show (producer)

CBC Radio One Drive Home Show (producer)

CBC Newsworld

Any particular program you are focussing on (e.g., Quirks and Quarks, The House).

If you get requests from two radio talk shows to appear, ensure that both know about it. With talk shows, the practice is generally "first come, first served," although individual producers may want to make different arrangements.

Is it Time to Retire the Traditional News Release?

The most successful news conference I was ever part of was the September 2003 news coverage in Saskatoon of the first human death in Canada from mad cow disease. We held the news conference at noon locally, but, as we expected, the news leaked out to the morning paper. We received calls from virtually all major news outlets and we advised them all that we would speak to the matter at noon, when our expert panel was assembled. In the interim, the media had access to accurate and credible information on websites like the Centres for Disease Control and Prevention in Atlanta, Lab Centre for Disease Control in Ottawa, and British Health. When the time for the news conference came, the media were fully briefed and knew the background material. Their questions were knowledgeable, informed and based on fact. Our news release, as far as I know, was never used. Stacks and stacks of photocopied backgrounders were left behind at the news conference site.

I've been thinking since then that much time is wasted in preparing artfully written, highly nuanced news releases, when we as practitioners could simply spit out the news, add a quote from a spokesperson, then add all the relevant information and resources in a backgrounder. The notion of the news release is that by writing it as news, it has a chance of being published verbatim. This happens in small-town weeklies, but nowhere else. No self-respecting reporter will use a release as is; they will take it as a lead for a story of their own. Why not focus then on giving reporters the angle, the contact person and the information, and skip the traditional news release format?

It's not just me. B.L. Ochman states, and I believe him, that he hasn't sent out a news release in 10 years but has successfully obtained national media coverage for his clients, primarily by writing pitch letters (more on this in the next chapter).[18] He notes,

> Editors don't need me or any other publicist to write their stories. They need me to point them in the direction of a good story, succinctly give them the facts as I see them, the sources I know and then get out of the way so they can write their stories.[19]

Video News Releases

Video News Releases (VNRs) are just that: broadcast-quality footage, however delivered intended for release to television stations. They typically contain a "story" in television format, complete with reporter, just as a news release imitates a news story. The story is 60 to 120 seconds in duration. It also contains a B-roll, which is additional footage a station can use depending on the angle it wishes to take. For example, the main VNR describes a new product or service and is promotional in tone; the B-roll might contain visuals of how the product is manufactured, how it is used and how it was financed (for the business media). Because of their extensive preparation and distribution time, VNRs lend themselves best to feature stories, particularly in the fields of entertainment, business and science. They can, however, be used for hard news or breaking stories; for example, the most-used VNR in 1993 was a series of four releases sent out by Pepsi in response to a rumour about product safety.[20]

Most advertising agencies can arrange to produce VNRs. They are costly to make (in the range of $20,000), duplicate and send out (about $6,500), but they are still cheaper than a national advertising campaign, for which the same amount of money might buy time on one major market alone. VNRs are used extensively by television, just as print news releases are used by all media. A 1992 survey indicated that all of the responding television stations used VNRs in their newscasts.[21] However, as with news releases, TV reporters use VNRs as a tip to their own story. The station will edit the release, particularly the B-roll, and adapt it to its own purposes.

News releases are the bread-and-butter of the media relations business. Even if you choose a different approach to contact the media, such as a news conference, it will still likely involve writing a news release. However, there are a number of other ways to deal with the media, which we will consider in the next few chapters.

Other Approaches to the Media

News conferences are good for dealing with several media at once or for getting news out quickly during a fast-moving or high-profile event. They should be used sparingly, though; most importantly, you should have real news if you expect media to attend.

The News Conference

Do not hold a news conference because you want a high-profile launch of your product or service. The newsworthiness of what you're saying should be more important than the level of profile you are seeking.

The efficiency of a news conference can be offset by some disadvantages. News conferences can exemplify pack journalism at its worse, as when one wrong-headed or partisan reporter decides to run off in his or her own direction at the news conference and all the other media follow. *The Canadian Reporter* describes it best:

> In general ... news conferences are where pack pressures show up in
> their most intense form. If you try to ask an open-ended question
> about topic B when the rest of the reporters want to talk about topic A,
> you'll feel their disapproval .... Individual reporters must guard against
> accepting uncritically the tone of the pack and the story evaluation of
> the pack.[1]

The risk of a news conference is that the pack might tear you or your spokesperson to pieces, especially if the issue is an emotional one. When we had the second death of teenager from meningococcal meningitis in two weeks, thus sparking fears of an epidemic for which there was no good vaccine, we chose to send out a factual news release, and only did one-on-one interviews. It was much more time consuming and the questions were still hard and demanding, but we managed to communicate the issue without causing a public panic.

Reporters generally prefer to ask their own questions and do not want to see other reporters taking advantage of their questions; if opportunity permits, they prefer to do one-on-one interviews with the main subject of the news conference after it's over. If time allows, be sure to schedule such opportunities.

Not having the time to ask questions is the greatest media complaint about news conferences. If in fact you are unable or unwilling to take questions, you may want to consider sending out a written statement instead. If you aren't going to take questions, you should advise the media ahead of time and give a reason why you won't accept questions. In that case, you might send out a media advisory such as this: "Joe Jones will make a brief media statement at four o'clock today at the Provincial Hotel to respond to the latest evidence given in the fish inquiry. Since the inquiry is still underway, he will not accept questions." This advises the broadcast media that they will get video and audio clips; the print media will simply take a copy of his statement.

According to an Angus Reid survey of reporters and editors, the most common criticisms of news conferences are as follows (more than one response was accepted):

no questions and answers/not enough time for questions	22 per cent
not newsworthy	14 per cent
equipment concerns	12 per cent
too long/too many speakers	11 per cent
disorganized/ambiguous information	8 per cent
no senior people present	7 per cent
no chance for one-on-one questions	6 per cent
no advance releases/notice	6 per cent
poorly timed/late starts	6 per cent
don't manipulate/tease/promote	5 per cent
too TV oriented	4 per cent
none/no complaints	8 per cent[2]

These answers provide a checklist for what not to do. But what is the practitioner supposed to *do*?

First, you must have a plan. The media relations event plan outlined in Chapter 7 provides a basic planning model and should be referred to before you set out on a news conference. Once you've figured out what you're doing and why, your key messages and your audience, you can get down to the nitty-gritty.

First, send out a media advisory. If you have the luxury of time, send it out two to three days in advance, so editors can add it to their schedule. For fast-breaking issues, you can give as little as an hour's notice, but it may mean calling media outlets directly to tell them you're holding the news conference or sending out notice on a commercial news release service. (Please note the same guideline for news conferences as for news releases: they are not to be called "press conferences.")

Tell editors what the conference will be about but don't give details. If it is specific to particular types of media (business, entertainment, sports), you can state this at the beginning: e.g., "Attention business editors." Do not call a news conference and tell reporters they must attend to find out what it is about: they will simply not attend and mark you as someone who knows very little about media. (I remember as the editor of an Edmonton weekly I would get a call every Wednesday inviting me to the Alberta Liberal party leader's news conference the following day. When I asked what it was about, I was told I would find out when I attended but it would be great news. When I asked what it had to do with my readers, the party contact couldn't explain. I never attended. After the fourth week I told the party contact in very clear and direct language not to call again or I would ensure the word *Liberal* would never appear in my paper).

On the other hand, don't reveal so much that the media will simply run with the information you've given them and obviate the need for a news conference. Be willing to accept media calls from editors trying to determine how newsworthy the subject is, but don't give them the substance of the story: no one will come to cover the story if another outlet has already run with it.

The media advisory

A media advisory is like an advance news release that calls media to your media conference. Media advisories don't require a special prose treatment. A typical advisory looks like this:

NEWS CONFERENCE
New process to boost production at Ourtown Mill
WHAT: Details of new mechanical process to increase production at
     company mill
WHO: CEO Bob Smith and head of production Joe Brown
WHEN: Thursday, Aug. 17, 10 a.m.
WHERE: Marvin's Mill, on Highway 13 two kilometres south of town
The company will provide a demonstration of the new technology and
     a plant tour will be available.
CONTACT: Tom Green, Media Relations, 555-1212, cell 222-2222,
     e-mail tgreen@ourtown.ca
—30—

Let's flesh out this example of the company mill. When the time for the media conference comes, the media person will introduce the speakers. The speakers will make their statements briefly, looking up from their notes for the cameras, and the demonstration will be held. (Always keep in mind the media's need for visuals, particularly action visuals). Once the formal part of the conference is over, the media person will allow time for reporters to ask questions. Before that, however, he or she will have prepared answers to some likely questions, such as, How much did the new machinery cost? How much will production and profit increase? Will there be layoffs? Are there environmental or regulatory concerns (e.g., zoning)? Has the process been tested anywhere else? The media person will have prepared a media kit with a news release, backgrounder and photos of the new process. Not much more is necessary. The media person should also have additional information on hand for those media who are interested, such as annual reports, technical specifications and so on. Don't drown the media with information they can't readily absorb. Give them the basics; then if they need more, provide it when they ask.

Media kits

Media kits can be used as part of a news conference or media event. Typically, a kit will contain a number of communications materials so that the reporters have all the information in one place. It usually contains a news release, backgrounder, speech/speaking notes of the speaker, perhaps questions and answers, perhaps a major report or document if that is the focus of the conference, and possibly photos. As stand-alone pieces, mailed or sent by courier en masse to the media, they will rarely be more effective than a simple news release. If the news release gets the attention you are seeking, you can then hand interested media the rest of the information you were intending to send out in the kit.

That said, one use for a stand-alone media kit is background information on a current issue. This use is the highest-rated value for media kits according to the Angus Reid survey of editors. However, it doesn't have to be sent as a kit but simply as a backgrounder—it can even be posted on your website and updated for a breaking, evolving story.

Locating the media conference

Before you call the media to the conference, choose an appropriate location to host the conference. It should be apropos to subject matter of the conference and it should also comfortably accommodate the number of media personnel you expect to host.

The room is best set up classroom-style on a level floor. Boardrooms present a problem for camera people: it's difficult to separate the subject of the news conference from the media. Be aware of the backdrop behind the speakers. It doesn't have to be blue nor must it have the company logo on it. (Indeed, a logo will only encourage camera people and photographers to zoom in on the subject to avoid promoting the logo, although in a business story or a story involving the main business of a town, the logo might be used). Don't seat the subjects in front of a window or distracting backdrop (e.g., a computer screen with flashing lights); it's fine to have equipment present as long as it isn't in the same shot as the speaker.

The most important technical aspect of the news conference is to ensure broadcast journalists have good sound. If you have enough media in attendance, you can rent a media feed/sound board from most audiovisual companies. Your microphones feed directly into the board, and the reporters can patch in their tape recorders, guaranteeing good sound.

If you don't have a media feed, the media will cluster their own microphones around the speaker's mic, with their own flashes showing, e.g., CBC, CTV. This profusion of microphones makes a good argument for a media feed since the space in front the speaker will look cluttered. However, if there is no time for it, don't hold up a news conference while you look for a media feed. If you go without a media feed, have your speakers seated. Most media microphones are on stands and it is easier to set them up than to attach them to a floor mike.

Have people dress as they normally would for the business. A plant manager should look like a plant manager and the CEO should look like a CEO, but a regular worker doesn't have to be in a suit. If your subjects are comfortable with it, have them stand while delivering the statement and taking the questions, and remind them to maintain good posture. (Posture is also important if they are seated). As the media person, you should rehearse your speakers if there is time, offering them mock questions so they are prepared to give appropriate answers.

Co-ordinating the conference

Most of the work of the news conference is detail, but it still needs to be done. Here is a sample checklist for media events that can be planned in advance.[3]

· Book room and ensure parking, passes, coffee, etc., will be available.

· Brief front-office staff so they can direct media when they arrive, or have someone at the door to greet media if they need directions to the site of the news conference. Send out media advisory to all media (or targeted media if the issue warrants).

· Brief security, if appropriate.

· Brief management.

· Provide a written brief to participants so they can begin preparing for the news conference. (The written brief may include a statement, news release, backgrounder, and prepared questions and answers, all focussed on key messages; it may require approval from management/ the client).

It may be necessary to brief key stakeholders (such as staff, unions, politicians and shareholders, to name just a few) before the news conference. If some stakeholders are likely to be critical of the issue you are raising at the conference, brief them concurrently with the news conference, not before. Don't give them a reason to go to the media before you are ready.

If talk shows and editorial boards are part of your media plan, contact them and book your speakers. If there are beat reporters or trade-magazine reporters who are likely to take an interest in your subject, call them and see if they will want dedicated time after the news conference.

If there are key media you want to attend, contact them to confirm their attendance. A reminder call may be helpful for most media, but use some judgement: you may be bugging them more than anything.

Once the conference starts, your job as media person is managing the proceedings: keeping records of attendance and responding to individual reporters' requests for more information, one-on-one interviews and appearances on talk shows.

When the conference has wrapped up, monitor your media coverage. (You can hire media monitoring companies for this; see Chapter 6). Analyze the coverage. Were your message and information picked up as planned? If not, evaluate what didn't work and try to correct it. Measure your results against the goals you set for the news conference. Simple coverage isn't enough. You may need to do some research (polling, counting calls to the call centre, tracking sales increases, etc.) to determine the effectiveness of the conference, but it is all part of the media relations plan. If, for example, your goals were increased investor support, improved staff understanding of the new process, regulatory approval, increased sales, accountability and community relations, you must determine what you accomplished. Did the news conference help you achieve it?

As you can see from the amount of effort it takes to host a news conference, the event should reflect a genuinely newsworthy issue. If it doesn't, then Mike Ura's advice still stands: "If you can send out a news release, don't call a news conference." If you do hold a news conference and it works, you will have engineered a good deal of extensive and positive (i.e., fair and accurate) news, all in a very short time at very little cost other than your time and effort.

Technical Briefing/Backgrounder

The technical briefing is a variation of the news conference and often precedes it. Technical briefings are used with particularly complex issues that require extensive discussion with the media so they can understand the topic. The introduction of a new law, a budget or a new technical process, for example, may require technical briefing. At a typical briefing, experts in the field provide a detailed explanation, in layperson's language, of the issue. This commentary should normally be on the record, since media will want to cite an authority.

Much like a news conference, the technical briefing will consist of the briefing, usually on PowerPoint with supporting documentation, and a question period for clarity and understanding. After the technical portion is complete, a more senior person will conduct a traditional news conference and take questions of policy or politics. However, the expectation by that time is that the media will have a more solid and in-depth understanding of the issue than they would have had without the technical briefing. Technical briefings are best held in the morning, since afternoons are usually very rushed as reporters try to file for their deadlines.

A variation of the technical briefing is the budget lock-up, used by federal and provincial governments to announce their annual budgets. Reporters are given extensive briefings, lasting between two and six hours, on the coming budget in complete detail. Media often have opportunities to interview budget specialists individually as well as during the technical briefing. The lock-up allows them time to write complete and accurate stories. However, by agreement with the governments, neither the reporters nor their outlets will release any details on the budget until the Minister of Finance rises in the Legislature to begin delivering the budget speech, usually mid-afternoon of budget day. The media are in effect "locked up" until the minister rises. By that time, however, they will have been extensively briefed and can be relied on to report accurately on the budget, always a complex, technical issue.

The key to this arrangement is the written agreement between media and government. Normally only lock-ups are used in this instance, primarily because of the length of time it takes to brief reporters. Most technical briefings last between 30 and 60 minutes, followed by the news conference, so there is little worry about the media leaving the briefing to broadcast the news. The time is short enough that they can wait until they have the complete story, including the quotes from the key speaker.

The Scrum

The scrum is another variant of the news conference, often called for the same reason: to accommodate several media requests for an interview at once or to deal with fast-breaking situations where an immediate response is required. The scrum is less formal, without the attendant paperwork and extensive preparation of the news conference, although it requires its own preparation.

The scrum began as a political tool. After Question Period, ministers would meet the media in the halls and address the issues raised in the day's sitting. The minister or opposition member would show up, surrounded by microphones and cameras, and take questions from reporters who had witnessed the sitting and now had an opportunity to ask their own questions. The result of this kind of scrum tends to be a replay of the Question Period exchange, since both parties (government and opposition) will stick to the messages contained in their briefing notes, which were prepared before Question Period.

For non-politicians, scrums are useful for handling large numbers of reporters on short notice. It is the responsibility of the media person to get the word out to the media that a scrum is taking place, with details of time and place. Preparation for a scrum usually consists of orally preparing a few key messages and answers for questions. News releases are normally not prepared, and the only documentation provided is already existing materials that help support the scrum subject's argument or aid the media in better understanding the issue.

Media Stunts

Non-profit and advocacy groups in particular, who are usually short on budgets and long on creativity, have mastered the technique of putting on media stunts. While the old-fashioned press agents would use stunts to get their clients into the news or gossip columns (as today's entertainment publicists still do), today it is more likely that the perpetrators of stunts will be lobbyists and activists.

Greenpeace was a pioneer of the planned media stunt in Canada, putting small craft in the way of nuclear aircraft carriers to demonstrate for peace or chaining members to trees to provide awareness of the importance of the environment. Media presence is essential to these stunts: without the media, no one would know what the stunt was, let alone the issue.

Media have a soft spot for stunts, and stunts can be seen every day. They have become more elaborate and formalized than the traditional protest rally, in some cases growing from simple stunts to organized annual events and campaigns. For example, Mothers Against Drunk Driving (MADD) started with a few parents outraged by the loss of their children to drunk drivers, in an era when drunk driving was considered a minor misdemeanor, punishable by fine. From protests and meeting with politicians to vigils and petitions, a grassroots movement grew to an organization that is much more formal and has an ongoing, year-round presence.

The basic stunt is still a reasonably effective means of getting media attention, although, like other aspects of media relations, it must be done well to receive attention. The stunt has three basic components.

1. The visual element

Even if it's just a simple protest rally, the stunt shows something happening. A person talking to a news conference is just a talking head; the stunt shows people in action. The importance of the visual in helping to get a message out and remembered is borne out through research. A study of television news indicates that a strong visual element aids the viewer's recall of an issue.[4] A study six months after the first recorded death by hantavirus in northern Alberta indicated that, of all the media used to provide public education (recorded information line, physicians, radio, television, newspapers), the public recalled most the information received from visual media (television and newspapers) and least the amount received through oral media (radio and the information line, although not all respondents could gain access to the info line).[5]

In addition to its lasting impact and its educational value, a strong visual adds an emotional impact that words and statistics sometimes can't (e.g., a picture of a pipe pouring untreated chemicals into a river adds an element to an analytical observation of the effect of effluent on the environment). This impact leads to the second key element in a good media stunt.

2. Emotion appropriate to the issue

While outrage is common to many activists' stunts, many other emotions can be portrayed, ranging from sadness and reflection (the tenth anniversary of the Montreal massacre), to anger (MADD), to joy (anniversaries commemorating key dates or events, such as the Persons Case), to humour through satire (the Raging Grannies). Whatever emotion is evoked, however, should be the emotion stunt planners are trying to generate in their target audiences (e.g., outrage, sympathy, humour). This emotional consistency must also reflect the final element of a good stunt.

3. Thematic consistency between stunt and issue

The visual should communicate the theme in a good stunt. Pulling a giant condom over the Peace Tower in Ottawa would for most people bring to mind a safe sex/AIDS awareness issue, not a foreign aid issue. This is where the real creativity of media relations planning comes in, and where activists and advocacy groups can have a lot of fun.

The stunt should not be so dangerous that it risks lives. For example, a 1999 stunt in Banff National Park involved a protester perched on a complex of logs on a key park bridge. When one angry driver began to dismantle the structure, the safety of the protester was jeopardized and media attention focussed on her peril. She was not hurt, in the end, and the protest concluded, but the issue that drove the protest was lost in a badly handled stunt.

Readers who want more ideas on stunts and how to stage them should consult Jason Salzman's book *Making The News: A Guide for Nonprofits and Activists*.[6] Salzman provides a catalogue of media stunts that the activist should study — as should potential targets of activism.

Media Events

The more mainstream version of a media stunt is the media event. Such an event is the traditional ribbon cutting, grand opening or inauguration type of story, often characterized by a cheque being handed from donor to grateful recipient while shaking hands. The most frequent outcome of these events is the dreaded "grip and grin" shot of photojournalism cliché, an outcome that should be avoided as much as possible. Sometimes these types of events can be creatively staged—for example, ribbons can be cut by robots to commemorate the opening of a high-tech automated factory or a bulldozer can do the honours to announce the beginning of construction. Similarly, giant cheques can be handed out, or at least the cheque can be presented in front of the equipment the money is intended to purchase.

However, the practitioner is better advised to take media through the building to show how the process works, what the funding will purchase or who the event will benefit. For example, a cheque presentation ceremony from a service club to build a new park can feature a children's softball game as a demonstration of how the money will be used. Media tours of a new building, site or process are also standard. In the event of a national event, satellite media tours can also be arranged, allowing out-of-town media to see and get video of a distant site. In the absence of such technology—or if it is not possible for safety or logistical reasons to take media through a site—you can either provide your own video and distribute it or ask the media to form a pool, from which they will designate a photographer/camera person to get visuals at the site, then distribute them to everyone else. To do this, you must have written agreement from all media. (See also the discussion of crisis media in Chapter 14).

Another staple media event is simply to invite media to conferences, where they can cover key speakers and interview them afterwards. Speakers at conferences are usually high-profile people in their field who are comfortable with media and who welcome media attention. You should ensure speakers know media will be present and have them agree to participate in any pre- or post-conference media. Sometimes people in the news don't want to be there any more than they have to, for reasons ranging from a desire for privacy to bad previous experiences to security. (For example, British author Salman Rushdie often spoke to writers and human rights groups while he was under the threat of death from a fatwa issued by Ayatollah Khomeini for his book, the *Satanic Verses;* but his security advisors would not allow any publicity of the event outside the immediate group he was speaking to). Sometimes people deliberately choose a strategy of media avoidance, on the grounds that avoidance does them more good than harm (thus, in mid 2001 Canadian Alliance leader Stockwell Day rarely spoke to media as it fuelled dissent in his troubled party).

Another, more formal event is a national day, week or month that organizations publicly declare to be theirs. There is no control over these declarations—any group can declare any date its own for any purposes. Thus, if March is National Water Dowsing Month, dowsers can hold parades, demonstrate new dowsing techniques, issue technical papers, hold conferences, submit petitions to government or hold other such events, and ask for media attention at the same time. While the media is generally averse to doing something for every date (there are far too many of them for legitimate coverage), if a newsworthy event can be arranged during the date (e.g., announcing new research on cancer during cancer month), it will increase the likelihood of coverage. A few, such as the annual Terry Fox run or Jerry Lewis' Labour Day telethon, are annual events that focus on the amount of money raised for the cause.

A media event can be put together quickly or can be a multi-year effort (such as preparing a major sporting event such as the Olympics or national art exhibitions). In the case of major undertakings, full-time media relations staff will be hired months or years ahead of time to organize the event, which may include handling broadcasting rights, organizing satellite coverage, managing post-event media conferences or marshalling a small army of volunteers to deal with the media during the event. Whatever the case, planning for a media event should go back to first principles. What is the purpose of the media event, and how can you evaluate whether you have achieved what you set out to do?

Direct Contact

So far, we've looked at contacting media through third-party intervention. It is also possible to call a reporter directly and to target media individually instead of contacting them all. Editors and reporters are responsive to direct contact, as long as it is relevant and focussed. This section looks at some of the issues in contacting individual journalists.

Editors and reporters

If you have a story of particular interest to specific media (e.g., seniors, the aboriginal community) or particular reporters, you can call them directly and ask if they are interested in what you have. If you're in a larger market, with several beat reporters from different media following the same story, you should contact them all. Beware of playing favourites, since the media you aren't favouring are not going to take kindly to you or your issue when they find out you've been giving their opposition information and leads you haven't been sharing with them. However, if a beat reporter calls you and clearly has more information than his competition, you should not share that; the business you conduct with one reporter should stay with that reporter. If you know a reporter is going to do a story on you and you anticipate it will be negative, you may want to get the story out first yourself. However, this may be overreaction; you may want to let the story play out first and see if it draws any other interest before making a bigger deal of it by releasing it yourself.

At any rate, if you call an editor or reporter, keep your presentation simple and above board. Don't ask for favours and don't drop hints that you might provide more information if the reporter plays along (remember your ethics; see Chapter 3). As always, once you approach the media you must be prepared to have them follow up on your tip, and they may not always do so in the manner you hope.

If you get turned down, don't try a heavy-duty sell job to get your story covered: you likely will find even more resistance in response. Either shop the story around to other media who might be interested or look for a different way of getting coverage for it. You could also wait until there is a change of editors or reporters. News is a very volatile business, and beat reporters are transferred every couple of years; the next one may be interested in your story. Direct contact is one arena where it pays to monitor news and reporters. Many media outlets routinely send out news releases when they transfer or hire new editors or anchors; you want to keep current on who is making the news decisions at the key media outlets and media drivers in your market. Meanwhile, if you don't have a contact name, approach the editor of a newspaper (or sub-editor, such as sports or entertainment) or the news editor of a radio station. Making your approach early in the day is better, before the daily story meeting.

Columnists

Columnists usually welcome feedback and additional information from readers, although this interaction doesn't always make its way into future columns. Bearing in mind that columnists write regularly, you should contact them if you feel they've missed information or perspectives that would be useful in a future column. Many newspaper columnists, particularly in national papers, now have e-mail addresses, which allows for almost instant response to a column. The downside to e-mail, however, is the columnist may have a huge e-mail correspondence he or she can't get around to responding to, in which case a letter or phone call might have a better chance of getting attention.

Editorial boards

Daily newspapers have editorial boards, which are composed of editors who actually write editorials (they often have other duties as well). They are willing to have people in the news come in and provide them with background information on their issue or organization. Some organizations that are frequently in the news (such as government or a city's major business) hold annual meetings with the editorial board. Others meet with the editorial board when they have an issue in the news, while still others meet with the board when they are doing a major media launch of a product or issue. In the latter case, the editorial board meeting is one of a number of scheduled media items (e.g., news conference, media tours, etc).

A simple phone call requesting to speak to the editorial board is usually all that is needed, particularly if you are already in the news. For national newspapers, a more formal letter asking for the opportunity is necessary. In either case, simply call the newspaper and ask for the editorial board.

The rules for meeting with the editorial board are straightforward. If the board meets with you (usually three or four editors constitute the editorial board), you will (with some exceptions) be on the record. A reporter may also be in attendance, and you may find a story resulting from your meeting. You will have a chance to brief them on your organization or issue; if your briefing is going to be longer than a 10-minute oral presentation, let them know in advance so enough time can be scheduled. After you've briefed them, provide a handout or media kit for further reference. From that point on, the meeting is open-ended and will last as long as you and they are interested. The board will ask questions, but because they are editors and editorial writers, the questions may be more philosophical (e.g., Why are you doing this? Have you considered other options?) than the typical W's and H's of hard news reporters.

From the meeting you may get a favourable editorial, or the information may be stored away for future use. You may also get a call sometime later asking for addition information and further follow-up.

Feature stories

Feature stories, sometime called human interest stories, are distinguished by their length, their ability to go into detail, their narrative form and their lack of "newsiness." Feature stories are staples of news but require special efforts to place. As one study indicated, news releases for feature stories were among the least likely to be used by the media.[7] However, feature stories can be pitched in other forms.

One of the more likely forms is a simple phone call to a reporter or outlet likely to be interested. This approach is particularly effective if you can get a newspaper to do a feature, since broadcast media may follow up on it. Another means of getting feature news coverage is to send out a regular tip sheet to media. For example, at the Edmonton Board of Health I sent out an annual "health calendar" to all local media, which outlined the various health days, weeks and months of the coming year (e.g., Mental Health Week, AIDS Awareness Day), giving local contact information for each event. This calendar allowed media to schedule health features in advance throughout the year. If you're working on a national scale, it may be more helpful to provide a monthly or weekly calendar of upcoming events. Tip sheets can be sent to all media, key media or targeted media.

Another way to get feature attention is the pitch letter, which is usually sent exclusively to one key media outlet. It is a one-page outline stating what your idea is, why the audience would be interested and who the contact is. You can also include some background material about the issue or personality involved or a reference to your website. Unlike the omnibus tip sheet, the pitch letter typically offers first use to the outlet that receives it:

An effective pitch letter will develop several story outlines or themes and tailor these proposals to the editor and the publication. The story should be proposed on a first exclusive basis, meaning that the periodical that initially published the story will be the only one to carry it.[8]

After waiting a reasonable interval, call the reporter, editor or producer to whom you sent the letter and ask whether they received it and if they are interested. (Unless you have an event or a speaker appearing at a certain time, pitch letters for feature stories are generally not time sensitive). If the contact is genuinely not interested, feel free to offer the same idea to other media.

Pitch letters are also effective for getting on talk shows and broadcast magazines (e.g., *This Morning* with Shelagh Rogers on CBC Radio One). Here's a sample pitch letter to a producer of a local radio show targeted to young adults. Note that for this kind of contact, you must know the name of the person who books guests for the show.

Dear Ms. Smith:

Next Tuesday, acclaimed entrepreneur Bob Jones will be in town to address the graduating class of the Centralia Institute of Technology on how to start a dot.com company—and survive! Mr. Jones has appeared on many talk shows, and his topic has resonated with young people who are wondering if there is any future in the New Media, and with their parents. Unlike many in the recent tech wreck, Mr. Jones has prospered on the Internet, and he is enthusiastic in sharing his experience, particularly with youth.

He would be glad to appear on your show next Tuesday, prior to his speech, which starts at 4 p.m. He can visit the host in studio or to do a phone-in interview. If it fits your schedule, he can do an interview prior to Tuesday from his home in Halifax.

I have attached a couple of recent articles on Mr. Jones; if you'd like more information, please see his website: www.rentageek.com.

I look forward to discussing this with you further.

Henriette Kelsey
555-1212; cell 222-2222
E-mail: henrikelsey@bobmail.ca

The letter must be brief, should highlight why the listeners would be interested (e.g., approaching a youth-oriented station because new media is of interest to youth) and must provide enough information that the producer can get a sense of the topic and the guest (having a guest who is media-savvy is a strong selling point). The same subject can be pitched to a number of different media outlets in the same market, according to their interest. The business editor of the local paper would be more interested in the business angle, a local computer newsletter would be more interested in the software application and the local CBC morning/drive home shows may be interested simply as a general-interest item (bearing in mind that if you pitching to two CBC radio shows, or two departments within the same newspaper, you should advise both shows, or both departments, to avoid double-planting).

Talk and magazine shows

Talk shows and magazine shows allow for extended discussion of your issue or story, particularly if you have a high-profile individual or someone who is currently in the news to speak about it. You may draw interest from talk and magazine shows with your standard news release or tip sheet; another way to solicit attention is through a pitch letter. If the story is timely, a phone call or series of phone calls may be necessary. For both talk shows and magazine shows, address your calls and letters to the show producer, not the host.

Special interest shows and specialty cable

If you think you have a story idea that a regular public affairs or special interest show (such as CBC Radio's *Quirks and Quarks* or a program on Discovery Channel, or local equivalent) would be interested in, send off a pitch letter to the producer. If you're outside Toronto looking for attention from a national show, there may be some value to hiring a national or Toronto-based public relations firm to help. (Use an Ottawa-based firm if you're looking for coverage from an Ottawa-based political show). These firms often specialize in placing stories on national and prominent local talk shows (e.g., Rafe Mair in Vancouver). Before you proceed, get a firm written estimate of how much this service will cost and the likelihood of coverage; placement could be a very expensive proposition, and you should have some confidence the type of exposure you will receive will merit the time and cost. However, in their defence, national PR firms have extensive experience dealing with this kind of media and may get you access that a simple pitch letter, no matter how artfully contrived, cannot give you.

This chapter has discussed a number of ways of approaching and dealing with existing media. The next chapter looks at some options for you to create your own media.

Do-It-Yourself Media

10

The media are sometimes accused of acting like a filter, taking the story from its source and rearranging it to fit the peculiar traditions of newswriting. Whether or not that accusation is justified is a subject for another book. But one way to avoid the filtering effect of media is to tell your own story, using some of the means that media provide. One general comment I will make is that in using do-it-yourself media, particularly new media (website/blog), users should look at the model of the mainstream media, and learn the value of a good editor. It's a truism in media that writers can't edit their own work; they are too close to it and need a critical but attentive intermediary to ensure clarity of thought, accuracy, structure and style. All new media writers should make sure a qualified editor takes a look at their work before submitting it to mainstream media or sending it to an unsuspecting world.

Op-Eds

Op-eds refer to the contents of the page opposite the editorial page. In both dailies and weeklies the editorial page usually appears on the last interior left-hand page of the first section. The page opposite, to the right of the editorial, is the op-ed page, featuring columnists, letters, commentary and guest contributions, particularly contributions from people in the news.

A column on the op-ed page gives you an opportunity to tell your story from your perspective, without the interpretation of a reporter or editor. (Of course, your piece will be edited for length, consistency and style, and the editor will keep a keen eye on anything that may be defamatory or libellous). Generally speaking, your column should be written in media-friendly language, but not in the straight news style. You can address the piece to the reader and write as if you were trying to convince someone of your point of view. If you or your client can't write in a media-friendly style, don't expect the editor to rewrite your column for you; the writing is your job, and you should take responsibility for doing it right. If you can't do it, hire a writer to do it for you. If the writing is weak, the column will not likely be accepted for publication.

To get into the op-ed page, contact the editor. (The editor's name usually appears on the page; otherwise, contact the editor whose name appears on the masthead). Identify yourself and explain that you would like to write an op-ed piece for the paper. Then explain what the piece is about, its general argument or point of view. Be ready to give good reasons why readers would be interested. If the editor is not interested, ask if he or she would publish your piece as a letter to the editor. (In general, letters to the editor are shorter and are written in response to recent news items that have appeared in the paper).

Don't bother submitting your column on speculation, hoping the editor will be interested; find out first whether there is interest. If the editor is not interested, look for other opportunities to get your message out. If you get the OK, be prepared to write 500 to 800 words. (Ask in advance if there is a word limit or any other consideration you need to know about before starting to write). Aim for a reasonable tone and state a good case; don't be partisan or argumentative—these stances are more appropriate to a letter to the editor. A guest column, like a newspaper column, should be fair in its outlook and based on evidence; be prepared to defend your column to the editor when you've written it and to provide supporting documentation on request.

The readership of both the editorial and op-ed pages of a newspaper is estimated to be low, but they have one key audience: reporters and producers, who scan them regularly to keep abreast of issues and to find story ideas. An op-ed piece also provides you with an opportunity to make your key audiences aware of your issue; having a guest column run on the op-ed page indicates that your story has legitimate news value and that the media (who shape public opinion) feel your point of view is interesting and newsworthy.

Don't expect favourable coverage from a newspaper just because it carried your column, and don't expect the paper to ask you to write another one unless your story stays in the news and develops further twists. However, a well planned guest column gives you a chance to tell your story, pretty much exactly as you want it.

Your column should identify you by name (even if it is ghostwritten) and affiliation, so that the reader knows your perspective. Before writing your column, read the columns in that newspaper carefully and try to find out how their columns meet the needs of the newspaper's readers—and how you can do the same. Study the style of editorial columns. Guest columns may be edited to fit the paper's style, language and usage; in general, the person who writes the newspaper's own editorials also edits the op-ed pieces. Try to follow that writing style.

Letters to the Editor

Letters to the editor tend to be short, to the point and written in response to a recent story that appeared in the paper to which you are writing. Letters may provide correction, illumination or criticism, depending on why you feel it is important to write. Most commonly, a letter to the editor simply points out an error or misunderstanding, or presents a different interpretation of the issue at hand.

Unlike an op-ed column, you should write your letter to the editor first, then send it by fax or e-mail to the newspaper. Send your letter on the day the story that prompted you to write the letter appears. Ideally, you want your letter to appear the following day, to get your message out early in the event of a breaking or continuing story.

Here are some guidelines for writing a letter to the editor:[1]

- Keep it short (100 to 150 words).
- Limit it to one subject.
- Have one main point and make it explicit (e.g., "The city should not discount transit fares for seniors").
- If you're writing on behalf of an organization, say so.
- Include your name, address and phone number. Many newspapers want to verify that you are truly the author and may have further questions for you.

Community Cable Programming

Community cable offers you the chance to be your own broadcaster. Community cable brings original broadcasting to the air 24 hours a day, seven days a week, particularly on issues of importance to the community in which the cable company has a license to operate. Standards vary from company to company. A small rural cable outlet may be glad to broadcast bingo or give you a talk show; all you have to do is show up and exhibit a willingness to learn and improve. Larger, metropolitan stations operate more like private television stations and may demand high technical standards of broadcasting and a marketing plan. However, both offer the opportunity for you to create your own television show, or at least a segment within a larger show, often exactly the way you want it (within the limitations of law and taste).

The best way to start is to call your local cable company and ask for the director of programming (or director of community programming). Ask about the station's policies on allowing interested people or groups to produce a show. They will likely ask what you have in mind, so you will need to give that some thought ahead of time.[2] Are you looking for a regular weekly show or a one-time special? Do you want to participate in a segment of an existing show? Who is your target audience? Do you have any experience in producing television? Can you provide a pool of volunteers who are willing to be trained in camera operation, sound, lighting, scriptwriting and makeup? The most important issue at this stage is that you have an idea that meets the interests or needs of the cable company and its viewers. Again, as with the newspaper columns, spend some time watching the community channel to see what it typically broadcasts and talk to some show producers to learn from their experience of pitching an idea and getting it on air.

Community cable television is worth exploring, particularly for voluntary and non-profit groups. In addition to the immediate exposure opportunity, it also provides you the chance to produce segments on topics of interest to you (e.g., recycling, tuning up your car, women's self-defence). In addition to being broadcast on the cable channel, these shows or segments can be recorded and used for other promotional or educational events, such as workshops or meetings your target audience may be attending.

If in fact you can make a go of community cable, bear in mind that these channels don't have ratings. It is simply assumed that their viewership is low. Therefore, if you are going to produce a cable show, spend some effort promoting it to your target audience. The advantage of community cable is that you are your own broadcaster; the disadvantage is that your viewership is low unless you actively promote yourself.

Advertorials

Advertorials are more common in newspapers, although a variation—public-interest advertising—can be found in broadcast media. An advertorial is a paid advertisement that looks like an editorial and generally takes a strong view on an issue, often in response to criticism from advocacy groups or the public at large. Advertorials are often a last resort when a company or agency feels it hasn't been able to get its message out through regular media relations; they afford a chance to state the party's case without criticism or filtering.

Advertorials are arranged through the advertising branch of a newspaper. The advertiser often asks the branch to keep the ad confidential until it runs. If reporters from the paper get an early look at it, they may call the company for comment, then call opposition groups for comment, and the advertorial may appear in the paper along with an extensive news story criticizing it. Advertising representatives keep an item confidential on request. Reporters and editors typically don't know or care what advertising is appearing in the paper the next day. Even as the paper is composed and news copy is laid out side-by-side with ad copy, the ad space is often left blank with a note "ABC company ad." The ad will be inserted later, just as the paper goes to press.

A variant of the advertorial is public-service advertising, in which a company or agency attempts to improve its image and counter negative news through positive ads, as part of an overall campaign. For example, a forestry company may prepare a series of public-service ads supporting sound environmental practices. The relative effectiveness of this is unknown. Newspapers and broadcast media can often tell you how many people saw an ad, but can rarely say how effective the ad was or whether it affected public opinion. Discovering that often requires focussed, individual research by the company placing the ad.

Both advertorials and public service advertisements cost money. The exact cost of the message depends on the size of the ad, the number of times it runs and the publication in which it appears. Rates vary from newspaper to newspaper and are typically set according to the size of the readership, just as broadcast media vary their rates from program to program according to the numbers of viewers they have.

Ad Features

Newspapers will often run advertising features, which highlight what appear to be news stories. The feature will usually have a theme—for example, the 125th anniversary of the City of Winnipeg, grand opening of a new store in town or kickoff to cancer month. The ad feature contains a number of "news" stories related to the topic of the ad feature, supported by ads from key suppliers or supporters of the institution or agency being featured. Ad features are typically set apart from the rest of the newspaper, either in their own pull-out section, or on a separate page with the words "ad feature" running across the top.

This near-news feature comes from the advertising department, which often initiates the feature to boost sales, especially during slow months or holiday seasons. However, the ad department is open to businesses and community groups to approach them and ask for an ad feature. The group must ensure a basic amount of advertising or have a good marketing plan that will lead to significant advertising.

In a business opening, for example, the business owner will want the ad feature to run when the business opens. He will likely commit to a large ad himself and will supply the ad department with a list of the suppliers who helped build the business ("Congratulations to Bob's Best Breads, from Lucci Plumbing and Electrical") or from ongoing suppliers ("Bob's Breads are made with Bobbo Flour, exclusive supplier to the Bob chain"). What the business owner gets is a good deal of prominence and an opportunity to write the "news" copy that accompanies the feature (it can also be written by the newspaper—either advertising or news will handle this). The owner can also normally review the feature in advance of publication.

The ad feature can be a good way to get your story out the way you want it, providing you can bring in enough advertising to make it pay. If you are arranging an insert or special flyer for the ad feature, you may also be able to negotiate a print overrun to produce extra copies, which you can then use for other marketing and promotional opportunities.

Media Sponsorships

More and more often, news media sponsor special events, either as a community service or to promote themselves to key audiences. Promotion is important when there are several media of the same type in the same market, all competing for audience and ad revenues. By associating themselves with popular public events, outlets promote themselves as good corporate citizens worthy of public support. Broadcast media in particular like to cover or sponsor community events, to demonstrate their commitment to the community (which they can then take to the CRTC as proof of community service when it comes time for licence renewal).

Television and radio stations regularly send station personalities (talkshow hosts, anchor people and weather people—but rarely reporters) to community events, usually in a van emblazoned with the station's call letters. Community-events coverage is seen as a form of mutual benefit, providing publicity for the local events and demonstrating the station's commitment to the community.

Media sponsorships can be negotiated for everything from a peewee softball tournament to a major arts or cultural event. Sponsorship might extend to signage, print references, broadcast references, recognition from organizers at the start of the event and recognition in a program. A large-scale example is Edmonton's Fringe Festival. The Fringe is the highlight of a crowded schedule of summer events in the city, and draws hundreds of thousands of visitors over ten days. Toronto's Caribana Festival is briefer but also draws huge crowds. The media sponsors get special treatment from event organizers in return for the right to be called media sponsor.

You can negotiate media sponsorship through the community relations department of the media outlet you think will reach your target audience. In general, your biggest selling point is either a very large audience that will provide maximum exposure or a very targeted audience that matches the outlet's desired demographic. For example, if you are trying to get media sponsorship to promote a motorcycle safety program, you are more likely to get support from a hard-rock station targeted to 15–25-year-old urban males than you are from a country and western station targeted to older rural listeners.

Another selling point in negotiating media sponsorships is image. You might focus on either the specific positive image associated with a successful existing event or the overall image that will accrue to the media outlet for supporting a worthwhile community event. In exchange, you might offer exclusivity: that outlet will be the only media sponsoring the event. At very large, established events, you can get separate sponsors for each of the radio, television and newspaper coverage — media generally see competition, particularly for advertising dollars, only from media in the same business. (For major sports events, such as golf tournaments and auto races, it is possible to sell media sponsorships, but this transaction is closer to advertising than to media relations. Here we're assuming that you are looking for publicity and are willing to work with local media to get it).

Exclusivity, however, does not mean you can deny other media from attending and covering the event. If you host a car rally and something interesting happens, other media may show up. However, only the media outlet sponsoring the event is allowed to call itself a sponsor and identify with the event. Exclusivity also does not mean boosterism: if the event is badly organized, has a low turnout or proves a dud, the news portion of that media outlet may describe it as such.

What you as the communicator get from media sponsorship is the affiliation of the media outlet with the event. This affiliation may lend credibility to the event, particularly if the media outlet is popular with your audience. But even better, the media outlet will actively promote your event. This might mean free advertising or on-air promotion from broadcasters, including being booked on talk shows. Once you have a media sponsor in principle, you must sit down with the community relations people and negotiate an agreement. It can be as simple as a one-page memo or as complex as a formal contract, depending on the magnitude of the event. What you want to make clear, however, is how often, when and where the outlet will promote the event, and what the event organizers have to do in return (e.g., provide free tickets for on-air promotion, allow the station van to appear at the entrance to the site, hang a banner on the stage). The quid pro quo can include prime space for cameras and microphones and waiver of copyright to allow broadcasters to air original material; it may also extend to such mundane issues as free parking, free passes, free event "goodies" (hats, T-shirts and so on) or invitations to the opening reception.

A wise strategy is to make a list of all the things you could provide to the media and a list of all the things you want from the media; then begin horse-trading. Since you will have prepared detailed communications and media relations plans in advance, keep checking back with your goals as you go through the negotiation process, to remind yourself what you set out to achieve.

To keep your sponsors happy, and to live up to your side of the bargain, get everything in writing with as much explicit detail as possible. (As we've already discussed, if the media is showing up with a van to take pictures, you don't want to make the relationship more complicated than it needs to be). Perhaps you can name a staffer or volunteer whose only job is to be the liaison with the media sponsor. (Other staff or volunteers can work with the rest of the media, if any). Keep a checklist of everything you and the sponsor have agreed to do, and ensure that everything is done. Throughout the event, be sure to recognize your media sponsors and other sponsors, even beyond what you have agreed to: they are making it possible for you to carry out your work.

At large events, you may need to provide accreditation so that media can gain access to event sites, media rooms (for writing and filing stories) and quiet interview spaces. For a more detailed outline to organize a major media event, or deal with major media sponsors, you may want to read *Marketing Public Relations: The Hows That Make It Work*.[3]

Public Service Announcements

Public service announcements (PSAs) are free, brief announcements that radio and televisions stations play to fill time, usually between programs. The Canadian Radio-television and Telecommunication Commission (CRTC) expects all radio and television stations to run a certain amount of free advertising as a public service. To maintain its licence, each station keeps a PSA log to demonstrate that it has fulfilled its obligations. Written PSAs can be faxed or mailed to broadcasters. Be sure your item is clearly labelled as a PSA or directed to the PSA editor on the envelope or cover sheet; the community relations department, not the newsroom, usually determines which PSAs run.

If written, a PSA must be short. A headline at the top will allow the PSA editor to determine what it's about and whether it should run; don't expect the headline to be read on the air. You have 10 to 20 seconds of air time, so keep your information short and focussed on the most critical elements. PSAs are normally aired as people drive to or from work or while they're doing the dishes; your listeners or viewers won't be taking notes. Here is an example of a typical PSA:

PSA: Ourtown Beavers Rummage Sale

Ourtown Beavers are holding a rummage sale this Thursday at 2 p.m. at the old Community Hall. Everyone is welcome to come and find a bargain. That's Thursday at 2 p.m. for the Beavers' rummage sale.

—30—

For more info, please contact:
Marcia Castor
555-1212, e-mail mcastor@ourtown.org

You should include a contact name on the PSA, just as you would with a news release. Media will occasionally follow up on PSAs for news stories, particularly on slow days and in smaller communities. Do not, however, include a phone number in the PSA message itself: listeners/viewers cannot remember a phone number from a 10–to 20-second PSA.

The disadvantage to PSAs is that the station runs them when it wishes, usually when there are no paid ads, which usually means outside of peak hours. On the positive side, PSAs are almost free to create and simple to submit, and they are easily worth the effort as a low-cost, low-risk type of media relations.

A more sophisticated approach is to create your own video or audio PSA. For this, you need the help of an audiovisual consultant or public relations firm, which will involve some cost. (However, don't incur more costs than you would take to undertake an advertising campaign: if you have that kind of budget, you are better off placing real ads). The media prefer to have something ready-made that sounds and looks professional, so if your PSA is well done, it may have a long shelf life.

Another option is to ask a media outlet for its co-operation in creating a professional-looking, professional-sounding PSA with you. The PSA would be used only by that outlet (you can offer exclusivity again), but because it is produced in-house, you have a better chance of having it run by that station. It might also be used over a longer period of time, allowing for greater exposure opportunities.

Community Billboards

Community billboards are the newspaper version of PSAs. Many newspapers, particularly weeklies, run small notices at no charge in a special section. Despite their apparently low profile, these items can have very high readership, particularly in community weeklies. This type of feature is so popular in some newspapers that they charge a small fee for it; it's generally worth it for the type of focussed exposure you can get at essentially the cost of a classified ad.

Self-Publishing: The Newsletter

One of the forgotten media is the newsletter. If you really want to have your own newspaper, it is relatively easy and inexpensive to create one. Before embarking on a newsletter, ask yourself the same questions you would for any other do-it-yourself media undertaking: who is my audience? How does this fit into my overall communications plan or strategy, and what will a newsletter accomplish for me? Even a basic newsletter requires time, attention and money; for the investment required to do a newsletter, you should know clearly what benefit it will provide.

Every major word processing package allows the user to set copy in columns, and specialty desktop publishing software is available for the more ambitious. If you want to undertake newsletter publishing in a serious way, take a course in design or graphics. The software itself won't help you; you must understand the basic principles of design if you're going to create an attractive, readable newsletter.

A newsletter requires some investment of time and resources, but it allows you to speak directly to your audience and permits a degree of two-way communication. It's important to acquire and maintain a mailing list that reaches your target audience (there are dedicated software programs for this task as well). To keep your mailing costs down, talk to Canada Post about rates for various services and how long it takes for delivery. Also talk to a print representative (look under Printers in the Yellow Pages) or your local copy shop to discuss your options for reproduction, graphics, colour, paper stock, binding and trim size — you might be surprised how far you can stretch a newsletter budget with a little creativity.

Self-Publishing: The Website

Websites are an established means of communications. Every major and minor business has one, as do governments at all levels, non-profit agencies, advocacy groups, many individuals and some lunatics. Nevertheless, the penetration of computers in society and the development of user-friendly software have made it possible for anyone to have a website. In a 2006 CRTC report, 75 per cent of Canadian households had a personal computer, up from 49 per cent in 1998.[4] Nearly 25 per cent of Canadians spend more than 25 hours a week on the Internet.[5] The Internet and the website are now established technologies and established media. Once your website is on the Internet, anyone can access it, but it is one of hundreds of millions of websites vying for attention.

For the serious media relations practitioner, a website allows the media to retrieve key information immediately. Many websites now feature a media room or news room. This page directs media to areas of particular interest (news releases, annual reports, statistical data, etc.), which they can view directly without contacting you or the media relations office. The website can save time and, if properly updated and maintained, is of ongoing value as a media resource. Its value as an electronic form of self-publishing is difficult to asses, but potentially great.

However, websites often don't provide what media want: simple information. Instead, reporters may be overloaded by hype and flash. A survey of US journalists found that their major reasons for visiting a website are as follows:

1. Find a PR contact (name and telephone number).

2. Check basic facts about a company (spelling of an executive's name, his/her age, headquarters location, etc.). (These queries are easily handled in a section called Frequently Asked Questions [FAQs] or by posting the latest annual report in the media room).

3. Discover the company's own spin on events.

4. Check financial information.

5. Download images to use as illustrations in stories.[6]

A lot of flash can crash journalists' computers, particularly freelancers who are using older equipment. The same survey indicated that journalists want a contact name and phone number, not an anonymous e-mail address for the webmaster. Journalists don't want to ask questions by e-mail; they still prefer a human contact, whom they can cite in the story if necessary.

The corporate world unfortunately reflects the frustrations of the journalists in the above survey. Many websites lack a contact name and phone number in the media/news room, and the site may be loaded with elements that require high-end equipment.

Websites take time, money and effort to create and maintain (enthusiastic volunteers, particularly IT students looking for work experience, can be of great help to the non-profit and advocacy sectors). Software and opensource products are available to establish websites. Since there is no 'standard' user, navigation software or hardware, basic usability standards and guidelines for website design are available; a simple Internet search will bring up information about usability standards for developers, designers and communicators to help guide you as you build your site. Some of the basic principles that apply to media room design apply to the design of the entire site:

1. Focus on information (statistics, FAQs, annual reports, summaries of programs/services or issues).

2. Have contact people prominently identified with phone numbers.

3. In order to accommodate as wide a range of users as possible, keep your site simple and have your developer follow World Wide Web Consortium, (W3C) usability standards wherever possible; if you deal with or want to deal with media and the public on a regular basis, you should be able to accommodate all users, including, for example, the visually or hearing impaired.

4. Update the page regularly. (This is generally the biggest failing of webmasters, particularly in the non-profit sector. If the website isn't updated regularly once it is designed and launched, users stop visiting it and the investment made in creating the website is lost).

5. Ensure security.

6. If possible (and relevant), add photos or art (e.g., your logo) in easily downloadable formats.

7. Ensure any critical comments you make on the website fall within the provincial laws on defamation and libel: websites are subject to defamation laws.

As with a newsletter, the value of the website should match the resources it takes to maintain it. However, the value of a website goes beyond communicating with the media. Statistics Canada reported in July 2001 that 51 per cent of Canadian households had a least one member who was a regular Internet user.[7] This figure is up from 42 per cent in 1999. Clearly, more and more Canadians are comfortable accessing the Internet for information; the website should be one of the alternatives to media you consider to reach your audience.

Blogs

"In the strictest sense, a blog is someone's online record of the websites he or she visits.... . They have been around since the early days of the Internet."[8] What changed is that new software and online sources have made it easier for people to build their own website (Andrew Smales of Toronto is credited with inventing the first defined blog software in July 1999).[9] Together with improvements in Internet search technology, particularly Google, it is now easier to not only write your own blog, but for other people to find it.

There will be a more detailed analysis of the current (2007) value of blogs as communications tools in Chapter 16. For now, as a source of your own media, blogs can make it a lot easier to get your message out. The main point, as with your website, is to make sure you continue to update it (usually every two or three days is enough as you build your fan base). And promote it, through some of the traditional media or through e-mails to your friends and colleagues. Don't rely on the world to find you; tell the world, more particularly the audience you are trying to reach) where you are and how they can reach you.

Internet Mailing Lists

Maintaining an Internet mailing list (sometimes called a listserv) can be more troublesome. A mailing list is something like an electronic newsletter and is usually focussed by interest (e.g., MS patient support, women's folk music, left-wing political advocacy, discussion of local plants, etc.); information for joining a mailing list is often provided as part of a website. If dynamic discussion is permitted, mailing lists can become virtual communities. A non-interactive list (on which only the list owner can send messages to subscribers) can be a great way to distribute information to many people at once but can also feel like targeted advertising to the subscribers.

A person joins a mailing list by sending a request to the list owner (sometimes automated with a software program, such as Majordomo); the person's e-mail address is then added to the subscriber list. When a subscriber has something to say, he or she sends the message to the list and it is distributed to all the addresses on the subscriber list. Mailing lists may be moderated, in which the list owner (the moderator) receives and approves messages before they are sent on to subscribers, or unmoderated, in which messages are sent freely by the operating software. Moderated lists are normally a more controlled environment, while unmoderated lists frequently erupt in wars of words (called flames), which may drive all but the hostile parties from the list.

The key to mailing lists is the motivation of the subscriber. You cannot add someone's name to a mailing list without permission (to do so is a form of spamming, and it's bad Internet practice), so you must have a topic of sufficient interest to draw subscribers. However, once the software is in place and subscribers have joined, a mailing list can be another low-cost, low-risk form of do-it-yourself media.

The last two chapters have examined in some detail how to get media attention and how to produce your own media. The next step is to consider what to do once you succeed: handling the media calls and interviews.

The Interview

11

At this point, we're at step seven of the nine-step media relations plan. Let's quickly recap the steps we've covered over the past several chapters.

1. Define the problem and conduct a situational analysis.

2. Set goals and get approval to develop a media program.

3. Research media coverage of you, your organization or your issue.

4. Develop media policy and procedures.

5. Get media training.

6. Approach the media.

7. Do the interview and supply the information.

8. Evaluate coverage.

9. Revise and update the plan.

Whether you take a planned approach such as this step-by-step system or conduct media relations on the fly, at some point you are going to have to talk to the media—usually in the form of an interview.

Overview and Limitations

The interview is the single most important aspect of media relations. News releases don't get reprinted verbatim, and reporters don't synthesize reports and facts into stories without asking for comment. Given that one of the key aspects of newsworthiness is how something affects people, the most common way for a reporter to build a story is to talk to a person, whether it's a person affected by an issue, a person responsible for an issue or simply a person who understands and can explain an issue. News is about people, and that fact means reporters will want to talk to people.

That process of talking is called an interview, which means, at its essence, "to meet with someone to get information."[1] However, that basic definition belies a complex and sometimes flawed process. At the best of times, with the best people, a simple exchange of information can be misinterpreted, misconstrued or just plain missed. In a news interview, with acute time pressure on one participant and anxiety-inducing dread on the other, the chance of making mistakes is even higher. The news interview is an artificial form of human interaction. One party asks questions, one party answers, the whole process militating against the kind of interactive, back-and-forth exchange and exploration of ideas that normal conversation allows.

The dread some interview subjects feel is quite real and amply documented. For example, a survey of US hospital CEOs shows that while the biggest problem they have in dealing with the media is the kind of media ambivalence we discussed in Chapter 3, their three next biggest complaints relate to difficulties in the interview process:

Greatest problems in dealing with the media:

1. Media misunderstand or lack information on health care or hospitals: 29.9%

2. I do not know how to say things: 26.6%

3. I am quoted out of context: 21.2%

4. I lack media training or experience: 13.1%[2]

Many CEOs—highly educated, managerially skilled leaders of major corporations—find the interview process the most problematic aspect about dealing with the media. Underlying this concern is likely a sense of lack of control. Managers are hired, among other things, for their ability to control people and make things happen. Interviews tend to be largely uncontrolled, or are controlled by the questioner, not the subject; for a personality used to leading and directing, this turnabout can be distressing, frightening, frustrating or even infuriating. (The subject's desire to control the message regardless of the context is called "source control" and is practised most often by politicians). Thus, if you are coaching or supporting someone who is preparing to do an interview, imagine yourself in the spotlight and offer that person sympathy and support.

Reporters also find the interview problematic. Working in a volatile environment and trying desperately to master fact and detail under time pressure, reporters often find that interviews pose a conflict between their desire to get information and opinion, and the source's desire to get out a positive message, regardless of the question. Because of this inherent clash, journalists have described interviews as "the most perilous and unreliable" way to get information.[3] Or, to put it another way, "None of us, as journalists or social scientists, trust the report of a single interview."[4] To get around unreliability, reporters look for external, objective verification of statements through fact, data or third-party corroboration; reporters also look for, and challenge, the logical consistency of the statements the interview subject is making.

Despite the limitations of the interview as a means of exchanging information or engaging in meaningful dialogue, it is still the fundamental tool of both the reporter and the media relations practitioner. It forms the crux of the relationship and will often determine the type and nature of the subsequent coverage.

Thus, to start with, we will look at some examples of how not to do an interview. Then we will look at some of the principles behind successful interviews, along with some variations according to different interview formats (e.g., hard news versus talk show). Finally, we will look at how to handle unfair and leading questions. The philosophical themes underpinning this chapter are intended to guide you and your client through a successful interview. Ultimately, you want to be prepared for it, know why you are doing it and have enough sense of the reporter's needs to provide information and good quotes. You must also recognize your need to get your message out, in a way that accommodates both you and the reporter. The best result from an interview is positive coverage in media—that is, a fair and accurate treatment of you and your issue.

How Not To Do an Interview

Generally speaking, there are five ways to do a bad interview and jeopardize your relationship with the media, your target audiences and your client/employer. Let's examine the failures and the problems they create one at a time.

Failure 1: Don't ask for and agree to the ground rules

When you take the call from the media, you should ask a few questions before you agree to do an interview. (That is, of course, unless you sent out a news release or other media item soliciting media attention; in that case, you should be ready to respond on the spot. If you are not, you should not have sent it out. One way to irritate a reporter and jeopardize a relationship is to seek out media attention, then be unable or unwilling to respond when it comes). If you're not expecting a media call, be sure the reporter supplies some basic information before you answer any questions.

Who are you and what media do you represent? This question rarely needs to be asked, but sometimes you may find yourself dealing with a novice reporter or someone who doesn't have a professional background, such as a newsletter editor or community cable volunteer. Introductions matter; be sure you know who you're talking to and the questioner knows, in turn, who you are.

What are you calling about? Again, the media will rarely call and start peppering you with questions right off the bat. The reporter will normally say something like this: "It's Jenny Smits from CCKK radio. I'm calling about a story we're following about the effect of gamma rays on man-in-the-moon marigolds. Is that something you can help us out with?" It is fair to ask not only what the topic of the interview is but also what documentation has motivated the call (such as a news release from the man-in-the-moon marigold society decrying the risk of nuclear power to their favourite plant). The reporter should be willing to supply this information before the interview so you can prepare to speak appropriately to the topic.

What would you like from me/us? This question narrows down whether the reporter is looking for basic information, which you can provide by fax or referring to your website, or for commentary and opinion. This question also helps you determine whether the reporter is making a straightforward request that you or a researcher can answer, or whether you need a CEO, minister or specialist to respond.

Do you need any specific information? This question helps narrow the inquiry down further. Reporters will sometimes send over a set of specific questions they want answered or list of information they are seeking. Do not, however, use this reasonable question as a lever to demand that the reporter send over detailed questions before you agree to talk to them. There must be some willingness on your part to let the reporter ask questions as the issue develops and he/she absorbs the information; asking for a list of specific questions before you agree to be interviewed is one of two ways to convince reporters you know absolutely nothing about media. (The other is to ask to see and approve their story before it goes to print).

In some cases, you may be asked to provide a set of questions for an interviewer to ask. This request is generally restricted to understaffed talk shows, which can't afford researchers. Be warned, however, that even if they ask for a list of stock questions, they are not bound to use it.

When do you need it? Sometimes reporters need the information right away; other times they're seeking materials for a feature they're working on during slow periods. Reporters will often tell you how quickly they need your response, but if they don't, ask: this knowledge will help determine your schedule and that of your spokesperson. The timeline may also lead to some negotiation. For example, you may say, "Our man-in-the-moon marigold specialist is tied up at a conference out of town today, but should be back tomorrow. Can it wait that long?" If the situation is urgent, you may need to find your specialist, pull him or her out of the conference and arrange a phone interview. Or you may simply have to tell the reporter your key spokesperson is unavailable and the reporter will have to wait: "Our specialist is giving expert testimony today and tomorrow at a civil trial, and cannot speak until she has completed her testimony. We really don't know how long that will be but I can call back when she is available." The worst the media will report, if you've made an honest effort, is that a spokesperson "was unavailable for comment." If you don't respond to the call, however, you may learn that "calls to the office went unreturned."

What format is it going to be? This question is for broadcast media who ask you or your client to appear on a show. Specific questions to follow up with include the following:

· Is it live or taped?
· How long will the interview be?
· Will you use the whole piece or edit it?
· Will other people be appearing on the same program/interview?
· Will you be interviewing other people involved with this issue?
  (This information is particularly important if you are involved in a
  contentious issue, such as labour relations; for example, if you are a
  union representative, you want to ask whether management will also
  be interviewed).
· Is it open-line format? Will I be expected to take questions from callers?
· Will I have time to make a statement or state my point of view before
  the questions come? (This request can often be accommodated by a
  question from the host and generally occurs at the beginning of an
  interview to set the stage for the questions. However, be sure you have a
  chance to state your view in your own words).

In general, appearances on talk shows and interview programs can be negotiated. In some cases, organizations set out issues they will and will not address. For example, the John Howard Society, which operates a number of prison and community programs, is often glad to speak about its work. However, discussions on the *Young Offenders Act* are generally contentious and fruitless. John Howard spokespersons often tell reporters explicitly that they will not discuss young offenders, but are glad to take all questions in other areas.

In this kind of negotiation, if the outlet does not agree to your terms, you can decline the request. If the outlet wants to touch on another area, you can negotiate exactly in what manner it will do so. However, in this kind of negotiation, unless you have specifically solicited media attention on the particular topic, you are perfectly within your rights to decline the interview. You are also within your rights to refuse to do an interview pitting you and someone else against each other, particularly if you don't want to have that kind of adversarial relationship. In a negotiation like this, you must keep your focus and remember why you wanted to do media in the first place: if the request doesn't meet your purpose or reflect your values, say no and state why you refuse. You can say no to the media, particularly if you feel you or your organization will likely be harmed by the encounter.

Once again, most professional journalists will supply this information when they call, but you or your client might be taken by surprise if you don't establish a basic relationship and some ground rules right from the start.

Failure 2: Be unprepared

This point should be so obvious as to go without stating, but unprepared interviews occur frequently enough that it deserves underlining. Don't do an interview, particularly a live interview, if you are not prepared for it. Preparation includes having key messages ready and practising answers to potential questions. It also means having all the information you will need to support your case readily at hand. Further, it means recalling what your purpose was in agreeing to do the interview. Prepare according to your experience and the type of interview. If the interviewer is a familiar beat reporter asking for simple facts, you don't need to spend much time in preparation. If it's an investigative show such as *The Fifth Estate* or *W5*, expect to spend several days in preparation.

Failure 3: Forget why you are doing the interview

It is possible to be so prepared for an interview that you are overprepared, so preoccupied with specific messages and questions that you can't remember why you are doing the interview in the first place. Keeping in mind the larger perspective will help you during the interview, particularly if you feel yourself getting bogged down in minutiae and excessive detail. When you feel overwhelmed, don't just fall back to a key message. If your key message pops up out of context, you may look like you're evading the question or trying to control the interview.

You agreed to do the interview in the first place because you need the profile, want to convince people of your point of view, are performing a public service, are trying to communicate with shareholders or any other goal-directed reason. While you may want to do media because you're bored and you like being on television, you should have a better reason than that. Remind yourself of your reasons before you do the interview, to help you keep things in perspective as the interview proceeds.

Failure 4: Fight for control

As I noted earlier in this chapter, the media are sensitive about their independence and strongly resist source control. Control may take many forms: reiterating key messages regardless of the question; speaking beyond the interview to the target audience (and often ignoring the question to reiterate key messages); controlling the setting of the interview; or exercising control by offering subtle deals (which basically comes down to "Be good to me and I'll be good to you"). Deals and negotiations with media are fine; they should, however, be explicit and made in good faith, so that both parties know what they are getting into and the legitimate needs of both parties can be met.

Practitioners and interview subjects should be careful of trying to exert too much source control. The media react against it, viewing it as essentially dishonest, an attempt to put a positive spin on negative news. Getting into control battles with reporters during an interview is risky business, more likely to backfire than to succeed. Don't forget that media generally have the last word. As we discussed earlier, personalities with a need to command and control will only get frustrated trying to deal with the media. As Vice-President Dick Cheney put it: "I did not look on the press as an asset in doing what I had to do. Frankly, I looked on it as a problem to be managed." If you're not comfortable with the lack of control you have over the media, look for alternative means of communications.

As I commented earlier, politicians are generally the most aggressive practitioners of source control, as the following example demonstrates. This exchange is drawn from an interview of US Senator Ted Kennedy by Bryant Gumble on NBC's *Today Show*. Gumble wants to talk about an incident with Kennedy's nephew over Easter; Kennedy doesn't.

> GUMBLE: But what about you, Senator, will you be able to...
> KENNEDY: Well, we'll be battling along, and I think we've got a good program. I think we've had good meetings with our colleagues, in the Senate and also in our conversations with the leadership: Senator Foley, Rich Gephardt, and Danny Rostenkowski, Henry Waxman and many others. And I think we'll have a good program and I believe the American people are well ahead of the politicians

on this one. After we pass that program, people, I think, are going to say why did it take so long?

GUMBLE: Senator, do you think the view of the American people of Senator Ted Kennedy has changed?

KENNEDY: Well, I'll have to worry about what their health insurance issues are. And I think they understand that they got some real important problems and I think we have a program that can address them and I look forward to the debate and the discussions.

GUMBLE: Senator, are you not going to talk about the Easter...

KENNEDY: Well, I'm glad to talk about whatever you'd like to. I'd like to talk about health insurance but I'm glad, Bryant, to talk about anything you'd like to.

GUMBLE: Sir—

KENNEDY: I enjoyed your speech up there in Providence College where you spoke up there and my son graduated.

GUMBLE: Thank you very much Senator. Let me ask you a couple of quick questions if I might. You have obviously taken a public relations pounding as a result of the Easter incident. What's your view of the way the media has handled this alleged incident and your role in it?

KENNEDY: Well, I've been in public life for some 30 years. I think I've enjoyed more favorable stories than others, but I believe by and large I've been fairly treated and look forward to the continued work in the Senate.[5]

Rene Henry commented on this exchange:

Senator Kennedy continued to give positive answers and get the message across to viewers that he wanted to give, whether or not they were answers to questions being asked by the reporter. The important thing [for him] is to stay in charge of the interview.[6]

Whatever feeling of control Senator Kennedy may have had in the interview was more than offset by what the viewers saw: a politician who not only refused to answer the questions of a popular TV host, but in fact ignored the questions altogether, preferring instead to deliver mini-speeches and homilies that had nothing to do with what the reporter asked. The Senator looked and sounded evasive—and typically political, to the public perception. You must ask yourself or your client: is that how we want to appear to the public?

Bear in mind that the public generally awards politicians very low credibility; partisan groups, such as environmentalists, businesspeople and unions, have only slightly more (refer back to the credibility chart in Chapter 2; politicians are at the bottom of the list). If in fact you choose to exercise this tactic in a media interview, remember that it puts you in the company of people who have very little credibility with the public, let alone with the media. Remember, too, the types of professions which are more credible: health and university people. Among other things, these speakers have or can refer to objective evidence to support their statements, and are often viewed as acting more in the public interest than in their own.

There may be times when the partisan road is the only one to take, and thus a road you choose to take, particularly if you are in the middle of a contentious, high-profile public debate. No matter how partisan you are, though, you had better have more going for you than just a few key messages that you reiterate without regard to the questions.

Failure 5: Stick too closely to formulas

Media trainers will often recommend that interview subjects answer questions by formula. While this advice is intended to help the subject understand the unique nature of a media interview, taken to extremes or dogmatically applied, it can backfire and make the subject appear as if he or she is deliberately ignoring questions.

One favourite formula is to make 30-second mini speeches for television interviews.[7] It's bad advice, however. Mini speeches are not as appropriate to TV interviews as are short, pertinent responses: watching a talking head bark at you in 30-second bursts is rather off-putting. Another technique, which is occasionally helpful, is to answer a question with a question.[8] Use this tactic judiciously. As a response to every question, it would be maddening; as an occasional rhetorical device, it might provide some insight into your decision-making.

More helpful is the "bridging" technique.[9] In this process you first answer the question put to you, find a way of making a transition or connection to your key message (bridging), then state your key message. Bridging is an effective way to accommodate both the reporter's issue (answering the question put to you) and your issue (getting your key message out). However, don't use the bridging technique every time. After a while the technique shows and people realize you are using technique to communicate (the audience shouldn't see your technique any more than reporters should let the audience see theirs). The recommended formula for how much time to spend on each aspect of the answer (15-second response to question, 10-second bridge, 15-second key message) can be more distracting than helpful. Given the anxiety and artificiality involved with doing media interviews, you or your spokesperson should concentrate most on the question asked and having a good answer for it, rather than trying to remember the formula and how much time you should be spending on each part of it.

A further risk to a formula, beyond its distracting qualities and its sometimes questionable relevance to the interview, is that if it is uncreatively or too insistently applied, it can backfire, leading to disaster. For example, one theory of media states that you should have a single overriding communications objective (SOCO).[10] While I support the notion of purpose and simplicity when it comes to media relations, taking this theory to its extreme can result in some stilted exchanges, such as the example that follows.

A reporter for CBC-TV's *Marketplace* was investigating a story about why all the chemicals in a pesticide are not listed on the label. (The unlisted ingredients are called inert because they do not directly kill the pests—those chemicals are called active ingredients; the inert ingredients are those added for secondary reasons, such as giving an aroma to the pesticide or helping it spray). The reporter had spoken to an apparent victim of environmental contamination, a scientist who had cited the carcinogenic risks of some common "inert" pesticide chemicals and an advocate who had contributed a couple of quick, provocative sound bites ("These are secret killers; this is a conspiracy of silence"). The following is the exchange between the reporter and a spokesperson from Agriculture Canada, who kept on message, regardless of the question:

REPORTER [lead-in]: We wanted to speak to someone in charge of the pesticide policy about this. Instead, Ottawa put forward ... an information officer. And a strange thing happened. She gave us the same answer 26 times, no matter what the question.

COMMUNICATOR: Pesticides, by nature, are toxic. They are meant to control a living organism. Pesticides, when used according to label directions, can be used safely.

REPORTER: I have here a Canadian government report which lists Canada's 50 most toxic chemicals, and a full one-third are inerts. Shouldn't we be concerned?

VOICE-OVER: When we repeatedly presented her with evidence from both inside and outside the government about the toxicity of some of these inerts, her answer was...

COMMUNICATOR: Pesticides are poisons. They are meant to be used to control a living organism. When pesticides are used according to label directions, they can be used safely.

REPORTER: I can find out what's in a box of cookies, things that might be harmful to my health, but I can't find out what's in a box of pesticides. You're not telling us; isn't that irresponsible?

COMMUNICATOR: Pesticides by nature are toxic...

REPORTER: OK, we've heard this before...

COMMUNICATOR: ...and they're meant to be used according to label directions.[11]

This interview is even more painful to watch than it is to read. The result is that the environmentalists' view prevails in the story, in large part because no other relevant point of view was introduced. This point can't be made too often: if you choose to limit to a simplistic key message the information you give to the media—or choose not to tell your story at all—they will go elsewhere for information and the resulting story could result in the loss of your reputation. While there are times when you should say no to the media (as discussed elsewhere in this chapter) or restrict information that you are willing to release (for legal or confidentiality reasons), nevertheless, you should ask yourself: if I decline to speak to the media or refuse to disclose information to them, what are the chances that this decision will result in a damaging or misleading story?

As the above exchange shows, while the SOCO theory is sound and comes highly recommended, it and other formulas should be applied with a leaven of common sense and an appreciation for the actual question asked.

How To Conduct an Interview: Basic Guidelines

Once you've discussed the interview with the reporter and are ready to do it (if in fact you haven't done it already), here a few rules to follow, beyond simply responding to questions.

Be accessible

Once again, this point should go without saying, but it is important to stay focussed on it because media identify it as a major barrier to effective media relations. A 1976 study showed that "... PR people are not immediately reachable by phone more than 50 per cent of the time."[12] A recent Ipsos Reid study confirms that accessibility is still an area in which corporations can improve when dealing with the media.[13]

Be honest, open and frank

This point should speak for itself. Honesty does not mean full disclosure, however, or providing the reporter with information outside the scope of the interview topic. You may have agreed to avoid some topics, and you may be under legal or ethical constraints in terms of what information you can provide.

If there are reasons for not answering a question, state them rather than simply replying "no comment." Media understand and can work with such statements as "I can't speak to that because it is before the courts," "That is proprietary information and we don't want to disclose it to our competition" and "Patient confidentiality means I can't talk about the specifics of this case."

Address bad news

There's no use spending a lot of time and energy denying the obvious. If your company's stock has fallen, your fundraising campaign falls short or things simply didn't work out the way you had hoped, be open about it. Don't be unrealistically positive (e.g., "The fact that we have to lay off 100 people will give them all the opportunity they need to pursue new career directions"). Speak to the situation directly ("We're having a bad year because the Asian market has fallen, and we have to lay off 100 staff") and sensitively ("We recognize this is bad news for the staff affected"). If it is possible to be optimistic that the situation will change, say so; but be careful it doesn't come out as spin doctoring and doesn't misrepresent the situation ("We will be calling those staff back once the economic situation has improved; when that will be I don't know because so much depends on external situations").

Be on the record all the time

Barring an ethical situation in which you feel morally obligated to provide media with information they should know but are in danger of risking your job or contract by doing so, you should never go off the record. You should not tell the media anything if you are unwilling to do so publicly. If there are circumstances that constrain you from being fully open, state them, but it should not be necessary to go off the record.

Also bear in mind that when you bump into a reporter at a hockey game or in the supermarket, you are on the record. Reporters will always be alert to a good story regardless of where they hear it, and if you say one thing in a social situation and another in a work situation, it will destroy your credibility with them. Regardless of how close you are to a reporter or how casual the social interaction, bear in mind that if you are practising media relations you are always on the job and always liable to be quoted.

This circumspection applies to other people as well. In small communities or in small professional circles, reporters may hear third-hand something you've said that contradicts what you've told reporters. A basic principle to follow is never tell a reporter anything you wouldn't tell anybody else, and never speak with anyone about information you wouldn't want to see printed in a newspaper.

Some people believe that good communications practitioners must have strong contacts in the media. This belief is mistaken and reflects a minority view, however. The news business is volatile, making the development of such relationships difficult, and many reporters are suspicious of communicators who want to mix with them socially as well as professionally. Certainly such mingling does happen, but it reflects old-school communications.

Call back if necessary

Often, the interview is over before you realize you forgot something key or have finally found a way to explain a difficult concept easily and simply. Don't be afraid to call the reporter back if you feel the new point is important enough. Reporters will sometimes do the same with you if they begin to write the story and find they are missing a piece of information that will make the story clearer.

Have fun

So traumatic is the interview for most people that they forget it can actually be an enjoyable experience. The joy can come from simply getting media attention for yourself or your issue; from finally being able to correct a public misconception; from helping your audience gain critical information or insight; or simply from being treated as an expert whose views are considered important enough to generate media attention. Having fun doesn't mean that you've lost sight of what you're doing or that you can be unprepared. It simply means that you can—and should—go into an interview situation feeling confident, prepared and ready to see all the results of your planning and preparation come to fruition.

Attributes of a Good Interview

The most satisfactory interview is one that accommodates both your needs and the interviewer's, one that leaves both of you feeling a sense of accomplishment and satisfaction. This section looks at some of the characteristics of a good interview.

Be engaged, be focussed

There are many formulaic "tips" for handling the interview or media relations (see above).[14] Again, beware of slavish adherence to formulas (including mine): the interview subject needs to be engaged in the interview and focussed on his or her message. Handling both the information and the communication formula at the same time is more art than mechanical exercise.

We have stressed the second issue—focus—repeatedly through the last few chapters. Focus simply refers to you knowing what you are there for and what you want to say. Engagement, however, is rarely discussed by media advisors. Engagement simply means that you are actively involved in the interview, are paying close attention to the questions and are picking up on the body language and non-verbal communication of the interview—all the things you would normally do when engaged in an interesting discussion with another person. In the course of a normal interview, as with a normal conversation, you will have time to make your point; meanwhile, answer the particular question the reporter is asking before you head off into key messages. Be confident that you will be heard and act confidently—remind yourself that the media wanted to talk to you in the first place. Unfortunately, subjects, particularly novice subjects, too often come to the interview with a passive attitude that basically boils down to "answer the questions and get this over with as soon as possible."

Remind yourself that you want to be interviewed, that you sought out and agreed to this interview. Even if you are responding to contentious and difficult issues, the interview is your chance to tell your story. Starting with that attitude, engage with the interviewer. You won't be able to rant or orate, but by paying attention, you can help ensure that the reporter gets the information and opinion he or she needs. Within that framework, you can find opportunities to get your message out.

To help meet the balance of engagement and focus, you must bring some essential attitudes to the interview process.

Be accurate

This is yet another point that should not need to be stated, but it is crucial. Beyond simply knowing what you're talking about, you should be ready to say "I don't know" if in fact you don't; guessing and speculating can be disastrous, particularly if the reporter has done his or her homework and has more accurate information than you have. For many subjects, saying "I don't know" feels like an admission of failure; in fact, it is simply part of being honest and open. If there is a reason you don't know something, state it (e.g., "We haven't completed testing yet, and until we do we won't know what caused this situation to arise"). However, the information you do give must be accurate and should be verifiable.

Act like an authority

This advice doesn't mean that you should be authoritarian (overbearing and dictatorial), but rather that you should look, act and sound like an authority (knowledgeable and reliable) on the subject. At base, the media want to talk to you because they have defined you as a newsworthy person whose views are relevant and interesting (remember, they're working on behalf of their audience). They want you to come across as an expert because it adds depth and seriousness to the story. So act like an expert. Show confidence during the interview that you are the right person to discuss the topic.

If you are really not an expert or authority, you should refer the reporter elsewhere or find someone in the organization who is better qualified than you to speak to the matter.

Present a case

It's not enough to give a reporter a set of facts and expect the story to write itself. You must have a point of view. Express it, then back it up with fact, reason or argument (in the sense of debate, not confrontation). You can make a case as a partisan person (e.g., a lawyer or union leader arguing your case in the public) or as an objective party concerned with public welfare (e.g., an academic who researches the issue at hand and has data to share). While some days your interview topic may be as basic as how many tonnes of potatoes PEI produces in a year, in most cases you must frame your information with a good argument.

Bring emotion relevant to the issue

Unless you are simply providing factual or statistical information, you may be involved in an area where it is reasonable to express emotion. If you are advocating increased funding for health concerns, such as SIDS or cancer, for example, you may want to express your passionate conviction that the parents and loved ones of victims need more support. If you are introducing a hot new toy or piece of software to the market, you can do so with a sense of humour and fun. If you are embroiled in a bitter public debate, it is normal to speak with a sense of anger and outrage about your opponent's stand—and the media may even want to goad you into it.

Of course, emotion may not be appropriate to every situation. Civil servants are not expected to get personally involved in issues. Likewise, researchers, physicians and social workers often maintain an attitude of professional distance from the people they deal with; by not becoming emotionally involved, they increase the likelihood of providing better service.

Whatever the case, if emotion is appropriate to the issue at hand, feel free to express it. It is one element of an interview, and you should give some attention to it in your preparation. Showing some emotion or concern also humanizes you and your issue, and allows a means of connecting with the audience.

Use a visual

Chapter 9 discussed the importance of a visual element in helping the audience remember a story. Visuals also can aid tremendously in explaining a complex process or issue quickly and simply, and saving a good deal of narrative description. There is some validity, after all, to the expression that a picture is worth a thousand words.

Television and newspaper reporters look for visuals as key parts of the story. The visual sometimes may simply be you as photographed during the interview, or it may be you doing something active or demonstrative of your place in the story, such as preparing picket signs in anticipation of a strike. The visual sometimes consists of a tour of a site or facility, or may be a re-enactment of an item that can't otherwise be shown (e.g., IV drug users' syringes at a needle exchange).

Some visuals don't lend themselves to a story at all and shouldn't be introduced if they are going to distract from the issue. However, just as you keep a verbal key message in mind as you go into an interview, consider whether you have a visual element that will help demonstrate or support your story.

Make a good physical presentation

Presentation refers to your physical appearance and ability to speak well during an interview. While presentation may be important, its absence is more noticeable. If you speak, dress and act as you normally would at work or while making a presentation, you should have no problem. However, if you have the other necessary attributes going for you—if you are confident about being in the interview, are prepared and engaged in the dialogue while focussing on your message—presentation tends to take care of itself. Worrying about presentation more than about the important attributes you should bring to an interview can be counterproductive. As one media trainer put it: "It won't matter that your shoes are shined if your foot is in your mouth."[15]

As for what to wear, consider an interview to be part of your daily routine: dress and act as you would when you are on the job. You don't need to dress up or down, although you should pay attention to basic grooming: hair combed, clothes clean, shirt tucked in, tie knotted and so on. Avoid excessive or distracting clothing or jewellery unless you're in show business and that's part of the act. Don't worry about studio makeup; wear what you normally wear, if anything, but bear in mind this advice: "Make-up? Don't worry about it. There is no make-up in outdoors interviews, and in a studio you may find someone to apply it. If you try to do it yourself, you'll look weird."[16]

In addition to your physical presentation, give a thought to the physical location of the interview. If the interview is for television, doing it close to the scene of the action (if there is any action) is always recommended: it adds dynamism and interest to the interview. If you're an emergency physician, being interviewed in the emergency room is good; if you're a software manufacturer, the plant or the lab is a great setting. Standing up outside is preferred if you can manage it; it puts you on the same level as the reporter, who will do his or her standup outside to close the interview. If you're sitting down, particularly in a studio, lean forward slightly in your chair; it will make you look more engaged.

Wherever you do the interview, get used to being close to the reporter, who will likely want to be close to you. Part of the need for closeness is that the reporter is holding a microphone near your face to get the best sound. Closeness is also part of media tradition. "Up close and personal" may be a cliché in this age of long-range mics and zoom lenses, but reporters often prefer to follow it anyway, so they can appear close to the action, which in many cases is you.

Use your key messages

Remember that for most interviews (broadcast interviews in particular), you need one key message. Although some trainers recommend three key messages, it's usually two too many, particularly for a basic 30-second radio/TV story. Stay focussed on your key message and ensure it gets out.

Be ready to introduce your key message at a germane point in the interview, but don't be obsessive. Trying to get back to the key message from a question that points in another direction can be distracting and frustrating for the interviewer as well as the audience (in the case of a live interview). Reporters are pretty savvy about key messages, and some will baldly ask outright, "What is your key message?" to get the topic out of the way before doing the interview.

Don't overpractise key messages, soundbites and mini speeches unless you're running for some kind of political office or leadership position. And even then, many media practitioners (and a large segment of the public) are leery about the candidate who comes across as too slick. Here is some good advice for anyone going into an interview, politician or not:

A candidate can't be too smooth. If a communications effort is too smooth is just becomes that—a communications effort on the candidate's behalf rather than projection of the candidate himself. In the end, communications skills alone can't do it. I think that eventually the man himself must show himself.[17]

By all means have a six–to eight-second soundbite ready: it helps the broadcast audience in particular to remember complex issues. But don't depend on your soundbite alone to get you through. Even the briefest hard-news interview will last three or four minutes and will cover other issues than the one your soundbite encapsulates. Be ready for all of it.

One final suggestion: don't bother trying to compete with reporters, particularly television reporters, in terms of verbal skills and visual *éclat*. That's their job, not yours. Be who you are, be prepared and engaged, and you will do a great interview.

We've spent some time and detail on the interview, both preparing for it and engaging in it. It may not be necessary to invest in this much detail for every interview, but it is necessary to pay careful attention to each interview situation, whether you are in an organized, planned situation or flying by the seat of your pants in a crisis situation. The interview is the key element of your relationship with the media and will determine whether you achieve the results you want from your media relations plans. There is still more to consider, however. Experienced practitioners can often predict and prepare for recurring or common media questions, and that will be the focus of the next chapter.

The Interview Continued: Questions and Answers

12

After all the time you spend preparing what you want to say, you also need to prepare for some specific questions the media are likely to ask, good and bad. Up to a point, media practitioners can predict with fair accuracy what kinds of questions reporters are likely to ask, and interview subjects should be as prepared to answer these questions as they are to deliver their key message.

The Basic Answer Format

First, let's take a look at the most common way of answering media questions, particularly in live situations where the media are looking for quick answers.

You should remember that reporters and anchorpersons will likely be prepared for an interview, particularly in live interviews on air, such as a phone-in show or a public-affairs broadcast. CBC and talk shows will usually follow a script. Here is the CBC radio approach to handling interviews:

> All interviews on CBC radio shows are based around something called a "green." The green is the script for the interview, and it usually includes a "bill" (a couple of sentences that one can use to promo the interview coming up later in the show), an introduction, questions and thorough background information. This means the interview is less spontaneous than you might imagine, but it keeps things focused and allows the interview to have a dramatic arc, if you will.[1]

Conclusion first, explanation second

One of the hardest aspects to understand for people who are new to media is the notion of giving the conclusion first, then providing an explanation. This structure flies in the face of the way we were taught to write in school (propose the argument first, provide the evidence, then state the conclusion). However, reporters want you to get to the point first by answering their questions, then filling in the rest later. You still provide complete information; you simply have to reformat it to make it media-friendly. If you don't, you run the risk of appearing evasive and non-co-operative.

Let's work through an example. In a typical document, the question "What happened?" would be answered chronologically, reviewing the history of the event up to the moment of interest:

> We turned off the auxiliary power for routine scheduled maintenance but had a sudden, unexpected demand for power from the hospital that strained our overall capacity. We shifted available power to the hospital but had to sacrifice power elsewhere; we chose the suburb of Dullville as the place that likely had the least need for short-term power. The situation is now rectified and we have power throughout town.

In media, you provide the same answer, but do it backwards. Here's the answer to the question "What happened?" in a journalistic treatment:

> Our town's power was out because we had a greater need at the hospital. Our capacity was low because our auxiliary power was down for routine maintenance. We have power throughout the city now.

This version provides the same information as the first, but it is shortened and rephrased into conclusion first, explanation second to suit media expectations.

There may be times (such as a technical briefing, news conference or scrum) when you want to make a detailed statement first, presenting facts in chronological or narrative order. In general, however, once the interview gets underway, you should answer the reporter's questions directly, then provide the supporting information and detail.

Basic Questions

Now we're ready to look at some of the most common questions asked in news interviews, both good and bad.

Five W's and two H's

We discussed the five W's (who, what, when, where, why) and two H's (how, how much) of newsgathering earlier. You should anticipate and be able to answer these questions, or else have a good reason why you cannot. In general, *Why?* poses the most problem for practitioners and is hardest to answer. For example, AIDS researchers still don't know with certainty how this disease evolved and therefore say so; they often point out the need for further research before a definitive answer can be given. Similarly, if your company or municipality has had a mishap, you may not be able to give the reason immediately. One way to deal with this reality is to state you will provide an answer once you have completed an investigation.

The five W's and two H's can each be important depending on the nature of the story. For example, if the mayor has just won a humanitarian award, the *Who?* of the story will be most important. If a group of developers has received approval in principle to build a major new shopping mall, the *When?* and *Where?* might be most important. It is possible to anticipate the media's focus on an issue and either create your key message in anticipation of the media's likely interest or, if your key message is different, find a way of linking back to it from the media's questions (paying attention, as discussed in the last chapter, to ensure you address the question asked, not just to reiterate the key message).

What, why and what next?

In hard-news stories in particular, three basic questions predominate: *What happened? Why did it happen? What are you going to do about it?* These questions form a good starting point for media preparation; from there, you can prepare simple, easy-to-understand answers. Consider these questions not only as you prepare for an interview, but also as part of a statement to read at a news conference or scrum, or for inclusion in a news release.

The same questions are asked in bad-news stories (such as disasters, emergencies and plant closures). Since you know the media will ask these questions, you might as well address them yourself and develop your credibility as the kind of spokesperson or organization that can meet hard questions head on.

The question *What happened?* tends to be fact-oriented, trying to determine what lawyers refer to as "the facts of the case." If the facts are in dispute or unclear, make it clear that you are relating your understanding of the situation at this time. If it is a volatile situation, such as a strike, crisis or protest, underscore that these are the facts as you understand them at the moment; the situation may change.

The question *Why did it happen?* is the question that seeks to assign responsibility for blame, particularly if what happened was bad. For example, if the story is a major pileup on the 401, was the weather a factor, was the accident caused by poor driving or is that portion of the highway poorly designed? For legal reasons, be careful about ascribing blame or responsibility; as always, speak to what you know about, and avoid speculation. During the 1996 Summer Olympics in Atlanta, for example, a volunteer security guard found and reported a bomb at a popular party spot. Media speculation pointed to the security guard as the person who planted the bomb. After several lawsuits, the media had to apologize and pay restitution to the man: there was no evidence at all to implicate him, only media speculation. In this type of lawsuit, not only is the media liable, so are those quoted in the media, adding to that kind of unfair speculation.

The question *What are you going to do about it?* is an opportunity to take a positive angle on a bad-news issue. Although you must address bad news directly, you can move the issue forward by speaking to what you will do next to improve it. A variation of this question is *What next?* which, if the answer is out of your control or beyond the realm of your responsibility, may indicate another time to avoid speculating.

How does it feel?

Sometimes used to the point of absurdity and insensitivity (for example, how do you expect parents to feel about the death of their child?), this question is often used to elicit an emotional response. The question is used with some risk to a reporter. For example, coverage of the shooting death of a youth in northern Alberta provoked a great deal of hostility toward the media. Local residents perceived reporters who asked *How does it feel?* to be insensitive; they felt such questions were intrusive and boorish in the middle of a personal and local tragedy.[2] As an interview subject, you have the right to refuse to answer this question if it feels too personal or in bad taste. You can also decline if you are in a position or occupation where your personal feelings should not be part of your decision-making process (e.g., a police officer, social worker or researcher).

Standard Question Formats

The basic questions we've just reviewed are fairly standard, and you should learn to anticipate them as part of the preparation for an interview. The following question formats are adapted from *The Canadian Reporter*.[3] You may want to refer to them as you prepare for the interview to gauge how questions are likely to be asked. (Whether they will in fact be asked depends on the reporter, the type of interview and the subject).

Open-ended question

Particularly at the beginning of an interview, or in a feature or talk-show interview, the interviewer may ask you to summarize the situation: "Mr. Smith is our guest today. He has just invented an automatic mitt warmer. Mr. Smith, how did you come to invent this device?" The open-ended question is generous; take full advantage by telling your story simply but quickly. What you are doing is setting the scene for the interview, and a brief description is all you need.

Closed-ended question

A little more focussed, the closed-ended question is looking for a specific answer. The unvarnished answer to a closed-ended question is "yes" or "no" or "maybe"; your further comments will clarify the reason for your simple answer. Provide the answer first, then offer any background information (as in the "answer first, explanation second" formula). Questions like this tend to be phrased like this: "Will your automatic mitt warmer be durable enough to withstand a Canadian blizzard?"

Can you give an example?

In order to get as specific as possible, reporters often ask for an example: "Why would anyone need an electric mitt warmer?" Examples are a good way to explain complex or abstract information in a form the layperson can understand. The example question can also be answered using a personal anecdote or story, which helps to humanize the news item. For example, "I first became interested in mitt warmers when I noticed my five-year-old son had his fist balled up inside his mitt, because his mitt couldn't protect against really cold temperatures."

Leading question

The Canadian Reporter explains a leading question like this: "[It] prods sources to say what you want them to say—and is generally a bad technique."[4] An example of a leading question might be something like this: "Does the lack of government funding for a research project like yours prove we lack a national program for research and development worthy of the name?" A leading question often signals that the reporter has a specific issue in mind to develop or an axe to grind; it also may mean that the reporter is repeating a criticism or comment he heard in a previous story. In any case, leading questions are usually bad ones.

Reporters can ask a number of bad, unfair and wrong-headed questions in an interview; some of the main ones will be discussed below. However, the best way to handle a leading question is to refuse to be led where you do not wish to go or do not belong. Your response might be something like this: "I invented the mitt warmer out of my own resources; I'd rather do it that way than worry about government funding."

Some people say...

Reporters must often get the opposition point of view into an interview but don't want to appear to take sides. This question proposes a conflicting perspective to the interview subject and demands a response: "Some people say that your mitt warmer will ruin the knitwear industry in Quebec. How do you respond to that?"

When asked an oppositional question, you can choose to be as aggressive or dismissive as you wish. Just be sure to direct your attention to the opposition, not to the interviewer, particularly on live or talk shows. People generally tune in to these programs because of the host, not because of the interview subjects, and they don't take kindly to criticism toward the person they just tuned in to watch or hear. Thus, a response like "Jane, you incredible twit, this won't have any effect whatsoever" will lose your audience (Jane won't be too receptive either), whereas "People who say that don't know what they're talking about; this will only help the knitwear industry" puts accountability where it belongs, on the opposition, not on the reporter asking the question.

I don't get it...

Notwithstanding your best intentions—and the reporter's—sometimes the information is too complex or the interview goes down a strange road. This question is usually politely phrased to help get the interview back on track: "I'm sorry, but I'm still not clear on how your automatic mitts rely on solar power. Could you explain that again for me?" Such a question is relatively straightforward to respond to, but you shouldn't just repeat what you've been saying, since that clearly isn't working. Look for a different explanation, use an analogy or example, demonstrate how it works, if possible, or consider how you might explain your information to friends or family who aren't as expert as you are.

What the heck are you talking about?

This is the reply you will get if you still can't explain your subject. The interviewer is getting very frustrated. Perhaps your language is too complicated and jargon-laden; you need to take responsibility if you aren't explaining your issue clearly. If you are not clear on where the confusion lies, it is quite reasonable to ask the reporter what element in particular he or she is troubled by. Be patient and, whatever you do, don't be patronizing if in fact the reporter has tripped up on what to you is obvious. Clearly, if a professional reporter who is somewhat informed about the issue still doesn't understand it, it's not that obvious.

Double-barrelled question

This is when the reporter asks two or more questions in one volley: "Are you marketing this to Asia? Do you think Christmas sales will be high? Will many people be put out of work because of it?" As *The Canadian Reporter* notes,

"[A double-barrelled question is] considered hazardous since it allows the source to choose which part of the question to answer."[5] Such an exchange gives you, the interview subject, the advantage: pick the easiest, or most beneficial, question to answer.

So what you're saying is...

Listen carefully to this question. It could be an attempt to put words in your mouth unfairly; it could also be a genuine attempt to encapsulate what you're trying to say. Reporters are skilled in synthesis, summary and simplification, and they often use these skills to get a clearer understanding of an issue. If this question is pitched to you, listen carefully to the rephrasing. If it generally and fairly summarizes what you're trying to express, say yes. If it doesn't, say no, but then try to answer with a summary that does accurately reflect the issue.

In summary...

Toward the end of a long interview, or after discussing a complex issue, a reporter (particularly a print reporter) may offer a summary of the key points discussed, more as an accuracy check than anything else. This question might be expressed as "OK, I think I understand the principles behind the automatic mitt warmer, but let's go over them one more time to be sure."

This kind of checking and rechecking is unlikely to happen in a live broadcast interview, where the interviewer is more likely to be prepared to discuss the issue. If it does happen, the interview subject usually must take responsibility for not being able to enunciate the issue clearly and simply.

Anything else you'd like to say?

As we have already noted, reporters are not usually experts in the topic under discussion, and after their questions are done, they will often provide an opportunity for the interviewee to raise any issues the reporter may have missed. If the answer is no, say so and thank the reporter for the opportunity, if it has been a good interview. If the answer is yes, try to be reasonably brief. If later you remember something you should have mentioned but forgot, you can always call the reporter back.

If this question is not asked at the end of the interview and you think there are still issues that need to be raised, you can ask for the opportunity to add more. (The exception to this advice is in live broadcasts. In that situation, you must be careful to ensure you get your points across; you don't have a second chance as you do in print or recorded interviews). The exchange might go something like this: "I think that's everything; thank you for your time."

"Thank you; there's just one final point I'd like to mention that I think you might be interested in: the mitt warmer is completely biodegradable after its solar cells give out."

Be wary of over-preparing to the point that you try to anticipate every conceivable question. You may become so preoccupied with trying to remember everything that you forget to stay engaged with the reporter. For example, I once helped a physician prepare for a talk show interview on the safety of baby walkers. A very conscientious man, he prepared as best he could, trying to anticipate all the possible questions, good and bad. He was so prepared for everything, he forgot the obvious, and the first question threw him off: "Doctor Yacoub, what is a baby walker?"

Unfair Questions

You shouldn't spend much time preparing for bad and unfair questions. Most of the questions will be straightforward, if occasionally abrupt ("thank you for agreeing to talk to me; why are you shutting down the plant and throwing hundreds of families out of work?"). However, bad and unfair questions happen, so it is important to be able to recognize them and be ready to deal with them when they do. In most cases, the correct response is simply sticking to your guns. If you are right, you have exercised your judgement as best you can (remember "Good communications cannot overcome bad judgement"), and if you are well prepared, unfair or malicious questions can mostly be ignored.

Leading question

As we discussed above, when you are offered a leading question, stick to your agenda, not the reporter's. If the reporter is trying to show that something else is going on other than what you're talking about, let him or her prove it; otherwise, stick to what you know and what you are confident about.

The insinuation

Underlying the reporter's question is a negative, sometimes nasty, insinuation: "How long has your plant continued to violate pollution controls?," "Why have you consistently opposed medicare?" or "When did you stop beating your wife?" When you receive a insinuation-laden query, address the assumption behind the question: for example, "Our record on pollution control is fine; the Ministry has not filed a complaint in 10 years" or "I have always supported medicare and always will."

The assumption

Related to the insinuation, the assumption is less of an attack and more of an unfounded guess. Reporters are often calling to check their assumptions, so give them credit for checking the story before going ahead with it. For example, the question might be, "Why were the guards in the jailhouse punishing the prisoner by taking him down as hard as they did?" The answer clarifies the situation without arguing with the assumption: "Actually, the inmate was armed, intoxicated and threatening violence to other prisoners and staff. He had to be subdued quickly and effectively before he harmed someone, or harmed himself." Don't get into a dispute over the reporter's phrasing; it sounds like denial and may be reported as such ("Staff denied that the prisoner was being punished, and claimed he was subdued because he was threatening violence"). While technically accurate, the use of the word "deny" is inherently dirty in media: it carries with it a presupposition of guilt and the whiff of a cover-up (see below).

Instead, state the situation as you understand it, and if you are confident in your knowledge, stick to it regardless of further questions, e.g., "Witnesses say the guards used excessive force; wasn't this just punishment?" "Since the witnesses were guards and inmates, and they have all sworn that the prisoner was menacing and dangerous, we did what we did to protect the lives of inmates and staff, who were in immediate danger."

The denial question

There is something about the word deny that implies guilt, and the word should be avoided altogether. Sometimes a denial question comes in direct form: "Do you deny you were punishing the prisoner and used excessive force?" If you respond, "We deny it; we used appropriate force to defuse the situation," you provide the reporter (and others if you're in a news conference or scrum) the opportunity to use the word "deny" in a story or headline. "Authorities deny excessive force" may be technically correct, but it leaves an impression of guilt or wrong-doing in the minds of readers.

To answer a denial question, simply keep stating your position in your own words. If the media persist in using the word deny, don't give in; the question is unprofessional, cheap and unfair, and you don't have to respond to it. Keep the high road and insist on using your language to describe the situation: "We took the inmate down because he was armed, intoxicated and threatening; we did so to protect the lives of staff and inmates."

Cheap shots and ad hominem attacks

These comments tend to be posed more often at politicians than at other figures. The relationship between reporters and politicians is one of the most toxic in the world of media relations. Even politicians, however, have a right to be treated with courtesy. Comments such as "You must believe in the tooth fairy if you think anyone is going to believe a cock-and-bull story like that" and "No one could possibly believe a line like that" are unthinkably rude but unfortunately common in the world of politics.

Don't rise to the bait and blow off steam at a reporter or your opposition. It may make for cheap and easy media, but it won't help you get your point across. Be assertive, be confident and be strong. Responses structured to communicate "This is what I believe and this is why I believe it" positively and effectively counter any cheap shots.

Fitting Questions to Format

The nature of the news interview varies greatly, depending on the issue, the medium, the format of the show, the deadline and the personalities of the main characters:

> In broadcasting, there is a vast distance between the quick, outside-the-meeting scrum; the thoughtful half-hour interview show, done in-studio; and the off-air news interview. The scrum demands paparazzi skills seldom spoken of in journalism schools, especially leather lungs and leather sensitivities. The in-studio encounter demands high levels of knowledge and self-possession. The off-air news interview demands skill and efforts very like those of a print reporter, including background preparation, a clear guideline, corroboration and review.[6]

The types of question you will be asked in an interview often depend on the type of interview you're doing. Part of your preparation should be to find out what kind of interview you'll be doing, which will help you anticipate the types of questions you are likely to receive.

Hard news

Generally, hard-news interviewing is focussed on the five W's and two H's: fact-based, quick and intense. Try not to let rapid-fire questions distract you from listening to the question, understanding it and responding to it.

Practising for the hard-news interview (or any interview, for that matter) is a good idea. It's best to work with someone who is experienced with media, whether as a subject, a communications practitioner or a former reporter.

Unless they have the appropriate background, friends and colleagues tend not to give a real-life experience and lack the aggressiveness a good hard-news reporter should have. If the issue is important and you don't have sufficient experience, it may be a good investment to contact a communications or public relations firm with expertise in media relations, and ask them to provide mock interviews until you feel ready for the real thing.

Feature news

The feature news interview comes close to being an educational opportunity, in which you have the time to go over an issue in detail, provide a good deal of background and supporting material, and direct the reporter to the sources. Don't let the more laid-back nature of this type of interview cause you to take it for granted. You're still on the record and are dealing with media, regardless of how comfortable you might feel. While you have the opportunity in this kind of interview to get to know the reporter better, don't assume familiarity or friendship; the interview is a business relationship, and you need to stay focussed and engaged with this type of reporter as you would with a hard-news reporter.

Backgrounder

What distinguishes the backgrounder from the feature is that you are less likely to appear in the story; in fact, the story may never be done. The reporter may simply be trying to get better acquainted with an issue by asking for more information that he or she can use as reference material.

Just the same, you are still on the record in a backgrounder. You may, however, be able to negotiate a "not for attribution" agreement with the reporter and media outlet. In such an arrangement, you provide information and commentary on an issue and may be quoted, but not directly, as in "Department officials today made clear that current regulations forbidding air transportation monopolies continue to apply." "Not for attribution" means you won't be publicly quoted; the reporter may have to tell his or her editor or colleagues who you are, however, just so they have some confidence in the source of the information.

Investigative reporting

Investigative reporters are digging into something they assume has gone wrong. You have a number of choices when approached by an investigative journalist: the area is so high-risk that blanket recommendations are difficult to provide.

If you or your organization has done something wrong and it is a matter of record, recognize it, apologize for it and move forward. Richard Nixon inadvertently demonstrated this lesson during Watergate. If he had taken responsibility and apologized, he might have avoided impeachment. More recently, Alberta's former Premier Ralph Klein invoked the notwithstanding clause of the constitution to deny people who were wrongly sterilized the right to sue the government; instead he mandated a uniform $25,000 to compensate for the loss of right to sue. The outcry was so great he withdrew his proposal within 24 hours and apologized to all concerned. While he recognized he had taken bad legal advice, he also recognized it was his decision to make. Despite his mistake and the insensitivity it showed, Klein's quick action to account for his decision was well received by the public, and his popularity remained high.

Sometimes it's easier to be wrong than to become involved in a situation of great murkiness and debate, where "wrong" may be a matter of opinion more than anything else. Contract law, for example, is complex and subject to a large amount of case law. It often takes a court to prove whether or not a wrong was done. In such a case, if an investigative journalist approaches you, you may want to begin by seeking legal advice.

Meanwhile, if you haven't done wrong, say so and prove it. While the onus legally is on the accuser to prove the wrong, if the media charge or question you for doing wrong and you have documentation that proves otherwise, show it. If in fact you have proof to document a situation, it may make the whole issue of an investigative report unnecessary.

If you agree to do an interview with an investigative reporter, take greater precautions than you normally would and protect yourself against excessive zealousness. Depending on what your role in the issue is (you may, after all, have sought the involvement of the media to further your cause), you may want to take some or all of the following steps:

· Contact a lawyer

· Ask to see all the reporter's documentation

· Indicate you will not be ambushed during the interview with documents that you have not had a chance to review[7]

· Insist on having a witness sit in on the interview with you

· Audiotape or videotape the interview, so you will have the same record as the reporter has

· Prepare and submit to the reporter all the documentation you have that supports your point of view (preferably third-party documentation)

· Consent to give the interview only if you can be interviewed in a setting of your choosing and if the reporter or camera operator agrees not to use video techniques that might portray you visually as guilty (e.g., harsh or diminished lighting, shooting from above).

A brief word on seeking legal advice. Lawyers specialize in different areas. If you are concerned about potential libel, consult a lawyer who is expert in that field. If you are taking legal advice, remember that lawyers are experts in law, not communications. Be careful of taking communications advice from a lawyer, just as you would be careful about seeking legal advice from a communicator. As Mulroney proved in the Airbus case, it is best to get advice from both, appropriate to their areas of expertise.[8]

While the investigative interview can be the most stressful, it is also the least common. As with most things, you shouldn't try to conduct media relations according to the worst possible outcome. Taking steps such as consulting with lawyers, arguing about camera angles and treatment, demanding to see documentation and recording interviews so you have a copy is prudent, but should be done only when needed and not as a matter of routine. Generally speaking, such steps should be taken when you have good cause to believe, either through past behaviour or current media request, that you need to protect yourself. These resorts should be your last choice, not your first, in practising media relations.

Crisis interviewing

Being interviewed during a crisis (such as an ice storm, airline crash or forest fire) often comes down to answering four basic questions.

What's going on?   This question can be enormously difficult to answer during a crisis. During the 1987 tornado that devastated Edmonton, reporters demanded a casualty count immediately. However, the situation was so uncertain, and new touch-down sites were still being found, that it wasn't until the day after the crisis that a reasonable estimate could be given. While this was enormously frustrating to the media, in fact it was as fast as authorities could respond, particularly at a time when the priority was sorting through collapsed buildings looking for survivors.

What happened? How did it happen?   Sometimes the answer to this question is easy ("A tornado"). Sometimes it may take years for the cause of a disaster to be known (for example, the cause of the crash of Swissair Flight 111 over Peggy's Cove took two years to investigate).

What are you doing about it?   As a crisis moves from the acute phase to the recovery phase, media attention shifts from what is going on to what the authorities are doing. The longer a situation goes on (e.g., the ice storm of eastern Canada in 1997), the more likely this type of media questioning, and eventually criticism, will be directed at authorities.

One thing to keep in mind is that the same facts do not always add up to the same opinion or outlook, particularly in times of crisis. If you are a subject expert known for a certain point of view, you may be consulted to provide a point-counterpoint perspective; if this is the case, you may need to be judicious in what you say, to avoid unintentionally hurting or provoking people.

How can people help? What can people do? The media often perform public service during a crisis, broadcasting calls for volunteers and equipment, asking people to stay away from the site, directing people to aid centres and so forth. In a crisis, you can ask for media help to get a message out and usually expect full co-operation.

Talk shows/open lines

On a talk show or call-in program, you can't predict what kind of calls you are going to get. Therefore, be flexible and be respectful of all callers and the host. While the callers (or the host) may be aggressive and hostile, one reason people tune in to these shows is to hear precisely this kind of questioning. Your ability to handle difficult questions with grace will help to determine whether people believe you and your point of view. This advice particularly applies to your response to the host. People tune in because they want to hear him or her, not you, so don't try to upstage, argue, belittle or be funnier than the host. Pay attention to the questions, stand your ground and be willing to engage in lively debate; on a talk or call-in show, you have more room for give and take, for humour, arguing your case and generally having fun, than you do in a standard news interview. It helps if you are an extrovert and like a good argument; if you don't, it may be better to find a spokesperson who is more appropriate to this format.

To prepare for this kind of interview, watch or listen to the show before you go on it. Get used to the host's approach and to the types of callers. The open line tends to be the most unpredictable type of interview, so don't over-prepare your answers and be willing to change direction if the situation calls for it.

Live television

A live television interview may happen during the news hour, in which case it will be brief, or as part of a talk show, in which case you will have more time. Pay more attention to your appearance but don't go overboard. Depending on the importance of the topic, you may want to practise appearing before a camera; if the subject is casual, you likely won't need to. You need to know the type and format of the show before appearing on it. It may be hard-hitting public affairs broadcasting or a light feature interview; prepare as appropriate.

Behaving in an Interview

The same rules apply for the print interview as for the broadcast interview. Just because you're speaking to a newspaper reporter instead of a television reporter doesn't mean you have a licence to be slovenly, distracted or confused. Dress as you professionally dress and behave as you professionally behave; remember that in addition to your quotes, the reporter is making judgements, directly or indirectly, on your body language and non-verbal communications.

The Telephone Interview

If you practise media relations a good deal, you'll discover the telephone interview represents the most common kind of questioning, particularly if you have developed a reputation for being a good source. The phone interview tends to be fact-focussed and brief, along the lines of a hard-news interview. But because you can't see the interviewer, it can be awkward at times; both parties usually prefer doing interviews face to face, but sometimes the phone is the only practical way.

Do the phone interview in a room that's quiet, where you're not likely to be disturbed by your colleagues or family (you may be doing this from home). Take notes while you talk, but try to stay focussed on the interview and the questions. You wouldn't play computer solitaire or try to write something in the middle of any other type of interview, but a phone interview makes it easier for you to be distracted. Stay focussed and do nothing except give the interview.

A Few Thoughts on the Media Interview

One of the reviewers of the first edition of this book had this to say about my description of the interview process: "(*In the News*) is especially enlightening in the dissection of the media interview, representing the interviewer/interviewee relationship almost as an elaborate form of courtship."[9]

Sometimes there is an element of courtship between the interviewer and the interviewee; the former trying to seduce clarity and a good clip out of the subject and the latter trying to use the process to a purpose: getting his or her key message out.

There is an essential element of ritual and elaboration to the media interview. It has unstated but understood rules on both sides of the equation. One party gets to ask questions, the other party doesn't. One party has information the other lacks, but can't simply tell them; it has to be elicited through question and answer. Though written information can be supplied, and often the subject has provided all the information in a news release and backgrounder, still the interview takes place as if the reporter had never seen the release and was breaking this as an original story. Though reporter and interview subject may chat informally before and after the interview, once it is on the rituals must be observed.

Journalism schools try to teach students to find other ways to get information (the Internet, Computer Assisted Reporting, to be discussed in more detail later), and even public opinion polling. Yet, the interview tends to be the crux of the reporter/communicator equation and worth spending two chapters to go through. This is where the rubber hits the road for most communicators. This is your best chance to get your message out.

But it's not for everybody. Academics and scientists in particular hate a process that doesn't allow them to simply tell the media what's going on (a technical briefing, though, is good for this kind of information-giving) and instead have to put up with a rigid and formulaic "Q and A" format. It is an arcane, culturally embedded practice of media. If your spokesperson finds it too objectionable and simple-minded, please take the burden of doing interviews off them, and onto someone who's willing to fulfill the sociocultural dance that is the media interview.

Done!

After all this planning and preparation, the interview will be over. As discussed, if you think of something after the interview you should have added, feel free to call the reporter back; make sure it's significant, though, or you'll just look like a pest.

After the interview, you should monitor the news coverage and analyze whether you came across as intended and whether your key messages were covered. Since people tend to be their own worst critics, ask a good friend or trusted co-worker how they thought the final story looked; it is far more often good than bad.

If you want, you can call the reporter afterward and thank him or her, but be a bit careful. Some media interpret thank-you calls as an attempt to influence further stories. However, if you think the reporter did a good job and you got what you wanted—fair and accurate coverage—it doesn't hurt to thank the reporter. They get more criticisms than thanks, and if your appreciation is genuine, they may take it that way. Don't assume that a pat on the reporter's back guarantees positive media coverage forever, though: every media opportunity is new and should be approached with the same care as the last one.

And although the subhead says "Done!," we're only talking about the interview. Remember this is part of a nine-part planning model, and we still have two steps to complete: evaluation of media coverage and revision of your media program, if necessary. If in your analysis you note errors in the coverage, you'll have to be ready to deal with them as well. Please refer to Chapter 15 for more information on the fine art of complaining about the media.

According to our nine-point planning model, we have only two aspects left to review: evaluation and revision. Whether you're working on a one-time project (e.g., opening a building, announcing a new product) or developing a longer-term relationship with media (e.g., cultivating business media contacts, you need a way to evaluate both the coverage you receive and what this coverage indicates for future media relations.

Evaluation

The two basic measures of media coverage are quantity of coverage and quality of coverage. Quantity is easy to determine. You can clip newspapers, commercial firms can monitor and provide tapes or transcripts of broadcast coverage, and many TV and radio scripts can be pulled from the Internet. All this coverage can be tallied and analyzed. It is particularly helpful to have a benchmark with which to compare your evaluation, a period prior to the implementation of the plan or campaign (see Chapter 7 for discussion of preparing an evaluation in advance of your media event).

Looking at the coverage of your agency or issue gives you a sense of media interest over time. The most important element to evaluate is whether you achieved the program goal you established at the beginning of the planning process. You should go right back to the plan, the issues that made you decide to engage the media and the goal you set for yourself. Ideally, effective media relations will achieve something for you and your organization: new members, an increase in sales, a change in public opinion, votes, whatever was your original goal.

Sometimes the measure is simply media presence; for example, governments have an obligation to be accountable and usually measure the volume of accurate information about their programs as an indicator that citizens are well informed. Sometimes the measure is an absence of bad news: issues managers often work hard to ensure that some issues are not covered in the media until the company is better positioned for them. (For example, a company might try to meet the needs of advocacy groups before they head off to the media to complain about company practices. McDonald's changed from styrofoam clamshell packages to paper in response to environmental criticism and received positive media coverage for doing so).

The first step is to determine whether you received any coverage at all. If you made an announcement of general interest, did you get most of the media outlets to cover it? If you targeted specific media, did you get the beat reporters you were looking for? If you didn't get the amount of coverage you hoped for, what was the reason? You may have to be critical of your own messaging or the particular way you approached the media. On the other hand, the lack of coverage may be due to factors beyond your control. (For example, after the terrorist attack against the US on September 11, 2001, the volume of news releases issued by Canada NewsWire and Marketwire was markedly reduced; everyone knew there would be no coverage of any other issue for several days after the tragedy).

A related issue is whether the media included your perspective in a particular story in which several people or organizations are mentioned. One of the more annoying media practices, to both unions and management, is when reporters talk to only one side in a labour dispute and do not talk to the other. Such a practice requires corrective action, by a direct call to the editor advising who the reporter should be contacting from your side in such cases.

A sample evaluation

If you are in the news, a simple way to evaluate media effectiveness is to look at exactly what the media covered. For example, in 1990/91, 356 stories in the *Edmonton Sun* and *Edmonton Journal* mentioned the Edmonton Board of Health (compared to roughly 22 in 1987/88). I prepared a breakdown of coverage according to the type of news item, as follows:

News: 271 (76 per cent)

Features: 34 (9.5 per cent)

Columns: 34 (9.5 per cent)

Editorials: 3 (1 per cent)

Letters: 8 (2 per cent)

Other (including ad features and photo captions): 6 (2 per cent)

Total opinion (columns plus editorials plus letters): 45 (12.5 per cent)

My analysis showed that the ratio of hard news to features and opinion was roughly six to one, which was consistent year over year.

When I compared the story analysis to the Edmonton Board of Health organization chart, I found the division that received the most media attention (largest number of stories) was Environmental Health: 60 per cent of total news coverage, up from its usual ratio of 50 per cent. That year, Environmental Health was dealing with a high-profile landfill issue, so this increase was predictable. Next in terms of coverage was the Communicable Disease division, down from 25 per cent to 12 per cent. This category was always difficult to predict because the occurrence of communicable disease, which was the Board's responsibility to control, is itself unpredictable. The third most discussed issue (11 per cent) was budget and contracts, since the agency faced a nurses' strike that year.

Other divisions received less media attention, which led to some discussion about whether we should apply more effort to getting coverage for major programs such as Home Care and Dental Health. At that time, however, Home Care was facing severe capacity issues and didn't want more media attention for fear it would increase demand. And other programs, such as Dental Health, simply didn't see any particular program benefit to news coverage and so wished to continue to react to news requests on an item-by-item basis.

Quantity vs. Quality

Quantity of coverage is one measure, but quality is another. After all, Richard Nixon had plenty of coverage during the Watergate scandal, but almost all of it was harshly critical. After you've counted the stories, analyze their content and placement. Probably the single most important thing you want to know is this: did the media transmit to their audiences the key message(s) you wanted to say? Key messages are important, and you can easily evaluate coverage in terms of whether your key message was mentioned. If it wasn't, you may need to change your message or think about why the media presented a different message. Was yours unclear, too complex, not sexy enough? You may have to apply some judgement here; some organizations, such as academia and research agencies, are wary of dumbing down key messages to the point of trivia.

If your message did get across, was it prominent enough to be recognized, or was it buried? Where did your story appear, at the top of the news or at the end? Was the information about you accurate, or does it require correction? (See Chapter 15 on how to handle corrections). What was the tone of the coverage: supportive, critical or neutral? The evaluation of tone is a subjective matter, and you should ensure those around you have samples of the coverage so they can verify or argue with your conclusions.

Let's look again at my Edmonton Board of Health example. Once I had reviewed the areas of the agency that had been covered, I looked at how media handled the stories. Here are my conclusions:

> As always, the media generally continue to provide consistent, objective coverage of the Board of Health. The sole exception was a ... column stating that the Board was incapable of handling environmental issues more complicated than traditional [health] inspector concerns. This is the first directly, solely negative comment we've received since a 1989 letter to the editor criticizing our handling of a flu outbreak at a nursing home. We have been criticized by others in the past ... but media coverage has always represented our point of view in contrast, which constitutes fair, objective journalism. Consequently, over the past four years we are running 820 to two in terms of fair, balanced coverage over negative media.[1]

The root of this outstanding coverage stems in part from the communications plan (including content analysis, media policy and procedures, media training and an ongoing relationship with city media), but in larger part goes back to the very first principle enunciated in this book: good communications cannot overcome bad judgement.

The Edmonton Board of Health had contentious, high-profile issues to deal with that year. Besides the controversial landfill site, the Board was involved with a nurses' strike, was offering a needle-exchange program in the inner city (to reduce the spread of HIV/AIDS) and had to deal with periodic outbreaks of dangerous diseases such as meningitis and tuberculosis. As we faced these issues, the Board and staff adopted the stance of "What is the best thing we can do?" rather than "How will this play in the media?." By putting professional judgement first and media relations second, Board staff and management had confidence to explain their decisions to the media without worrying about controlling their spin. While we certainly paid careful attention to how to explain a decision to reporters and how to put an issue forward to the media, more time was spent on the matters themselves.

Another way to analyze media coverage is to divide commentary into three categories: positive, neutral and negative. Notwithstanding media attempts at objectivity, coverage is sometimes biased. Coverage of Terry Fox was unfailingly noble and heroic, whereas coverage of Brian Mulroney's second term was aggressively hostile. According to this model, positive coverage is defined as more supportive of your view than of others' position; negative coverage is, of course, the opposite. Such bias can be seen more clearly when you are in an adversarial situation, such as a strike. Media coverage can certainly show bias. A headline such as "Union demands fair treatment" implies the union isn't getting it, while the headline "Union demands excessive—CEO" gives the management's point of view greater prominence.[2] Care must be taken using this method, so that it accurately reflects news coverage and demonstrates "positive" or "negative" according to fair measures (without resorting to spin).

In their evaluation of news coverage, particularly positive or "good" news, practitioners often equate the coverage with the equal value of having advertised that news, to demonstrate the dollar value of media relations and its cost effectiveness. For example, the City of Edmonton would summarize its positive newspaper stories quarterly, then estimate how much that amount of media space would have cost in advertising, at normal advertising rates. For example, in 1993, receiving a 25-cm story in the *Edmonton Examiner* would be the equivalent of buying $189.24 in advertising from the *Examiner,* at the rate of $1.82 a line.[3] In one three-month period the city estimated it received $30,000 in equivalent-cost advertising from the print media in the city. Whether news stories equate to paid advertising is unknown; there is also some question whether people read a newspaper for the news or the ads. Personally, I don't think news coverage can be equated with advertising. They are two separate worlds and shouldn't be used as comparators.

Another element to look at is outcome versus activity. Does media activity cause any tangible difference to your client or your organization? Let's say you are trying to use the media to recruit members to your organization. If you get a lot of media attention but do not actually gain any new members, what have you achieved? The best way to evaluate media coverage is to examine the results. If you are trying to change public opinion on an issue, for example, you should know the public's opinion (through a survey) as you go into your campaign and should be able to show a change in opinion (through, say, a subsequent survey) after your planned media effort.

Measuring Achievement of Goals

Your analysis of media coverage provides some information that can be used in future media or campaign efforts. However, by itself it doesn't address the key issue: did you achieve the goals and objectives you set out to achieve?

The overall communications goal of the Edmonton Board of Health was to improve accountability. As a publicly funded agency that provided a public service, it needed to be accountable to the citizens it served. It produced an annual report, but ongoing media coverage kept it in the public eye in a more meaningful—and thus more accountable—way. The Board also had objectives, which either stemmed from the communications plan or were the result of more project-specific plans. For example, we wanted to increase the number of high-risk people, particularly seniors, who received flu immunizations in the fall. Using media, we did so, but found that media alone was not enough. We then shifted toward building alliances with seniors' organizations to get more seniors out.

In later years, our attendance at flu clinics continued to grow, and we continued to promote them through the media, but we also promoted them through advertising and work with the seniors' organizations. Finally, as our clinics had increasing numbers of seniors attending every year, we were unable to state exactly how much was due to media coverage and how much was due to other aspects of the campaign. This is not uncommon in multifaceted PR campaigns of any type. However, at the end of the campaign or project, if you can point to overall success, you can at least share in it—there is usually enough credit to go around. If you have the resources and the time, you can go back after a campaign is over and research in more depth where your target audience's information came from and what motivated them to make the decisions they did.

Revise as Necessary

After you've had a chance to review your plan and your objectives, you should revise the plan as necessary on the basis of your evaluation. Generally speaking, if you're doing an ongoing communications or media plan, you should review it annually. If you are managing a one-time special project, review it and note any changes or improvements to make for the next time you do something similar.

Depending on your evaluation, your revision may be as simple as saying "we achieved our goals" and continuing to follow the same model in future media relations. On the other hand, it may be as drastic as saying "scrap media relations, we need to look at advertising." (For example, in Chapter 1 I provided an example of a case in which very positive media stories did not result in any increase in clientele for a program; accordingly, the focus of the plan was changed to a direct-mail campaign to increase program intake).

Usually, though, revisions are minor adjustments, with a view to improving coverage, in either quantity or quality, the next time. If the coverage was, in your view, flawed or incomplete, your revision may be to raise the issue with the media. (See Chapter 15 for a more complete discussion of complaining to the media). If your message wasn't getting through to the media, you may have to refine it to make it more media-friendly. Are your spokespersons (including yourself) effective and moving? You may need more media training or may need to find people who can better present the issue or the organization.

A revision need not be negative. If, for example, you found a talk-show host who is sympathetic to your issue, note it and make plans to cultivate that relationship. A positive editorial or column should be noted, with a view to building on that good press.

You should look not only at the plan itself but at the environment, to see what's changed that you will need to consider for the next time. For example, there may be new opportunities as new digital channels arrive and are looking for programming. TV news shows and newspapers sometimes change format and focus to reflect their audience. (For example, CNN made a dramatic change to its Headline News Service, trying to reach a younger audience with shorter, sharper stories, newer, younger news readers and an Internet look. [4] However, it is losing ground to the right-wing Fox News).

Your revisions may end up with a request for more funds or resources to get media coverage, as well as changes to the media plan. You are much more likely to get a positive response if your evaluation is sound and focussed on achieving tangible, measurable benefits to the organization.

At this point, we've reviewed the complete planning process. Up to now, we have looked at a number of key issues in media relations, including identifying individuals who make good spokespeople, learning how the media work and discussing how to plan and implement a media relations program. For the most part, we have looked at dealing with mainstream media and media issues. In the next chapter we will explore specialty media and unique media situations.

Special Media, Special Cases

14

Some media have a specialized focus, which gives them a "take" on news coverage that differs slightly from the mainstream media. Such a focus may include business reporting, sports, entertainment and government/politics. Reporters on these beats treat a sports hero, for example, much differently than a politician.

If your target audience is the business crowd or sports fans, these media can be helpful in getting your message out; they tend not to be as effective in communicating your message to the mainstream. A number of Canadians, for example, have tuned out of politics and change the channel whenever a public-affairs show comes on. Nevertheless, the approaches special media make to their subject can vary dramatically, so you should have a sense of how to deal with them effectively.

Business Media

The business media have expanded considerably in the past decade, in part because a new generation began to invest in the stock market for the first time. Business now has its own 24-hour television channel BNN, and the *National Post* has morphed the *Financial Post* into a national newspaper that contains an extensive financial section. There are also a number of business and investment magazines (including two magazines carried by the dailies), syndicated and local radio shows, business columnists like Gordon Pape (who writes columns and books) and investment newsletters, whose subscribers support the cost of the newsletter in the hopes of getting detailed investment information.

Business news has traditionally focussed on the success of companies and corporations. In the 1990s, Canadians began to invest in mutual funds and the stock market in record numbers, as the baby-boom generation began preparing for retirement. Accordingly, a major focus of business reporting these days is on investment news: will the shares of a company rise or fall because of its business practices? How will the stock market fare? Should investors move from higher-risk stocks to lower-risk bonds? Until recently, these were the concerns of a small group of professional investors; today, they are the concerns of a great many Canadians. In fact, business news is often front-page news, so if you are trying to get into the mainstream media, one way to do so is by considering how your story affects business or employment.

Dealing with investors represents a specialized sub-field within communications called investor relations. Investor relations specialists have to meet not only the general needs of mainstream media but also the specialized needs of business media, who want more corporate information and specific financial detail (all this while juggling ongoing communications with current investors, managing direct communications with key investors such as pension and mutual fund managers, following government policy changes and dealing with regulators, both from the markets and from industry-specific boards). As with all communicators, investor relations specialists practise media relations within a broader context of communications. The practitioner must meet the broad-based, general interests of mainstream media while attending to the specificity of trade magazines and investor newsletters. There is considerable debate within the field as to whether investor relations should be in the Finance or Communications branch. Wherever placed, this specialist should have a solid understanding of business economics, rules of disclosure for publicly traded companies, and dealing with both business and mainstream media.

Approaching the business media is no different than approaching any other type of media: you need to know the outlet audience and find a way to present your issue as something of interest to it. Some elements are unique about business media, however. For one, business reporters tend to be better informed about financial issues than are general reporters; they are (or should be) able to read a financial report and understand the company's situation from it. They may also cover other issues that directly affect business, such as environmental protests, government hearings and labour disputes; as such, they have a broader base of interest than just strictly financial knowledge. Business reporters are particularly wary of appearing to be in a conflict of interest such as receiving gifts or perks from sources or favourably covering a company they have invested in.

Business reporters also have a stronger desire than most to speak to the person at the top—the CEO—and the media are usually the last people the CEO wants to speak to. Instead, the company may want to hire a formal spokesperson, or at least have the media relations person coach the CEO for an interview. Generally, the CEO should be in front of the media as part of the process of communicating the company's overall strategic plan, which is usually the CEO's major task.

Still, there are times when it is more appropriate for a spokesperson or media practitioner to deal with the media: to handle requests for information, clarification or background material, for example. To practise business media relations, you need a strong sense of corporate values and a clear, deep understanding of the business the company you are working for does. Media practitioners, like reporters, tend to come to their jobs as specialists in their field (communications, journalism) rather than as specialists in the industry in which they work (e.g., computers, health, charities, unions). In most situations, you will learn the industry after joining it.

Fortunately, corporate communications is more manageable than other types of media relations. In health and law, for example, it is unlikely that the communications practitioner will have an opportunity to become as knowledgeable as a doctor or lawyer (in fact, it is easier for a physician or lawyer to be trained as a good media contact than it is for a communicator to be trained in medicine or law). However, courses and programs on business are easily accessible through community colleges and extension faculties, and most companies are supportive about orienting new staff and consultants in the specifics of the company's business.

(For that matter, you should try as much as possible to become expert in the business of any company or agency you're working for, whether it be a non-profit community group, an advocacy group, a high-tech or traditional company or a government department. If you're a freelance communicator, you may want to choose a sector in which to concentrate your client base, so that you don't face a steep learning curve every time you take on a new project. Freelance book publicists are a good example of such specialization).

Typically, only medium and large companies have business communicators on staff. Small businesses tend not to have the resources or don't perceive themselves as having the need. (However, companies listed on the Toronto Stock Exchange must disclose material information on a timely basis, both broadly and simultaneously. In general, news must reach the financial media, regulators, shareholders and the investment community). Nevertheless, business media like to do stories on small business. Small businesses are often the subject of running items in the business media (e.g. New business in Ourtown), especially if they are in an unusual line or field (e.g. chimney sweep, pet hostel). If a company has an in-house communications department, the staff or consultant will typically work with a number of other departments in order to make communications to the business media consistent with communications to other key audiences. For instance, you would talk to sales and marketing staff about their work with customers; to human relations or internal communications staff about issues involving employees; to government or legal relations staff about government regulators; and to investor relations staff about investor concerns and needs.

Business media can be approached and dealt with using the tools we have discussed in previous chapters. However, you should recognize that business reporters are very knowledgeable and their focus is fairly tight. Try to gauge opportunities for the CEO or other high-profile company representatives to speak to media in order to gain an advantage or receive strategic attention; otherwise you yourself should be the contact.

Government and Politics

Most government and government-funded agencies (school boards, crown corporations, health regions) maintain a formal media relations function as part of their accountability to the public. In smaller communities and organizations this function will be managed by a senior person as part of a wider responsibility (e.g., town manager, school superintendent); most medium to large governments and agencies will have a person or department responsible for media relations. These people will usually be part of the administration and speak to decisions made at the administrative level. Publicly elected officials manage their own media relations (in provincial and federal government, political parties have their own media relations staff).

Thus, we must discuss the political and civil service functions of media relations separately. Practitioners on either side need to be aware of what is happening on the other side: civil service media relations staff need to be politically sensitive, although not partisan (governments change, after all), and political media relations staff need to know what the administration is doing and what current policies and procedures are, so that ministers and others can speak responsibly and accurately about them.

Political communications

As noted, the relationship between politicians and the media can be one of the most toxic in the field of media relations—and a widely quoted maxim on covering politics doesn't help: "The only way to look at a politician is down."[1] This is a distinctly unique view to its subject among beat reporters. Sports reporters, for example, don't look down on athletes nor do business reporters look down on business. They may challenge them or criticize their subjects on the beat for bad behavior (e.g., Enron and steroid use by pro baseball players).

Yet, there is a willingness to learn the beat and cultivate relationships with key members of the beat, but this is sometimes absent in political reporting.

The need on both sides of the relationship is obvious. Political reporting is one of the major types of newsgathering, and reporters need politicians to provide quotes and information on topics that affect the community at large. Politicians, on the other hand, rely on media to provide information to constituents about policies and programs, but rarely have access to funds to communicate with the constituents in other ways. Outside of occasional flyers, most of the advertising budget is earmarked for election campaigns.

One of the hallmarks of politics is its partisan nature. Politicians hold a set of beliefs which they try hard to convince the rest of the world to agree with; critics and naysayers are not encouraged. As with other partisan individuals (lobbyists or business and labour leaders, for example), politicians often view the media as a potential ally in getting the word out—or as a potential barrier to allowing the public to receive wisdom. Today's media consider themselves objective and non-partisan—a far cry from media coverage in the nineteenth and early twentieth century, when political parties owned newspapers and provided the party line to loyal readers. Like others who deal frequently with media, politicians see the media's mistakes and shortcomings more than most people do; this knowledge adds to their skepticism about dealing with reporters. Nevertheless, both parties need each other, although the approach will vary from politician to politician and personality to personality:

> Other players in the political world treat journalists with a mixture of benevolence, fear and contempt. Some politicians blatantly court their attention. Others treat reporters with disdain—but nonetheless never make a move without considering what kind of press it will get.[2]

Reporters covering politicians can be among the most aggressive and abrasive of all media. They can also be the most sophisticated, if they have spent some time on the beat and moved beyond the easy drama of the post-Question Period scrum. *The Canadian Reporter* describes the relationship thus:

> In general, reporters tend to offer political sources far less slack than they offer bureaucrats. Some work on the premise that everything a politician says is on the record unless the politician says specifically, in advance, that it's off the record. Others are less rigid, but are probably far more willing to promise confidentiality to bureaucrats.[3]

In general, reporters prefer to get their quotes from the political level and their facts from the bureaucracy. This arrangement gives politicians leeway to express their personal and partisan opinions, while bureaucrats can support or clarify a comment with more detailed information.

Civil service communications

If the media view of political life can be caustic, their view of bureaucratic life can be dismissive. Reporters tend to perceive bureaucrats, when they aren't simply disconnected from what's going on, as barriers to information.

Communicators in the public service are often called information officers, public affairs officers or communications officers. *The Canadian Reporter* has this to say about them:

> Most government departments have information offices, but the people who staff them are seldom expert, or privy to the best information. For reporters, the key is to use information officers to best advantage: for information on background reading, access to documents or names of the best-informed experts. By and large, information officers like to deal with reporters without having to pass them on to higher-ups. By and large, reporters who are satisfied with what information officers give them are poorly informed. So the challenge is to pose the questions that will take you past the information office.[4]

Specialist information officers are called media relations officers. Unlike their public affairs counterparts, who will be involved with a number of different communications activities (such as writing and designing brochures and reports, producing audiovisual material, developing advertising or speechwriting), media relations officers deal only with media. Depending on the issues the department deals with, a practitioner of media relations could be defined with any of the terms used above.

Providing background information, documents and access to experts is the legitimate and traditional responsibility of the public service communicator. Depending on the level of knowledge of the information officer, and the nature of the administration he or she works in, the officer may act as an on-record source. However, the issue (suggested by the quotation above) of going to more knowledgeable sources than the information officer speaks to the need for the officer to be as expert as possible in the issues handled by his or her department.

The media's dismissive attitude speaks to the importance of having information communicated to the media by the most qualified and competent—and not simply the most available—person. To do so, the information officer (or more likely the media relations or communications manager) must work within the bureaucracy to encourage both specialists and senior administrators to deal with the media directly. It also points to the necessity, within formal bureaucracies, of having goal-oriented, research-based communications and media plans, policies and procedures. If these ideas sound bureaucratic, nevertheless they reflect the language and process in which bureaucracies work. In this environment in particular, the practice of media relations must reflect the culture and approach of the organizations it supports. Similarly, the philosophical and practical approach to media relations must fit the organization's culture, values and structure, be it government, business or non-profit.

One final word for the government communicator. *The Canadian Press Stylebook* devotes considerable space to government jargon, providing the following advice to reporters dealing with government: "Avoid using the jargon that often flows so freely from government news releases or officials' mouths. Jargon fails to convey information to those unfamiliar with the term and can even mislead."[5] Typically, such language has great meaning and subtlety among specialists and those acquainted with the issues, but no substance outside the bureaucracy. Try to put government diction into user-friendly language yourself, if only to prevent media from providing its own interpretation. Many governments are now sensitive to the need to write documents in plain English; documents written for the media should be written in the same style.

Entertainment Media

Entertainment media have experienced a boom in the past decade, and from time to time entertainment news breaks into the front pages. In a desperate attempt to attract young viewers, who are viewed as a prime buying demographic, Ben Mulroney has been unleashed by CTV, which has also brought us *Canadian Idol*. The blur many reporters fear between news and promotion is most keenly seen in this debate. Local CTV newscasts will hype *Canadian Idol* as if it was really news, when it is purely entertainment. The Canadian Association of Journalists is vigilent whenever it sees signs of advertising driving news coverage.[6] Most entertainment reporting, however, still happens in specialty media, such as E! channel on television, a wide array of magazines, and dedicated sections and special features in newspapers.

Entertainment media include movie, book, concert, art and theatre reviews; profiles of celebrities; interviews with stars of the moment and stars making local appearances; talk shows; stories on the entertainment business and stories on the lives of celebrities. (For example, the merger of TimeWarnerAOL to create an entertainment conglomerate was a story, as are stories of financial success [*Titanic*] and failure [*Heaven's Gate*] of entertainment ventures.) Entertainment columnists write about the business, current hits, personalities and pure gossip. In addition to the entertainment sections of the mainstream media, there are numerous television programs (*Entertainment Tonight* being the oldest), magazines and local newspapers. The Internet has also turned entertainment coverage over to the masses (or at least net-heads) who provide their own reviews and try to leak elements of blockbusters, such as the *Star Wars* movies. (One fan went so far as to re-edit the first segment of the *Star Wars* series online, then posted it for fans to discuss whether it was superior to the studio's version).

Entertainment media often work under conditions unlike mainstream media. Entertainment reporters are granted access to celebrities on strict conditions of how such people will be treated. For example, Monica Lewinsky was chased by several media outlets for her first interview after the Clinton scandal came out. In addition to setting a fee for her performance, she also obtained assurances that the interview would not focus on the salacious elements of her relationship with the President. The interview with Barbara Walters also indicated the overlap between news and entertainment: most of the information about the Lewinsky/Clinton relationship was well known by the time Monica began speaking to the media. In truth, the media's interest in Lewinsky was driven more by entertainment value than by traditional news value.

Most celebrity interviews that demand positive treatment in exchange for access cater to fans, who are more interested in gossip and soft news anyway. As many celebrities find out, such *quid pro quo* does not extend to hard news, and a drunk-driving, drug or assault charge puts the celebrity squarely in the public domain, as Mel Gibson found out in the summer of 2006 when he was arrested for drunk driving, then made what were interpreted as anti-Semitic remarks. A further limitation to this kind of clout is that it does not extend to getting a favourable review. In small media, reviews are written by reporters and editors; in large media, review writing is a specialist function (Roger Ebert doesn't cover anything except movies for his newspaper), and reviewers are expected to have some distance from the material being reviewed.

Negotiating with media is possible when you control access to a person or story the media want. For example, a teenager caned in Singapore for petty vandalism demanded and got 40 minutes over two nights on *NBC Dateline*. In the case of one network, a prominent person involved in a recent criminal case even secured the right to approve the script of the interview to ensure the tone was positive.[7] Such leverage is possible. However, it also comes close to chequebook journalism, in which a figure in the news agrees to sell his or her story to the media, on an exclusive basis, for a fee. (This practice is most common in tabloid journalism, particularly British tabloids).

Whether this kind of bargaining is even appropriate or necessary is another question. Reporters are increasingly less willing to make this kind of accommodation, and the relative effectiveness of a "positive" interview or story for a personality who is receiving bad press is doubtful. If there is a reason to distrust a certain reporter or outlet, access can simply be denied (after all, people in the public have the right to deal with the media they choose), and Canadian public personalities, who have more rights to privacy than do American ones, can deal with the media they prefer.

Traditionally, the bulk of the work of the media relations practitioner in entertainment is publicity, particularly to promote attendance at an event. Most standard media relations techniques are used, with special emphasis on media sponsors. Radio stations in particular are sought, and on-air promotions are particularly encouraged. Prior to events on the stage, the practitioner will send out a notice to media of a photo shoot. The shoot will provide video and still photographs to accompany reviews. To get reviews, complimentary tickets (called "comps") are distributed to most, if not all, media in the market, whether relevant or not.

Sports Media

Sports fills the largest non-news component of daily newspapers and television newscasts. Media relations in sports has some similarities to handling entertainment media. In both cases, practitioners control access to key figures; sports may also involve selling broadcast rights to radio and television stations, which in turn are expected to be generally supportive of the home team. Like entertainment reporters, sports reporters will also cover negative stories when they happen (e.g., a hockey player is charged with domestic assault). Off-the-field stories have drawn increasingly large readership, and sports stories have begun to resemble business stories (in their coverage of the economics of sports) and entertainment stories (in their coverage of personal scandals).

The media practitioner in an amateur sports organization spends much more time seeking the attention of sports reporters than does his or her counterpart in professional sports. At the professional level, the practitioner's first responsibility is to the television and radio stations that broadcast the team's games. Depending on the team, the station and the contract, the station may have negotiated rights for players to appear exclusively on the station's sports shows, and the broadcaster may get special rights over other media (e.g., naming the game's three stars). Meanwhile, the practitioner must balance this privilege against other reporters' legitimate needs for access to personalities, service and information.

In addition to providing ongoing information to feed the almost insatiable demand for sports news, practitioners must train athletes to speak to the media. Many athletes are uncomfortable with the media, expecting reporters to be as positive and supportive as fans are. Some of the biggest problems practitioners in sports have is not with reporters but with athletes and managers, who expect deferential reporting.

Sports reporting is typified by strong opinion and analysis. The avid fan will know the score from last night's game; he may even have seen it. What he's looking for is analysis of what happened, and access to the kind of information the public may not be privy to, such as a key player being unable to play the next game because of injury. Reporters are encouraged to comment on a team's or athlete's performance, and even game reports are typified by a strong, personal writing style. Unlike other types of media, which have separated the functions of reporting and reviewing, sports reporters often combine both skills, in a style called sports writing, which means in addition to fact they are interested in analysis, critique and perspective.

You will rarely be a spokesperson in this type of media relations, except in unusual situations when management or athletes are unable to comment for themselves or when you are required to speak for the owners. Sports media relations is generally a practice where media relations is used to help others out in front of the microphone or the camera.

Crisis Communications

We have already looked at crisis communications in terms of the typical questions an emergency prompts. Few people in the field specialize in crisis communications. Generally, crisis communicators are either people who practise other forms of communications or media relations, or people in other jobs (weather, medicine, municipal government) who have been called into media relations because of the crisis.

Most municipalities practise their disaster plans regularly, as do health agencies. Large private corporations also usually have disaster plans in place, particularly sensitive businesses such as petrochemicals and mining. The disaster plan outlines all responsibilities in a crisis, from emergency response to customer service, and part of every disaster plan is a media relations plan.

The media relations plan should include media relations managers, the media liaison, communications staff including the webmaster and media spokespersons; their backups; and all their phone numbers (home, business, cell, BlackBerry). All contacts should have access to backup cell phones and conventional phones. You should also have a list of key media contacts, particularly Canadian Press. In the very early days of a crisis, if no media contacts have been established, contacting CP will get your message out to all media. You should also have a list, with backups, of all your media support services, news release agencies (Canada NewsWire or Marketwire,) and advertising agencies (in the event you need to send out an ad during the crisis). Media rooms (places where media can gather to file stories and where news briefings and conferences can be held) should be designated and stocked with the materials reporters will need: a sound board, phone/computer jacks, pens, word processors, Internet access, fax machines, coffee and snacks. Media rooms are typically located near the crisis-management headquarters or emergency operations centre (EOC) but not at the emergency site itself if the crisis is site-specific (e.g., a mine disaster or train wreck).

When the crisis occurs at a specific site, the first media issue is to ensure security at the site so media don't interfere with rescue operations. In such a scenario, media will be on-site and at the EOC, and media at both locations need to be briefed; the briefing must be done either by the same person or with the same information. In multi-site disasters (e.g., the Red River floods or the Ice Storm of 1998), it is impossible to maintain this kind of control. Front-line staff—firefighters, rescue workers, police, ambulance staff—should be encouraged to deal with the crisis first and the media second. Reporters in the media room will often ask for interviews with front-line staff; managing these requests is a major job in itself, and the media relations manager must have enough staff or volunteers to handle the task. Such interviews need to be cleared with the EOC; once that clearance takes place, front-line staff are usually more willing to talk to the media than if they are approached directly.

In the early stages of a crisis, media briefings should be held hourly, on the hour, then less frequently as the crisis passes, until the crisis is over. Regular briefings will more or less handle on-site media, whose major question will be "What's going on?" Release as many details as possible at the early stage, bearing in mind the volatility and sensitivities implied by a crisis (for example, names of fatalities are usually withheld until families are notified, casualty figures are not released until legally verified, etc.). Information about how authorities are handling, or trying to handle, the process is helpful, and great care should be taken to ensure clarity of language given some of the emergency jargon that often comes with a disaster. (For example, the term "man down" in oil-well blowouts literally means just that: a man is reported being down on the ground. Reporters need to know the term does not necessarily mean a fatality or even an injury, and that specifics as to why the man is down will be forthcoming).

The most knowledgeable people at the disaster site should handle media briefings, with a media relations manager chairing the news conference and directing questions. Briefings are best handled by presenting a short statement of the current situation, followed by a statement by the specialist, who will speak to his or her area of expertise.

If the site is secure, media should be taken to it and allowed to speak to staff and professionals who are handling the situation. In some cases, it may not be possible to take a herd of reporters and cameras to a site; in that case, the media can be asked to establish a media pool and designate one camera person who will take shots, then share that footage with all media. A pool radio reporter can also be designated, to get sound to share with other media.

This arrangement will help to deal with on-site media. Off-site media from across Canada (and around the world, if the disaster is of significant size) may also need to be accommodated. Off-site media include television and radio magazine shows such as *Canada AM* and *As It Happens.* With the advent of 24-hour television news channels and all-news radio, it takes very little time for a crisis to move from local news to national and international media. In the event of multiple requests for interviews, work with local media first, then let them worry about how the information gets to international media. It is the local media you will be dealing with when the crisis is over, and you don't want to alienate them by seeming to ignore them in favour of their more glamorous colleagues.

A recent and tragic demonstration of some principles of crisis communications was the terrorist attack of September 11, 2001. With world attention focussed on the incident, authorities from the Mayor of New York to the President of the United States spoke, usually live, as the incident unfolded. The site of the disaster was cordoned off, although media tours were arranged once the sites were relatively secure. During the early days following the attack, major television networks cancelled regular programming and devoted themselves to the event (in addition to the 24-hour news channels). In Canada, something happened that hasn't been seen in almost 50 years: daily newspapers, almost all of which publish in the morning, put out extra editions in the afternoon.

One emerging technique for handling both breaking news stories and national or international media is to use the Internet. The organization's website can be a way to update key stakeholders (government, unions, regulators and so on) and the public about the events, providing you with a direct means of communications instead of relying solely on the media. Website updates should be prepared in conjunction with the EOC, to ensure that accurate information is put up; a notice can then be sent to national and international media through a private news release service. The website then requires regular updating and all notices should be dated and timed when posted, so media and the public alike can get a clear sense of new and old information.

One area that is often forgotten in a crisis situation is internal communications with staff and families of rescue workers. Internal communications with staff can be accommodated through an intranet or password-protected website that is not accessible outside the organization, through e-mail and print bulletins to staff, with newsletters for an extended crisis or in meetings with staff. Care must be taken with confidential company information and details about staff injuries or deaths (families are usually notified before such information is given). Post-crisis communications is also important: some kind of appreciation, whether it be as simple as a thank-you memo or as formal as a memorial, helps provide recognition and appreciation.

The media will generally be supportive of authorities early in a crisis and will often ask how they can assist, such as broadcasting appeals for food and furniture. (One month after the September 11 attack, people were still giving blood, even though there was no need for it, and hundreds of millions of dollars had been raised for the families of the victims). As the crisis evolves, more media attention will be paid to the management of the situation. At this point, the best advice to recall is the first principle of media relations: good communications cannot overcome bad judgement.

Internet and the New Media

It is unlikely that the new media will displace the old. When television became widely available, experts predicted it would kill radio; instead, radio adapted, and continues to thrive. Radio simply had to leave the world of national entertainment broadcasts (radio drama, comedy, variety and soap operas) to the new medium. Instead, radio focussed on music and news, and made the transition from network broadcasting to narrowcasting: providing music and information to highly segmented target audiences. Television will likely make a similar adaptation, depending on where the Internet goes.

As noted, 75 per cent of Canadian households have a personal computer. The Net is becoming more and more a regular part of media relations. NASA regularly posts pictures of its major explorations concurrent with release to the mainstream media. While viewers can watch the pictures on 24-hour television channels, they can also see them, usually in greater detail, on the Internet. When the Kenneth Starr report on the Monica Lewinsky scandal was released, the media immediately began to summarize it (having barely read it). Concurrently, it was posted on the Internet, giving immediate access to the entire 400-plus page document to anyone in the world. And today most media outlets, even small rural newspapers, maintain websites where their stories are filed. Sites such as Canoe.ca, maintained by the Sun newspaper chain, are free and extremely popular; other agencies, such as Canadian Press, try to sell access to their services.

With reporters spending two hours a day on the Internet, and more consumers using it, the media relations practitioner cannot afford not to be Internet savvy. A colleague of mine reports half the students in her journalism program want to write for the Internet, not mainstream media.

The Internet as a research tool is proving invaluable to reporters, communicators and students, though a caution needs to be made that just because items are on the Internet or in a blog doesn't mean that they are accurate or true. As noted, good reporters will often start from the Internet but will seek further verification, or contradiction, to get a fuller story. Students in particular should use the Internet this way, as a primary source which requires further verification from other sources.

While it can be helpful for the consumer of news to have direct, unfiltered access to information on the Internet, it has to be understood that the Internet can also be the source of pure rumour, speculation, innuendo and slander. Thus, a website like the Drudge Report can publish anything it likes; what is disturbing is that mainstream media may cite it without question as a source when they would not give the same credence to someone calling into the newsroom with a hot tip. Both the media practitioner and the reporter need the ability to filter through a morass of facts and innuendo to add perspective, context and priority for the news consumer. More on blogs, the Internet and the critical importance of a good editor in Chapter 16.

15

As we have discussed in earlier chapters, reporters make mistakes. Even among themselves, they believe their error rate is high. A study of reporters' accuracy in quoting witnesses at the Colin Thatcher trial in 1982 showed an astounding 25 per cent error rate. Reporters are often criticized by the public for making even more mistakes than they realize, although a good deal of this criticism is unfounded. Advocacy groups in particular believe the media are biased against them, ignore key messages or fail to understand the issue from the perspective of the advocate.

Scholars have proposed several different models of how media present news in practice.[1] For our purposes, however, we will confine our discussion to the issue of media error. Media error should not be confused with media bias. While the media claim objectivity as an integral principle, in truth pure objectivity is impossible. Objectivity is particularly prized in mainstream journalism, but it is generally practised in terms of fair, accurate and balanced treatment by reporters on any given issue. Of course, journalism goes through cycles when objectivity is replaced by subjectivity; the muckrakers of the early twentieth century had a definite point of view, as do modern magazine editors, columnists, editorialists and bloggers. For a brief time in the 1960s, the realization that absolute objectivity is impossible led to the "New Journalism" of Tom Wolfe and Hunter S. Thompson, in which the reporter's personal biases are displayed in the story.[2] Today, the practitioner of media relations needs to be aware of the ideological bias of target media. For example, the *National Post* is a more conservative newspaper than the *Toronto Star;* both reflect their political views in the stories they choose to cover and the manner in which they cover them. For the practitioner, however, what matters is that, whether or not media objectivity is possible, reporters nevertheless hold it as a value, and the practitioner can demand objectivity in news coverage of the issue as long as it is being handled as news.

Thus, if an error occurs, it is important to find its source. Was it the reporter's fault, or was the reporter given false or misleading information? If the reporter quotes someone who misrepresents your point of view, your quarrel is with that person, not the reporter, unless in quoting the other party the reporter refuses to acknowledge your point of view. However, reporters are not supposed to take sides in a dispute, and much of their writing is a matter of "he said, she said" journalism; readers are expected to make up their own minds.

If an error of fact occurs, it is critical to correct it—quickly. Reporters follow other reporters' stories, as we have discussed, and broadcast media keep files of newspaper clippings on major stories. All reporters keep their own files and notes, and if a mistake is not corrected quickly, it will be filed and continue to be perpetuated. The longer a fact goes uncorrected, the harder it is to get fixed. Among other points, reporters may argue that the error is now a matter of public record and cannot be changed.

To correct an error, first ensure that it is indeed an error of fact, or else a misrepresentation that leads to a false impression (at this point we will not address libel and defamation). Review your notes and media material. If the error is in what you have given out, correct yourself with the media. Send out a notice to all concerned, pointing out the error and that you were the source of it. If you have a reason for the error, state that as well (e.g., the error was based on old research which has since been disproved). While this admission will lose you some credibility points at the beginning, it will pay off in the long term; reporters need to know that your dedication to accuracy is as strong as theirs is. When an error occurs, the first thing the editor asks the reporter is whose error it was; if it's yours, you may save a reporter's job. (But don't expect gratitude. Owning up to an error should be as natural to you as it is expected to be of others).

If the error is not yours, you have to determine how important the error is and how you want it rectified. Given the ease with which error can occur in media, you may want to ignore it entirely, especially if it is trivial, unlikely to recur or your key message got through despite it. The next step up is a minor correction that you want the reporter to know about for the next time. For this, simply call the reporter, point out the error and ask that the error not be carried over into future stories.

If the error is important enough to call for a public correction, talk to the reporter about it. At this stage, you don't need to threaten lawsuits or other heavy-handed tactics. As noted earlier, the media are likely to be reluctant. The Columbia School of Journalism study of US newspaper editors indicated great reluctance to run corrections.[3] Nevertheless, the profession of journalism demands high attention to errors. *The Canadian Press Stylebook* finds the issue important enough to address twice. First:

Accuracy is fundamental. Discovery of a mistake calls for immediate correction. Corrections to stories already published or broadcast must not be grudging or stingy. They must be written in a spirit of genuinely wanting to right a wrong in the fairest and fullest manner.[4]

And again:

Admit errors promptly, frankly. Public distrust of the media is profound and troubling. The distrust is fed by inaccuracy, carelessness, indifference to public sentiment, automatic cynicism about those in public life, perceived bias or unfairness and other sins suggesting arrogance.

The power of news stories to injure can reach both the ordinary citizen and the corporate giant. CP's integrity and sensitivity demand that supervisors and staff respond sympathetically and quickly when an error has been made. It doesn't matter whether the complaint comes from a timid citizen or from a powerful figure's battery of lawyers.[5]

If you have spoken with the reporter about a significant error and are unhappy with the response, the next step is to go to the editor, producer or news director. Going above the reporter's head first is simply discourteous; in any job, the first place to bring a complaint is to the person responsible for it. If you are unsatisfied with the response, then take your case to the reporter's superior. Often a counter-offer will come back, such as an agreement to take the concern as a letter to the editor or, occasionally, as a follow-up story. Give this offer some thought; if all you want is a correction, it may be a reasonable way of doing so.

Media will run corrections, but they usually need to be pressed. For that pressure to work, you must have a clear-cut case of a major error that is misleading to the reader or audience. But, since you know the editor is likely to be reluctant to begin with, coming in with a heavy-handed attitude is likely only to meet increased resistance.

The reason for this reluctance is two-fold. First, there is the natural reluctance of any institution to admit error. Although media often rail against bureaucracies, they are, particularly larger outlets, major bureaucracies in themselves. Error means an attendant loss of face and possible disciplinary action (like any employee, a reporter is liable to be fired if he or she is not doing the job competently, and making errors is a basic sign of reporter incompetence). The second reason relates to the culture of the profession. As former editor Mark Harrison puts it, "This is a craft where ego is very important too. What you do every day is what your life is all about. And to be told that you've erred—I mean, it's automatic to go into a defensive mode."[6] Legendary CBS reporter Edward R. Murrow offered this perspective: "The press is not just thin-skinned, it has no skin."[7]

If, however, you are unsatisfied with the response of both reporter and editor, the next step is through a formal complaint mechanism, such as the provincial press council or newspaper ombudsman. Unfortunately, newspapers are more open to correcting errors than are the broadcast media, and have ways to resolve disputes over errors. Broadcasters are another matter, which we will look into in a moment.

Complaining About Newspapers

For print media, the quicker route is the ombudsman, although there are fewer ombudsmen than press councils. Some newspapers have an ombudsman, as does the CBC.[8] The ombudsman can be approached directly and will investigate all complaints. The mandate of the ombudsman includes any other aspect of media relations, and if you are concerned about balance, bias or use of language, the ombudsman will look into it. "Looking into it" doesn't mean compliance, but the ombudsman will at least investigate the concern and get back to you.

Most provinces have a press council, although membership is voluntary (the Sun chain, for example, does not belong). The press council is a more formal process, and may take up to six months to investigate a complaint. Its findings, if favourable to the complainant, will be printed in the offending newspaper, and that will constitute the correction.

If there is no intervening body and the editor is not being responsive, you can complain to the publisher, who is the CEO of a newspaper (the president in broadcast journalism). To proceed to this level, you must have a provable case. (If you want to go still higher, you can approach the board and the shareholders, although by this point you are really only looking to embarrass the offending newspaper). Once a complaint gets to the level of the publisher, many private-sector organizations will threaten to withdraw advertising; whether this move will be effective, or will simply serve as spite, is an important question. The answer comes down to clout: if you are a major advertiser, particularly in a small market, the media outlet will likely pay close attention; if you're not, the media may call your bluff. When you get to this point in the relationship, you must ask yourself whether you are ready to sever all ties with the outlet and whether your business or future coverage will suffer as a result of the decision. You may want to ask the Ann Landers question: are you better off with them than without them? If in fact you are better off with them, you may have to recognize the limitations of trying to complain about them. If not, you can refuse any further dealings with them (at least if you are a private person or company; governments have different options). Again, if you reach this point in the relationship, you need to ensure you have a solid case, one that you can defend to other media if need be. On occasion, when this point is reached, the aggrieved party may choose to do some advocacy advertising or advertorials of its own, putting forward its case.

Governments cannot go to that extreme, although political parties use advocacy advertising during election campaigns. Governments, particularly in their bureaucracy, have an obligation to be accountable to the people and provide information to the media as they would to any citizen, even if the media are being hostile to them. However, elected officials can use the power of office, sometimes called the bully pulpit, to get out their message over the heads of the media. They can speak to the people directly, they can mail out newsletters to constituents and they can address key stakeholder groups directly.

Politicians can and do criticize what they perceive as unfair treatment in the media and have greater leeway than do bureaucrats in choosing what media they deal with. However, given that this type of dispute also has a good chance of becoming a *cause célèbre* in itself, you need to have an absolutely bulletproof case of media error or egregious bias that you can defend to other media, to the public and on the floor of the legislature if necessary.

Politicians have tried to complain against particular reporters to the owners of the media outlet with varying degrees of success. *Toronto Sun* reporter Claire Hoy once filed suit against his own newspaper because, he claimed, Mulroney exerted political pressure on the *Sun*'s owners to have him transferred from his Ottawa beat to Toronto.[9] Such pressure didn't result in any improvement in Mulroney's approval ratings—and, ironically enough, he eventually became chair of the Sun Media Corporation.

Complaining About Broadcasters

Complaining to broadcast media is more difficult. The chain of command goes from television reporter to assignment editor, news producer to president. If none of these individuals are responsive to your concerns, there are few options outside the system. The Canadian Association of Broadcasters will look into complaints, but it is an advocacy group representing broadcasters; even if it accepts a complaint and views it as founded, it has no authority to force a broadcaster to correct the error. The Canadian Radio-television and Telecommunications Commission does not handle complaints directly. The best you can do is intervene when the broadcaster's licence comes up for renewal and argue their licence should not be renewed. This is unlikely to be successful, but may result again in some embarrassment to the offending station.

You can consider legal action, although this is expensive and time-consuming, and should only be done if the mistake is big enough to affect your reputation or that of your client. Never threaten to sue until you have sought legal counsel (you need to determine whether you have a case first). Even then, you may have the opportunity to negotiate a correction or retraction that will save a good deal of time and money. While some highly publicized cases indicate courts do rule against the media, a host of lesser-known cases wither on the legal vine, are thrown out or are simply lost. Legal action should be the last resort, used only when errors will clearly damage your reputation or that of your client. Not only do you have to prove wrong, you have to prove harm to yourself.

As we discussed in the first chapter, many practitioners and clients are ambivalent about dealing with the media. This ambivalence should not cloud your judgement when it comes to correcting media errors or contemplating legal action. When dealing with media errors, you can help your client or organization best by maintaining some objectivity, analyzing the options open for complaint and assessing the likely success of each option.

Up to now, we have only looked at correcting errors. Practitioners can also complain about rudeness, ineptitude, insensitivity and bias. Bear in mind, though, reporters may also have the same complaints about you. As with any type of business relations, basic rules of personal conduct can be expected, and demanded, by both parties. (Revisit Chapter 3 for a discussion of what constitutes a professional relationship on both sides of the issue).

This completes the most technical aspects of this book, the day-to-day practice of dealing with the news media, within the context of a strategic plan. It is absolutely essential to the practice of media relations, serving as the groundwork of the practice. Once the basics are mastered, however, it is time to consider some more complex aspects of media and communications, and their relative roles in shaping public opinion, and ultimately public policy. The next two chapters provide an introduction to the larger world of media, communications and society. Chapter 16 looks at emerging trends in media, particularly the evolving roles of new media and mainstream media. The final chapter considers whether quality journalism, and quality communications, are still relevant in the modern world.

TOWARDS A GREATER UNDERSTANDING OF MEDIA   THREE

Communications and Technology and their Influence on Society

Emerging Trends in Media and Media Relations

16

In 1999, when the first draft of the first edition was prepared, blog software was just becoming available, and the iPod was still in the labs at Apple Computer. Predicting future trends in media relations is a risky business, given the five-year average lifespan of a textbook. Nevertheless, there are some interesting transitions occuring now in media that can be identified and tracked for their impact on future media relations. What these are and how they affect the business and art of media relations is the theme of this chapter.

Computer Assisted Reporting (CAR)

CAR is gaining in popularity as a research tool, as reporters move from using simple search engines on the Internet to find information, to managing fields of data to determine patterns that aren't otherwise visible. Fred Vallance-Jones of the *Hamilton Spectator,* a Canadian Association of Journalists (CAJ) member, and CAR expert gives a mundane example of the power of CAR: He was curious about what the most popular name for a dog in the Hamilton area was. He got the data from the city dog license office, dumped it into a data-sorting program and quickly came up with the most popular name for a dog in Hamilton: Molson.

On a far more serious note, the *Toronto Star* gained access to police information in Toronto that pointed to one disturbing fact: statistically, it can be shown that Toronto police treat black people differently from white people. CBC Vancouver, working from several data bases, uncovered the fact that every few weeks there's a murder of a young Indo-Canadian man in Vancouver, attributed to a gang war that has been ongoing since the 1990s.

CAR is a powerful new investigative tool, and the CAJ provides regular workshops to its members on how to use it. CAR may offset the shrinking newsroom and can improve the quality of journalism. For communications practitioners, it leads to a different question: do you know what data bases your organization is using to store its core information and how publicly accessible they are? What do you file with regulators, for example, that anyone can access? What do your financials contain that a good business reporter could interpret for something newsworthy? There are companies that can carry out this kind of search for you. Communicators have a responsibility to fully understand not only what information their organization makes public, but also how that information could be interpreted and used.

The Shrinking Audience for Mainstream Media

As a rule of thumb, mainstream media (MSM) are those media that are basically non-digital, such as daily and community newspapers, general interest magazines, television and radio stations that can be viewed/heard over the air; new media (NM) is generally everything else, especially if it involves greater use of technology to access, such as the Internet, cable or satellite. Beyond the technology, MSM reflects traditional, middle class values, while new media emphasizes more defined attitudes—alternative media grew up in the 1960s, though some periodicals, such as *Georgia Straight, Rolling Stone* and *This Magazine* have moved more to the mainstream. Also, MSM and NM are generally characterized by the generation gap—NM, generally speaking, representing the under 35 generation, while MSM represents the values of older users. Finally, today's new media tend to offer very quick, brief items of interest—there aren't a lot of long essays on the Internet or in the blogosphere. The terseness of NM is best seen in cell phone text messaging, which reduces complex thought to a short collection of code and emoticons (e.g., lol, ;-)).

For some decades there has been rapidly increasing competition for the mainstream audience. For example, in 1980, 95 per cent of the US watched ABC, CBS or NBC news; what other choice did they have? In 2002, that number watching the Big Three shrunk to 32 per cent.[1]

Of particular concern to MSM owners and investors is that young people do not use mainstream media (young people are the most highly prized demographic because they have the most disposable income of any group). There is nothing new in this. Historically, young people have never been heavy newspaper readers and if so, confine themselves usually to sports and entertainment. When they get older and settle down, they develop a greater interest in politics everytime their local taxes come in, and when they begin to wonder about the quality of education for their children's neighbourhood school. Seniors with no children at home and no need to go to work can afford to spend an hour a day reading the local newspaper from end to end. One wonders as the baby boom generation moves off into retirement whether there could be an increase in the sale of daily newspapers as the retiree market expands, followed by a precipitous drop thereafter.

The question for marketers, and to some extent media relations practitioners, is whether that trend will continue, or will youth, as they get older, cling to whatever the next version of their iPod, laptop, cell phone or BlackBerry will be to get their news? MSM, which was very sceptical of the Internet in the 1990's, has dived into any new technology that comes along in the hope this audience will develop a love for their brand, and, that when they move from NM to MSM they will turn to their favorite brand on their television sets. Thus TSN encourages text messaging to vote for the player of the game, and makes its shows easily downloadable on iPods, in the hope that if and when young viewers move away from new to mainstream media, they will turn to TSN on their television sets.

As we've seen, both MSM and NM are very disdainful of each other, and there is often a general assumption that new media technology will replace old. The facts disprove this assumption. A 2006 report by Statistics Canada called *Our Lives in Digital Times* points out:

- The office computer was supposed to create the paperless office; instead, paper consumption has doubled in the past 20 years.
- E-mail was supposed to replace snail mail; the amount of mail going through Canada Post has increased marginally.
- Internet sales have increased; the overall total square footage and number of retail stores has also increased.
- The number of hard telephone lines doubled in Canada between 1983 and 2003, despite the omnipresence of cell phones.[2]

These trends tend to prove that new media technology doesn't displace old; it adds to existing media and existing media adapts to new media, as radio adapted to television by changing its programming.

The big, and as yet uncertain, question is whether and how mainstream news media will adapt. To some degree they have, by offering free subway dailies for commuters for example. As well, a recent CRTC study shows that more and more, Canadians are using the Internet to watch TV, listen to radio and access their news. TV and radio have adapted somewhat, by allowing access to their programing online, and by using webspace as adspace. So, while audience time on traditional TV is down, revenues are up as advertisers spend more dollars placing their advertisements online.[3]

In other ways they haven't as newspaper and mainstream television audiences continue to shrink.

Whether mainstream media can respond to new technological challenges is literally a billion dollar question. However, it means that media relations practitioners need to keep on top of new technology and how people use that technology. Podcasts and text messaging are new ways of delivering media to young audiences. Are BlackBerry and iPods simply replicative technology, a different base from which to get the same information, or will they generate a new culture and language of their own?

The Internet is here, still evolving and will have more surprises in store. All practitioners need to be sure they have an Internet presence that is easy to access and navigate and that delivers your message to its audiences appropriately, (e.g., podcasts, RSS feeds, e-bulletins, media rooms).

The Blogosphere and MSM

It's interesting that both MSM and NM have well developed feelings of disdain for the other, yet journalists use more blogs as sources for news on a daily basis, and NM, like blogs, get a good deal of their information from MSM and link to it.[4]

A disturbing trend in media is reporters finding information on the Internet and using it as a news source without verifying it first. Right now, in the middle of the first decade of this century, the blogosphere is a wild, unregulated place which closely resembles the early days of the Internet. Blogs appear and disappear, many are not updated regularly, preach to the converted, find themselves in legal trouble and, occasionally, produce first rate commentary (rarely do they generate original news). Scott White of *Canadian Press* notes that the vast majority of blogs are not visited more than once, and only a few on a regular basis (out of the blogosphere, 437 blogs have more than 1,000 visitors, and a mere 60 have a subscriber basis of more than 5,000).[5]

Part of the problem bloggers face is easy access to technology. Just because it's possible to create a blog, it's not always advisable unless the blogger has something of interest or value to say. Most don't. Yet another problem with the blog, as with many websites, is the lack of an intervening editor to challenge the writer and push him or her to a more thoughtful, better place. Carl Bernstein won a Pulitzer Prize in journalism with his partner Bob Woodward for their coverage of Watergate, in the 1970s. Looking back on the experience, Bernstein had this to say about the editor/writer experience:

> We had said publicly over the last several decades that for a reporter, all good work was done in defiance of management. That meant the reporter had to set his or her own course, had to push back against editors at times, to roam and be free to explore, to defy the conventional wisdom if necessary. It meant that reporters, whatever they covered, had to find the inside stories, get to the bottom of things, and find the

.... Deep Throats if possible. At the same time....reporters need editors. In the end we are collaborators and they make the final calls.

After all, that was what the Watergate reporting had been all about—partnerships. My partnership with Bob, and ours with (editor) Bradlee, and Bob's strange and incomplete partnership with Deep Throat. In all, it added up to a feeling of solidarity. Today's Internet bloggers and television's talking heads don't have that. No brakes. No one there to question, doubt or inspire. No editor."[6]

Thus, there is a risk when using bloggers as a source, as well as a concern that reporters will use them without checking to validate the information. From the practitioner's point of view, get on the Internet and on the blogosphere and find out what people are saying about you, your organization and your cause. If it's wrong, get it corrected. If you face resistance ("It's only a blog, I have a right to free speech,") get a lawyer and pursue it. You have a right to protect your reputation in public spaces and to have accurate information presented about you. Media relations is a high profile business; you have an obligation to ensure your profile is factually correct.

Lest it be thought I am against blogs per se, there are some early values of blogs as a communications tool and as a medium. First, they bring great eye witness reports. Soldiers in Iraq and Afghanistan brave military censorship to set up blogs of their experiences in combat. This is one of the flexibilities of new technology; it is sometimes behind the lines of a story before anyone.

Another strength of blogging is that blogs can act as a reality check on MSM and politicians and other figures. For example, CBS News reported on some absences in the younger President Bush's military service. It was a blogger who pointed out that the font used in the documentation was from a word processor, not a typewriter, a technology which was not available when the original document was made, casting doubt on the story.

New media also allows for direct commentary unhindered by the filter of MSM. For example, YouTube ran a quick clip showing a reservist shooting at a bulletproof vest on a dummy. After the bullets shredded the vest, the reservist turns to the camera and declares his senator voted against giving troops new vests. "Now it's our turn to vote against him," the soldier concludes.[7]

During the tragic Dawson College killings in Montreal in 2006, some of the footage carried live by the 24-hour television news networks was video from some of the cell phone cameras taken by students who were caught in the school before being evacuated.

The 2005/06 federal election in Canada featured a number of political blogs—official and otherwise—and we can expect to see the technology pushed further for partisan purposes.

There may be a role for the blogger to do what the journalist can't, which is to take sides on an issue. As the Missouri School of Journalism's Clyde Bentley says "The main difference between traditional journalism and citizen journalism is that traditional journalists are sent out to cover things they don't really care about... A citizen journalist is not out to cover something, but to share it."[8] If the blogger can share that experience and point of view in a manner that is well-written and well-thought out, blogs will add to the public and media discourse on important issues in society.

Meanwhile, let's explore in more detail one reason why reporters are giving so much attention to NM, and ignoring some of the guidelines that they were taught in journalism school, such as getting at least two sources on each story.

The Shrinking Newsroom

One clear trend in the past 15 years—and a worrisome one for the future—is the absolute decline in the number of working reporters in Canada, combined with an explosion of new media: a second national newspaper, 24-hour business, sports and news television channels, the rise of 24-hour news talk and sports AM radio stations, and of course the Internet. The end result is fewer reporters working for more and more media outlets. The numbers tell the story:

Here are the number of jobs Statistics Canada defines as being journalists, from the annual census over the past fifteen years:

1991	1996	2001
13,470	12,660	12,960

It's no surprise, then, that the 2003 Ipsos Reid study of editors and reporters put staffing and resources as their number one concern (44 per cent).[9] There is some hope; three times as many expected to hire staff as to cut staff (42 per cent versus 12 per cent).[10]

(Unfortunately, the results of the 2006 census were not available as this book went to press. Those interested might wish to follow up with StatsCan and see if the trend halted in 2006. Please ask for Occupation Code F023, Journalists).

In any case, the numbers are down, in part due to the severe recession of the early-to-mid 1990s, and in part to convergence (more on this later).

The net result is that there are fewer reporters working in news outlets than there were 20 years ago. This is not a phenomenon confined to Canada. From 1980 to 2006, Philadelphia lost over half its newspaper reporters.[11]

This only adds to the day-to-day stresses of the working reporter. Already under pressure to begin with, they have to fill the same space and time with half the staff. Hence, the practice of taking bloggers and others at their word in order to get a story out, instead of taking the time to check it out and talk to other sources, can be present. This is not a good thing for either the media relations practitioner or society as a whole. From the technical point of view, it might seem that the media will more readily accept our stories and use them without question. Unfortunately, there is the risk that they will do that with a competitor, and our point of view will be lost.

Again, from a practitioner's point of view, the phenomenon of un-screened news diminishes the value of using news to communicate in the first place. As noted much earlier in this book the value of using news to get your message out is that it has gone through some degree of third party scrutiny. If your message appears in the media, it carries greater credibility than, say, an ad, which the audience knows you have bought and paid for.

From the larger social view, if news media begin to replicate news from sources such as blogs, it will have no added value to the user whatso-ever. Consumers are very media savvy; they recognize news for what it is and advocacy/communications for what they are. If the line becomes too blurred between the two, society is worse off for it. At their best, news media provide a reality check to the messages that every advocate wants to get out; it is soci-ety's loss if that service vanishes through the physical incapacity of reporters to be as thorough as they need to be.

This leads us to convergence and its role in the shrinking news room. Convergence came with great hype as billions were spent in corporate Canada to merge television, newspapers, radio (to some degree) and the Internet. Most efforts have failed and had little result in terms of better news or improved access to news, though CanWest Global's effort to drive all their news off their website deserves some chance to prove itself. For example, at the IABC Canada Conference in 2003, Canadian Press (CP) took great pride in announcing its converged newsroom between broadcast, print and the Internet. When asked at the 2005 conference the status of that experience, CP replied that it was now working more in a co-operative model than a converged model.

The effect of convergence, or media mergers as they are better called now, is still to be seen. The most recent buyout prior to publication of this text is that of CHUM media by CTV BellGlobeMedia on July 12, 2006. Tucked away in the coverage of this news was this observation:

CHUM says it plans to cut 191 full-time and part-time positions across the country as it undergoes a complete reorganization of its television operations to "increase focus on services to local viewers."

The moves include switching Citytv stations in Calgary, Edmonton and Winnipeg from one-hour evening newscasts to a daily half-hour local news magazine show.

In addition, a morning show at a CHUM-owned A-channel in Victoria will be discontinued. Citytv Vancouver will cease its traditional newscasts and add resources to *Breakfast Television*.[12]

The layoffs included technical staff as well as reporters/editors. While CHUM states the plans were afoot for months, there seems to be no indication that CTV will reinstate the lost news programming.

For the news user, this is the loss of another voice in media, particularly a voice targeted at younger viewers.

For the media relations practitioner, convergence means more effort will have to be made to work with reporters than ever before. It has been a common complaint from practitioners that media ask us to do too much of their work for them. Unless this trend changes, it will be necessary for media relations practitioners to work more closely with reporters than in the past.

Meanwhile, in the middle of this chaos, CanWest Global and BellGlobeMedia continue to be profitable. The role of corporate profit versus social responsibility is a major issue in media business these days and it is time that large media corporations were brought into the debate.

Corporate Social Responsibility (CSR) as a Tool to Improve the Quality of News

Businesses and business leaders have shown themselves to have a greater responsibility to society than simply to generate profit for themselves and their shareholders. In the nineteenth century, Gilded Age American tycoons built free public libraries and established great foundations in their name to do public good, but these were generally individual philanthropic decisions.

In the early part of the twenty-first century, particularly after high-profile business scandals in Canada (Bre-X, Conrad Black) and the United States (WorldCom), the social responsibility of business to contribute in a more meaningful way to society was defined and named Corporate Social Responsibility. Particularly prominent in those businesses which are active in the environment, such as logging, mining and energy, CSR policy is now embedded into many Canadian and international corporations.[13] Professor Jared Diamond pursues the idea of CSR further, laying ultimate responsibilty with the public for the practices of media—"Our blaming of businesses also ignores the ultimate responsibility of the public for creating the conditions that let a business profit through hurting the public.... In the long run, it is the public, either directly or through its politicians, that has the power to make destructive environmental policies profitable and illegal, and to make sustainable environmental policies profitable."[14]

Is it possible to take the same approach with media corporations, and move from passive receivers of news to active participants who demand a higher standard of journalism from media, and a higher standard of communications from communicators? Unfortunately, it rarely happens, and the debate about the quality of news is confined to academic and professional circles. Part of the purpose of this book is to bring the notion of greater corporate responsibility for media owners and to communicators to a wider public.

While media companies have contributed to the communities around them, I wonder if the case can be made that their real contribution to CSR should be to hire more reporters, and improve the quality and quantity of news their outlets produce. For decades, the view of owners and managers of media has been that newsrooms and reporters are cost centres, i.e. reporters cost money whereas advertising, subscriptions and distribution of flyers bring money in. Actually, the facts fly in the face of the accountant's argument. The *Toronto Sun* was founded in the early 1970's from the flames of the deceased *Toronto Telegram*. Widely held to be irrelevant, if not downright irresponsible from the beginning, the *Sun* grew from strength to strength. One of main strengths was the writing of columnist Paul Rimstead, whose Rabelaisian, larger-than-life style of living drew legions of devoted fans and reflected the zeitgeist of Toronto at the time. Since his death, the paper has never been the same. Yes, reporters and columnists cost money, but they can also bring in money. In the modern parlance, content is king and proprietors of media need to give more thought to the quality of the content of their media, if not for reasons of CSR, then because that quality and attention to the values of their audiences, will bring in more money.

The battle between the accountants and the journalists over the integrity of news is old and ongoing. An excerpt from the 2006 Annual Report on the State of the News Media:

> The idealists have lost..... The most cogent explanation for why journalism in the public interest has lost leverage was probably offered by Polk Laffoon IV, the corporate spokesman for *Knight Ridder*. 'I wish there was an identifiable and strong correlation between quality journalism.... and newspaper sales,' he said. 'It isn't...that simple.' From here on, at many companies, the fight on behalf of the public interest will come

from the rank and file of the newsroom, with the news executive as mediator with the boardroom.[15]

This reflects the declinist point of view, as discussed in the introduction. The Neo-Pollyannist view, which I share, is that quality is in demand. For example, *The Globe and Mail* improved into a significantly better newspaper after the *Post* entered the scene (competition is a good thing for all media), adding more colour, more columnists and expanding its sections on arts and sports. Of all major newspapers in the Toronto battle for readers, it seems to have held its ground while others are in decline.

However, the *Post* and the *Globe* have moved their significant financial tables, of vital interest to investors, out of the newspaper and onto the Internet, where investors can delve into the data to their heart's delight. "All this will free up space for more business news, analysis and opinion," the *Post* claims.[16] Let's all hold them to it.

There is room in MSM for more commentary, analysis and opinion, as sports reporters have shown for some time. With 24-hour news on TV, radio and the Internet, it may be time for newspapers and other mainstream media to copy the *Post* and the *Globe* model, and vacate space normally devoted to pure facts and lists, (such as stock exchange information), and the notion they keep a public record, and move into space that adds more value and context to the user, and provides more context to the facts themselves (such as more stock analysis and commentary).

Then owners and operators of mainstream media and new media could both consider their roles in the delivery of quality news. More reporters and editors who have the time to delve into and challenge the information they are bombarded with daily can only result in a better-informed public.

Towards a Greater Understanding of Media, Communications and Technology

17

After several chapters of detail on the mechanics of media relations, let's step back a bit to consider some larger themes and some of the implications of how media and communications shape public opinion and the effect of technology on media and society. This chapter is simply an attempt to connect the reader to the broader and more thoughtful discussion on media theory. We look at three issues of current interest: is the medium still the message, as Marshall Mcluhan put forward; is Noam Chomsky correct in his view that MSM represents a corporate, capitalist view that fundamentally moves their own interests further; and is there a need for more research in communications? Finally, the book concludes with a short list of recommended reading which can lead to more in-depth discussions and thought about media, communications and society.

Is the Medium Still the Message?

The media truly became a topic of serious academic study with the theories of Marshal McLuhan, who famously opined that 'the medium is the message.' That might have been true in the 1950s, when the technology of media was primarily print and broadcast (and he focused primarily on the effect of broadcast media on society). From today's perspective, almost all media then was mainstream and it was pretty static, unlike now, where new technologies are emerging all the time, and there is very little capacity for people to absorb their impact before a newer technology comes along. Video tapes, for example, changed the way we viewed television because we could now choose what to watch and when, and not be dictated to by the timing of television programmers. Video is now obsolete, having been replaced by DVD, and PVR.

The 20-year timeline academics used to have to contemplate the effect of communications technology on society is not a present day luxury. It may have been a distraction anyway. For example, as per the previous discussion on the blogosphere, the technology is interesting but in the end irrelevant—unless someone has something of interest or value to say on a blog, it simply doesn't matter. In some ways, blogs and the Internet are a return to the original days of newspapers, when thanks to the development of cheap newsprint and better printing pressses, writers like Addison and Steele could sell their pamphlets for pennies in coffee houses. Their writing survived, while that of thousands of their contemporaries is lost to time. The difference is that Addison and Steele had something of value to say and could write well and engagingly. Coffee drinkers who bought pamphlets on a per copy basis began to value Addison and Steele's work; in effect, a reliable brand was established, not based on marketing or technology, but by the quality of their writing and thought and cheap easy access to it. Similarly, some blogs/websites will survive the test of time because they are well-written and interesting, while most will be forgotten. (Unfortunately, some good writing and commentary may be lost simply because it won't be discovered before the technology goes the way of the microfiche, becomes obsolete and is replaced).[1]

Thus, I would argue that we have gone full circle and the medium is no longer the message, particularly since almost everyone has access to the medium, whether it be a website or blog. Instead, it's time to argue that the idea is the message and we as a society have to move beyond the notion that just because it is possible to create a communications medium with new technology we are therefore changing society, and move to the notion that we should use a communications medium to communicate ideas in order to move society.

The moving of society to get it to a different point is less dependent on the technology than the ends for which that technology is used. Thomas L. Friedman in *The World is Flat* points out that computer technology is changing business and society around the world, and helping developing countries such as India connect to, profit from and improve their material and social well-being. He also points out that Al Qaeda used the same technology to develop an international web of terror aimed at creating a supra-national fundamentalist Islamic state.[2]

It is less the presence of a communications technology that moves society than the ideas and actions that are communicated and inspired through the use of that technology. The main difference between MSM and NM is the speed and reach of new media, and its ability to literally go around the world in an electronic second.

Do Mainstream Media Simply Represent Corporate, not Public, Values?

For years, Dr. Noam Chomsky has argued that MSM manufactures public consent that only supports corporate, capitalist values while overlooking any genuinely dissenting view. Are there now media that seriously challenge the views and values of MSM?

As noted, both MSM and NM disdain each other, yet each oddly connects to the other; mainstream media cites blogs as sources in their news, and blogs connect their readers to MSM sites. Blogs still haven't created stand-alone sites that are unique, alternative and have large audiences, such as the established independent websites like the *Drudge Report* and *The Onion*. Whether they will ever establish their own cadre of creative writers like Addison and Steele is still, in 2007, unproven. Much of the blogosphere is preaching to the converted, as activists visit mainly activist sites, businesses visit business sites, workers visit labour sites and so forth. Blogs are part of every political campaign, but whether they influence a vote is still uncertain.

Studies on mainstream media have shown the public is wary about who controls them and the effect of the establishment in colouring news stories. A 2003 study by the Canadian Media Research Consortium (representing journalism/communications programs at the University of British Columbia, York and Ryerson Universities and Université Laval) found that 76 per cent of Canadians believe reporters and news organizations are often influenced by powerful people and their interests.[3] These would be CEOs, governments, bureaucrats, powerful lobby groups and people with money. Furthermore, only 37 per cent said news reporting was "often" fair and balanced; 42 said "sometimes" fair and balanced and 15 per cent said "seldom." Only 59 per cent agree that mainstream media get the facts straight. Interestingly, only 31 per cent of Americans agree that media get the facts straight, illustrative of a far more partisan media and a contentious public issue—the war in Iraq.

So, those Canadians who consume the news (and many don't) tend to be sceptical of the quality of the news they receive. One key difference between mainstream and new media is that mainstream media have a cultural value of objectivity while new media tend to be partisan and present a particular point of view, whether personal or issue-based. The public generally want mainstream media to maintain its value of objectivity (outside its opinion pages of course).

CanWest Global's management is perceived as having an unhealthy effect on the quality of news in its newspapers, which under the Southam brand had a history of editorial independence, reflecting the values of the communities they represented. One of the oddities of mainstream media is that they are, outside of public broacasting, owned by capitalists whose primary concern is profit (there are exceptions like the *Toronto Star* which has a unique charter focusing on social progress, dating from a previous owner). Government reviews of mainstream media practices, like the Kent Commission of 1980, have studied MSM, particularly newspapers, and argued there should be a higher expectation on the value of news in society, and greater responsibility by owners to put more emphasis on news. Solutions, though, are hard to come by. Kent argued for greater government regulation of newspapers, which owners, journalists and believers in a free press found difficult to stomach.

The struggle between journalists and owners has been longstanding and, as we've seen, there are two schools of thought as to whether mainstream media are in irreversible decline (declinists) due to technology and desire for greater profits, or have the potential to recover, with an emphasis on the quality of the news, such as that provided by national newspapers like the *New York Times* and *The Globe and Mail* (neo-Pollyanists). One great difficulty in any kind of theorizing about media is that they are incredibly diverse and generalizations are problematic even between a daily urban newspaper, a national daily and a comunity weekly, let alone between print and broadcast or MSM versus NM. Furthermore, we've seen enlightened capitalists like Pierre Karl Péladeau and Conrad Black (who, regardless of what one may think of his business practices, did create a new national newspaper) incur significant business risk to support traditional, quality mainstream media.

Still, there seems to be public support for Chomsky's criticism of MSM, but no credible media alternative has yet developed to challenge MSM. However, the advent of the Internet has allowed the public to create their own sources of news, and bring the news of value to them rather than rely on an intermediary to do it for them. It is quite likely that the main competition to MSM is not new media like blogs, but the Internet itself, which is now so established it is hard to consider it any more as "new" media. It is entrenched in public and private life, and a major player in modern communications.

The question for MSM, and urban daily newspapers in particular, is whether they can adapt to new tastes and technology, as radio did, or whether they will wither and die, like telegraph communications. It is possible for traditional media to adapt and evolve, as radio did when television first emerged, again when FM radio emerged to challenge AM, and yet again when satellite radio arrived. *MacLean's* is still a successful magazine after several format changes in the face of technological challenges and changes in public taste. It is of interest that they focussed on the content of the material they carried, and not on simply adapting to new media; there is a lesson there for daily newspapers in particular.

Most MSM is hidebound in the beats it covers (courts, governments, police, sports, business etc.). Rarely are MSM looking at covering different news that could be of interest to its readers. Thus, about 50 US newspapers devote space and resources to covering the Baby Boomers demographic and the effect they continue to have on society as their numbers drive public and social policy.[4] Although MSM continues to survey and focus test their audiences, it never seems to result in any serious look at changing the focus or the content of the news they present.

The Value of Communicators in Society and the Need for More Research

As shown in the previous chapter, the absolute number of journalists in Canada has declined over 15 years, while the number of news outlets has increased. A similar examination of communicators shows a different picture:

	1991	1996	2001
Communicators	23,780	27,069	27,465

(Source: Stats Canada Census results, Code F024: professional occupations in public relations and communications).

Again, it will be interesting to check if the 2006 census shows this trend continues. Experience suggests to me that it will.

Meanwhile, I would argue from these statistics that society as a whole is putting a greater value on formally and professionally communicating with its various publics. One of the greater increases has been in non-profit charitable organizations along with academia, whose communicators are primarily fundraisers (it should be noted that the Stats Canada figures include all types of communicators—fundraisers, speechwriters, website designers etc.—as well as media relations specialists).

Unfortunately, while society is paying more attention to the value of communications/public relations, media is still getting greater attention from academia. In part this may be simply because media has a longer history. I trace the development of media relations back only as far as 1908, when the Pennsylvania Railroad hired Ivy Lee to be its press agent, working solely with news media to generate a more positive public image for the railroad in the era of the robber baron (other aspects of communications such as promotion date back to Phineas Barnum, and newspaper, radio and television advertising came about when the technologies were established). News media as we understand it goes back to the late 18th century, when cheap newsprint meant that pamphlets and broadsheets could be quickly and cheaply printed for sale.

So, our history is not as long as journalism's. Communications may be difficult to examine since much of the activities involved are hidden from the public. Communicators are intermediaries; we develop communication strategies and pieces for other people to use. A communicator may write a great speech that moves public opinion but the speech will be read by someone else, like a CEO or a politician. Still, as communications grows as a field in Canada and internationally, it could use the same scrutiny and study that media receive for many reasons, especially to help develop a better sense of how much the practice of communications shapes public opinion and public policy.

Further Reading

These are simply some thoughts from a practitioner to generate further attention to the wider, more philosophical world of technology, media and communications studies. I direct the interested reader to the Further Reading section which concludes this chapter, and this book, and thank all those who have taken the time, and interest, to read the book, and learn how to work with media to communicate to the public and key audiences.

This list was compiled by me and Professor Karen Wall of Athabasca University.

Journalism

The Elements of Journalism: What Newspeople Should Know and the Public Should Expect by Bill Kovach and Tom Rosentiel (Washington, D.C.: Committee of Concerned Journalists, 2000). Journalists are often the fiercest of media critics, seeing their own shortcomings more clearly than outsiders. This book addresses the shortcomings of media and suggests what needs to be done to improve the quality of reporting and journalism.

The Journalist and the Murderer by Janet Malcolm (New York: First Vintage Books, 1990) is a fascinating case study of the complex relationship between journalist and subject, through a psychoanalytical framework.

The Missing News: Filters and Blind Spots in Canada's Press by Robert A. Hackett and Richard Gruneau (Toronto: Garamond Press, 2000). Media can have a very traditional, if not hidebound, habit of what to cover (crime, government, sports, etc.). This book looks at some of the issues that don't get coverage in mainstream media, including labour, power and social inequality.

Sustaining Democracy: Journalism and the Politics of Objectivity by Robert A. Hackett and Yuezhi Zhao (Toronto: Garamond Press, 1998), examines media bias and objectivity.

Communications Theory

Communication Theory—Media, Technology and Society by David Holmes, (London: Sage Publications, 2005) offers an introduction to communication theory appropriate to the post-broadcast, interactive media environment.

Health in the Headlines: The Stories Behind the Stories by Stephen Klaidman (New York: Oxford University Press, 1991) looks at several cases of media coverage of complex health and environmental issues, with a view to understanding how the media manage complex and contentious scientific issues.

How to Watch TV News by Neil Postman and Steve Powers (Toronto: Penguin Books, 1992) provides a critical look at television news and shows how to become a more discerning viewer.

Manufacturing Consent: the Political Economy of the Mass Media by Edward S. Herman and Noam Chomsky (New York: Pantheon Books, 1988) is a classic, offering a more conceptual approach to media in general and its effect on modern society.

Propaganda by Jacques Ellul (Toronto: Random House of Canada, 1973) is a classic philosophical examination of the intersection between technology, media and society.

"Public Relations Bibliography," S. Ramsey, ed. (*Public Relations Review: A Journal of Research and Comment,* 2002). *The Public Relations Review* is the oldest journal devoted to articles that examine public relations in depth. Most of the articles are based on empirical research undertaken by professionals and academics in the field.

Public Relations: Strategies and Tactics by Dennis L. Wilcox, Phillip H. Ault, Warren K. Agee and Glen T. Cameron (Don Mills, Ontario: Longman, 2000) and *Effective Public Relations* by Scott M. Cutlip, Allen H. Center and Glen M. Broom (Upper Saddle River, New Jersey: Prentice-Hall, 2000) are standard American texts dealing with the wider world of communications and public relations.

Understanding Media: the Extensions of Man by Marshall McLuhan (Cambridge: MIT Press, 1994). This is perhaps Marshall McLuhan's best-known book and a seminal classic on media, culture and society.

Ethics

Culture Inc: the corporate takeover of public expression by H.I. Schiller (New York: Oxford University Press 1989), *Culture Inc.* exposes the agenda and methods of corporate cultural takeover.

Necessary Illusions: Thought Control in Democratic Societies by Noam Chomsky (Boston: South End Press, 1989). Based on the 1988 Massey Lectures, *Necessary Illusions* argues that, far from performing a watchdog role, the "free press" serves the needs of those in power.

"Toward a Professional Responsibility Theory of Public Relations Ethics," by K. Fitzpatrick and C. Gauthier (*Journal of Mass Media Ethics,* 2001): 16 (2 & 3), 193–212. This article addresses the theory of public relations ethics and the roles of a public relations practitioner as a professional, an institutional advocate, and the public conscience of institutions served.

Toxic Sludge is Good for You! Lies, Damn Lies and the Public Relations Industry by John Stauber and Sheldon Rampton (Monroe, Maine: Common Courage Press, 1995) provides a critical look at the business, and a reminder to practice ethically and professionally.

New Media

Jamming the Media: A Citizen's Guide to Reclaiming the Tools of Communication by Gareth Branwyn (San Francisco: Chronicle Books, 1997) a DIY guide to media with chapters on zines, ezines, public access TV, and media stunts.

The New Influencers by P. Gillin (Sanger: Quill Driver Books, 2006) looks at how Internet-based communications platforms like blogs and podcasts give individuals the power to reach global audiences without the restrictions of conventional channels or editors and the influence they bring to the market.

The Real World of Technology (revised edition) by Ursula Franklin (Toronto, House of Anansi Press, 1999). Franklin examines the impact of technology upon our lives and issues such as the dilution of privacy and intellectual property rights, and the influence of the Internet upon the craft of writing.

Blogs

For updates on media changes in Canada, please refer to:
http://mediarelationsincanada.wordpress.com

Notes

Introduction

1. See, for instance, Donna G. Albrecht, *Promoting Your Business with Free (or Almost Free) Publicity* (Upper Saddle River: Prentice-Hall, 1997).

2. See, for instance, Jason Salmon, *Making the News: A Guide for Nonprofits and Activists* (Boulder: Westview Press, 1998).

3. See, for instance, Kay Borden, *Bulletproof News Releases* (Marrietta: Franklin-Sarrett Publishers, 1994).

4. Mike Ura, *Making the News: A Guide to Using the Media* (Vancouver: West Coast Environmental Law Research Foundation, 1980): 22.

5. Angus Reid Group, *Canadian Media Review 1993: An Elite Survey of Editors and Journalists for Communications Professionals* (Toronto: Angus Reid Group, 1993).

6. Ura, 24.

7. See Bill Fox, *Spinwars: Politics and the News Media* (Toronto: Key Porter Books, 1999): 13–22.

ONE   **THEORY AND PRINCIPLES ON MEDIA RELATIONS**

1   **Why Media, Why News**

1. Philip Kotler and Gordon H.G. McDougall, *Principles of Marketing, Canadian Edition* (Scarborough: Prentice-Hall Canada Inc., 1983): 425.

2. "A small business in career upgrading," *Globe and Mail,* 14 November 1999, D6.

3. Michael J. Robinson and Andrew Kohut, "Believability in the Press," *Public Opinion Quarterly* 52 (Summer 1988): 174–88.

4. Anne R. Owen and James H. Karrh, "Video News Releases: Effect on Viewer Recall and Attitudes," *Public Relations Review* 22:4 (Winter 1996): 376.

5. David Blount and Glen T. Cameron, "VNRs and Air Checks: A Content Analysis of On-Air Use of Video News Releases," *Journalism and Mass Communication Quarterly* (Winter 1997); cited in Wilcox, Ault, Agee and Cameron, eds., *Public Relations Strategies and Tactics* (Don Mills: Longman, 2000): 532.

6. Gilbert Cranberg, "The editor-error equation," *The Columbia Journalism Review* 25 (March/April 1987): 40–44.

7. Neil Hickley, "CJR Poll: Handling corrections," *The Columbia Journalism Review* (July/August 1999), http://backissues.cjrarchives.org/year/.

8. Patrick McGee, "Did I really hear that?" http://www.prcanada.ca/CRISIS/DISFLUT.HTM, (accessed 3 May 2004).

9. Fox, 65.

10. *CP Stylebook,* 13.

11. Catherine McKercher and Carman Cumming, *The Canadian Reporter: News Writing and Reporting* (Toronto: Harcourt Brace & Company, 1998): 107.

12. A novelty can be made out of anything: e.g., pens, fridge magnets, coffee cups, balloons, key chains, clothing (t-shirts, jackets, caps, belt buckles), calendars, trophies, shopping bags, condoms, rulers, bookmarks, postcards, business cards and hot-air balloons. Check under Advertising Specialties in the Yellow Pages. Don't be afraid to be creative in this arena: sometimes it's the unlikeliest approach that takes hold best.

13. Colin Lindsay, *A Portrait of Seniors in Canada, Second Edition* (Ottawa: Statistics Canada, 1997): 122.

14. See, for example, Lester Potter, *The Communication Plan: The Heart of Strategic Planning* (San Francisco: International Association of Business Communicators, 1997), http://www.iabc.com.

2   Basic Principles of Media Relations

1. Fred Emery, *Watergate* (New York: Random House, 1994): 175.

2. Fox, 68.

3. Risk Communications is defined as "The transmission of information about health and environmental risks, their significance and the policies aimed at managing them." Davies, Covello and Allen, editors, *Risk Communication: Proceedings of the National Conference on Risk Communications, held in Washington D.C. January 29–31* (Washington, DC: The Conservation Foundation, 1987), back cover.

4. Vincent Covello, *Handbook on Risk Communication, presented by Dr. Vincent Covello, Director of the Center for Risk Communication in New York City,* (Calgary, Risk Communications conference handout, 1994).

5. McKercher and Cumming, 127.

6. Robert Martin, *Media Law* (Toronto: Irwin Law, 2003).

7. G. Stuart Adam, "The Thicket of Rules North of the Border," *Media Studies Journal* 12:1 (Winter 1998): 24–30.

8. Derek DeCloet and Sean Silcoff, "Air Canada probe extends to Bay St.," *National Post,* 28 July 2001, A1.

9. *Canadian Defamation Law,* http://www.duhaime.org/ca-defam.htm; (accessed 26 July 2001).

10. Shannon Proudfoot, "Internet blogs prompt rise in libel suits," *Regina Leader Post,* 18 March 2006, D12.

11. See, for example, Ed Shiller, *The Canadian Guide to Managing the Media,* second edition (Scarborough: Prentice-Hall, 1994).

12. "News bias assessed," *Edmonton Journal,* 6 December 1992, F1.

13. "News bias assessed."

14. Ruth Sulivan, "Rain Man and Joseph," Eric Schopler and Gary Mesibov, eds., *High Functioning Individuals with Autism* (New York: Plenium Press, 1992): 24.

15. Much of this section is informed by Randy Sumpter and James W. Tankard Jr., "The Spin Doctor: An Alternative Model of Public Relations," *The Public Relations Review* 20:1 (Spring 1994): 19–27.

16. Harry G. Frankfurt, *On Bullshit* (Princeton: Princeton University Press, 2005): 7, citing Max Black, *The Prevalence of Humbug* (Ithaca: Cornell University Press, 1985): 143.

17. Michael Specter, "The Media: After debate, the masters of 'spin' take the floor," *New York Times,* 18 February 1992, A16, cited in Sumpter and Tankard.

18. Arthur E. Rowse, "How to Build Support for War," *Columbia Journalism Review* 31 (September/October 1992): 28–29.

19. Rowse, 29.

20. Frankfurt, 61

21. See, for example, Bruce Porter, "The Scanlon Spin," *Columbia Journalism Review* 29 (September/October 1989): 49–54.

22. Sumpter and Tankard, 24.

3 Professional Relations

1. Brian Biggar, *PR Flacks and Media Hacks: Public Relations and the News Media* (Master of Journalism thesis, Carleton University School of Journalism and Communication Resource Centre): XI.

2. For more discussion on this point, see, for example, "Is the press any match for Powerhouse PR?" in the *Columbia Journalism Review,* (September/October 1992): 27–34.

3. All quotations from Biggar, 62–66.

4. Biggar, 55.

5. "Positive messages about PR outweigh negatives," *Communications World* (December 1992): 28.

6. Quoted in Katherine Dunn, "The Lies the Good Guys Tell," *Globe and Mail.*

7. Ernest Hemingway, *The Paris Review,* 1958. *Bartlett's Familiar Quotations,* 16th edition (Toronto: Little, Brown and Co., 1992): 72.

8. Style manuals began as simple guides for reporters to help them observe common language usage and spelling; they later developed into more comprehensive manuals that look at newsgathering techniques, and ethical and professional standards. While the *CP Stylebook* is the most common in the country, major newspapers and television chains also have their own style guides.

9. McKercher and Cumming, 383–85.

10. See Canadian Association of Journalists website, http://www.caj.ca/aims/index.html.

11. CPRS website: http://www.cprs.ca/cprscode.htm.

12. Wilma Matthews, *Effective Media relations: A practical guide for Communicators,* (San Francisco, IABC, 2000), preface.

4 Basics of Media: Who They Are

1. "More radio listeners tuning in to CBC," *Regina Leader Post,* 1 August 2003, A10.

2. Adapted from Susan Truitt, "At 6 a.m., it's morning lite," *Columbia Journalism Review* (November/December) 2000: 96–97.

3. Rosental Calmon-Alves, "Many newspaper sites still cling to once-a-day publish cycle," by Rosental Calmon-Alves, *USC Annenberg Online Journalism Review,* http://ojr.org/ojr/workplace/1090395903.php, (accessed 22 July 2004).

4. Julia Angwin, "Internet adoption hits the wall," *Globe and Mail,* 16 July 2001, B8.

5. "Post forcing shift in advertising revenue: buyers," *National Post,* 30 October 1999, D4.

6. Canadian Community Newspaper Association, *The Age of Community Newspapers,* Presentation, June 2004, Saskatchewan Government.

7. Robert Dykstra, *The Hometown Newspaper and Viability of News in the Community Press* (Unpublished master's thesis) Carleton University School of Journalism and Communications Resource Centre, Reference 775, 1998: iii.

8. Jane L. Thompson and Ellen Himelfarb, "TV that's so bad it's good," *National Post,* 13 February 1999, 13.

9. *Exurbs* refers to bedroom communities that surround a major city but have independent administration; synonymous with outlying communities.

5   Basics of Media: How They Work

1. Florian Sauvageau, "Surveying Attitudes," *Media Magazine,* (Winter 2000), http://www.caj.ca/mediamag/winter2000/media2000—15.html, (accessed 26 July 2001).

2. George Pollard, "Canadian Newsworkers; Cross Media Analysis of Professional and Personal Attributes," *Canadian Journal of Communications* 11:3 (1985), 269–86, cited in Debarats, 98.

3. Pollard, 98.

4. Barber and Rauhala, "The Canadian News Directors Study," *Canadian Journal of Communications* 30 (2005), 87.

5. Barber and Rauhala, 282.

6. McKercher and Cumming. xvii–xviii

7. A number of academic studies have demonstrated the influence of public relations on news. See Chapter 8 for more extensive discussion and reference on this issue.

8. Some examples can be found at http://www.nytimes.com/navigator or http://www.ryerson.ca/journalism/links/.

9. The reader who wishes to pursue this can start with Chapter 2, "What is News?" in Neil Postman and Steve Power's *How To Watch T.V. News* (Toronto: Penguin, 1992).

10. Ipsos Reid, *2003 Canadian Media Relations Review* (Toronto: Ipsos Reid, November 2003).

11. Quoted in Paul Near, *The Edmontonians,* February 1994.

12. McKercher and Cumming, 9–30.

13. Susan Craig, "Striking unions ask for Herald meetings," *Globe And Mail,* 15 November 1999, B3.

14. *CP Stylebook,* 12–15.

15. A recent survey of Canadian journalists concluded they shared the following values when it came to reporting: accuracy, getting information to the public quickly, letting ordinary people express their views, investigating activities of institutions and providing analysis of complex problems. See Sauvageau.

16. Doris Graber, "Seeing is remembering: How visuals contribute to learning from television," *Journal of Communications* 40:3 (Summer 1990): 134–55.

17. Graber, 138.

TWO THE PRACTICE OF MEDIA RELATIONS

6 Getting Started

1. The use of the term *proactive* is certainly troubled. As far as I can tell, the word proactive was developed by the bureaucracy to define the opposite to the word reactive, which is itself an antonym to the word active. Proactive is thus redundant, and is generally more accurate to speak of an active or activist approach to media relations. However, common usage must be recognized, if not respected, and thus I will use proactive throughout this text.

2. Bill Carney, "The value of Reactive Media Relations in Communicating Risk," (unpublished manuscript), 1994. Available on request from the author.

3. Ipsos Reid, 11.

4. Biggar, 62–66.

5. For example, for some time communicators felt that hard-line messages about drunk driving didn't work and softer, responsible drinking messages were preferable. However, after the campaigns began to reduce drunk driving among the general population, it was found that young drivers (statistically at highest risk of practicing dangerous driving) were not receptive to the softer messages. As a result, the messaging changed back to the hard-line, as seen in the "Bloody Idiot" campaign in western Canada, driving home with no subtlety the point that drunk driving kills and maims young people.

At some time, this message will have to be changed again, to keep up with changing attitudes.

7 The First Steps

1. Carol Roberts Legge and Molly Butler, *Situational Analysis: Fetal Alcohol Syndrome/Fetal Alcohol Effects and the Effects of other Substance Use During Pregnancy* (Ottawa: Health Canada, 2000); http://www.cds-sca.com, (accessed 26 July 2001).

2. Wilcox, Ault, Agee and Cameron, *Public Relations Strategies and Tactics* (Don Mills: Longman, 2000): 146–47.

3. The two major communications associations in Canada provide assistance and literature to members on communications planning: the Canadian Public Relations Society (CPRS) and the International Association of Business Communicators (IABC). Their websites are http://www.cprs.ca and http://www.iabc.com respectively, each of which has addresses and contacts for local chapters. You can also refer to Wilcox et al., *Public Relations Strategies and Tactics* or Cutlip et al., *Effective Public Relations.*

4. For a longer discussion on content analysis, see Walter K. Lindermann, "Content Analysis," *Public Relations Journal* (July 1993): 24–26. For an example, see Jianming Ma and Kai Hildebrandt, "Canadian Press Coverage of the Ethnic Chinese Community: A Content Analysis of The Toronto Star and the Vancouver Sun, 1970–1990," *Canadian Journal of Communications* 18 (1993): 479–96.

5. For more information, see Chuck Chakrapani and Kenneth R. Deal, *Marketing Research: Methods of Canadian Practice* (Scarborough: Prentice-Hall Canada, 1992).

6. Louise Lee and David Kiley, "Love Those Boomers," *BusinessWeek,* 24 October 2005; http://www.businessweek.com (accessed July 27, 2007).

7. Edmonton Board of Health policy manual, 1989. As a result of health reform, the Board of Health is now Capital Health Authority, Public Health Services.

8. Government of Canada, "Chapter One," *Treasury Board Manual* (Ottawa, 31 July 1994).

9. Government of Canada, 14.

10. For sample communications policies refer to Wilma Matthews, "What should I tell them? Why every organization should have an official policy for communicating," *Communications World* (May/June 2004): 52

11. Angus Reid; Biggar.

12. Ipsos Reid, 11.

13. Angus Reid.

14. This summary owes much to Michael M. Klepper, "Surviving the Spotlight: Selecting a Media Trainer," *Communications World* 9:10 (October 1992): 16–17.

15. Fox, 183–84.

8   Approaching the Media

1. More and more media mergers/takeovers are occurring, resulting in "convergence" in media, in which one umbrella company may own major daily newspapers, television networks, cable companies and major Internet sites. Thus, Bell Globemedia now owns CTV and the *Globe and Mail*; CanWest Global owns Global television network, many of the former Southam newspapers and the *National Post*. The effects of convergence are still to be seen, outside of creating profit by blending news and advertising operations from each of the media outlets the conglomerate owns.

In theory, convergence implies significant technological change. For example, BCE has announced Combobox, an all-in-one telephone, television and Internet service for homes. However, whether consumers want this technology remains to be seen; all previous pilot projects melding television and home computers have failed. The last media convergence, the blending of television and radio networks in the 1950s, did not see the two technologies become one. Instead, while television displaced radio as the dominant entertainment medium, it did not replace radio. In order to survive, radio changed itself dramatically, orienting itself to music and news, and leaving situation comedies, soap operas, dramas and quiz shows to the new medium of television. The same process may occur with home computers; consumers may want to keep their radio, television and computers as separate pieces of hardware, and the real change will come with programming.

Meanwhile, one early outcome of convergence may have a profound effect on news gathering and reporting. Television and radio stations are subject to regulation by the Canadian Radio-television and Telecommunications Commission (CRTC) on the theory that there are only so many spaces available for channels and a regulatory body is required to determine which companies get access to the airways. (The relevance of the CRTC itself has come into question since digital broadcasting now allows huge numbers of stations to go on the air.) Newspapers did not up to now face CRTC regulation, on the grounds that anyone can start a newspaper, as the six daily newspapers in Toronto have proven (the *National Post* gave Torontonians a fourth daily to choose from, in addition to the *Sun, Globe* and *Star,* two giveaway dailies for subway and transit users made Toronto the biggest market for daily newspapers in North America). Now that television networks own newspapers, however, reporters find themselves subject to regulation. Both CTV and Global received licenses to broadcast for seven years, but the licenses come with restriction. On the question of whether the television and newspaper newsrooms can be shared, the CRTC decided they must be separate but they can share news (i.e., a reporter from the newspaper side can also file a television report, and vice versa). The worry about this was defined by a recent *Globe and Mail* editorial:

> The decision to let broadcasters merge TV and newspaper newsrooms keeps alive the worry that people will soon see a reduction in the numbers of journalists interpreting news stories for Canadians. While that might not be a concern right now in cities such as Toronto or Ottawa, where there is a plethora of media outlets, it's a bigger worry in such places as Vancouver (where Global will now control all or part of three of the four daily newspapers available in that city, plus two television stations).
>
> The early signals aren't good. CanWest Global president Leonard Asper has been widely quoted as saying he envisions a future in which journalists "wake up, write a story for the Web, write a column, take their cameras, cover an event, and do a report for TV, and file a video clip for the Web."
>
> The business case for such a future is strong; one person doing the jobs of four clearly reduces labour costs. The impact it would have on the array of opinions Canadians are exposed to, and by extension the democracy we live in, would be more difficult to measure.

What does this mean for the practitioner of media relations? At first glance it hints at a future of overworked reporters who are under such pressure to file stories in multiple media that they will simply take a well-written news release and run with it unchallenged, thus making it all the easier to get your message into the media. On further reflection, though, one of the major values of communicating through the news media is that if the news release (or any of the other approaches to the media discussed in this chapter) is given the professional scrutiny a good journalist applies to all news releases, the resulting story carries that much more credibility. Will media stories of the near future be perceived by the public as credible, if the audience feels that newsrooms are simply recycling news releases as news? Practitioners should follow this recent ruling with great attention, to determine exactly what effect it will have on the media business and the communications business.

See Robert Fulford, "CRTC moves into the newsroom," the *National Post*, 3 August 2001, B1; and "The complications of convergence," the *Globe and Mail*, 4 August 2001, A12.

2. John P. Robinson and Mark R. Levy, "News Media and the Informed Public: A 1990s Update," *Journal of Communications* 46:2 (Spring 1996): 132.

3. Leo Bogart, "The Public's Use and Perceptions of Newspapers," *The Public Opinion Quarterly* 48:4 (Winter 1984): 709.

4. Lynne Walters and Timothy Walters, "Environment of Confidence: Daily Newspaper Use of Press Releases," *Public Relations Review* 18:1 (Spring 1992): 31.

5. Biggar, 39.

6. Ipsos Reid, 7.

7. Angus Reid

8. P. Morton and J Warren, "Acceptance Characteristics of Hometown Press Releases," *Public Relations Review* 18:4 (Winter 1992): 38.

9. Linda Morton, "How Newspapers Choose the Releases They Use," *Public Relations Review* 11:3 (Fall 1986): 22–27.

10. Tana Fletcher and Julia Rockler, *Getting Publicity: A Do-It-Yourself Guide for Small Business* (Vancouver: International Self-Counsel Press, 1990): 11.

11. Linda Morton and J. Warren, "News Elements and Editor's Choices," *Public Relations Review* 18:1 (Spring 1992): 47–51.

12. Many of these styles of lede are taken from Ken Metzler, *Newsgathering*, second edition (New Jersey: Prentice-Hall 1986): 47–51.

13. "Stories Not Getting Through? You Could be Trapped in a Media Bozo/ Jargon Filter," http://www.jargonfreeweb.com/newstory.html, (accessed 26 July 2001).

14. Ibid.

15. Simplifying language will aid clarity, but it can also lead to a lack of accuracy due to oversimplification. There are no true synonyms (words that mean the same thing) in English. The reason we have different words is because they provide a different description and meaning. "Red" is more commonly understood than "cerise," but red can have a range of shades

(fire-engine red, blood-red, pink, salmon, scarlet, crimson, etc.), while cerise can only be cerise. The trick for the writer is knowing how to balance clarity and accuracy without misconstruing either. One common way of doing this is to write a simple news release, with a more technical document attached; another is to conduct a technical briefing of the media (we'll look at this strategy in the next chapter).

16. *CP Stylebook,* 37.

17. The term "double planting" comes from Jeanette Smith, *The Publicity Kit* (New York: John Wiley and Sons, 1991): 40.

18. B.L. Ochman, "Press Releases are a Colossal Waste of Time: Mail the Media a Letter," Communications World Online, http://www.iabc.com/cw/private/cwb/2004/0604/waste.htm, (accessed 24 June, 2004).

19. Ibid.

20. Anne Owen and James Karrh, "Video News Releases; Effects on Viewer Recall and Attitudes," *Public Relations Review* 22:4 (Winter 1996): 371.

21. Owen and Karrh, 370.

9 Other Approaches to the Media

1. McKercher and Cumming, 191.

2. Angus Reid.

3. Developed from materials provided by Capital Health Authority, Edmonton, Alberta, 1996.

4. Doris Graber,"Seeing Is Remembering: How Visuals Contribute to Learning from Television News," Journal of Communications 40:3 (Summer 1990): 134–55.

5. Gerry Predy, Bill Carney, Joy Edwards, "Effectiveness of Recorded Messages to Communicate the Risk of Acquiring Hantavirus Pulmonary Syndrome," Canadian Journal of Public Health 88:4 (July/August 1997): 275–76.

6. Salzman.

7. Linda Morton, 26.

8. Rene Henry, Marketing Public Relations (Ames: Iowa State University Press, 1995): 94.

10 Do-It-Yourself Media

1. Developed from Ulli Diemer, "Don't forget to write," *Sources Hot Link* (Toronto: Sources, n.d.).

2. However, I wouldn't recommend you submit a formal proposal until you've found out if the cable outlet thinks your idea has some merit. And instead of seeing a proposal, some producers prefer you submit a sample video (they will usually give you access to the studio to do so) so they can get a sense of your abilities as well as a sense of what your show would look like on the screen.

3. Rene Henry. See especially Chapters 11 and 12.

4. Carley Weeks, "More and more Canadians are getting connected," *Regina Leader Post,* 21 July 1, 2006, D12.

5. Ibid.

6. Jakob Nielsen and Kara Pernice Coyne, "Corporate Websites Get a 'D' in PR," http://www.useit.com/alertbox/20010401.html, (accessed April 2001).

7. Canadian Press, "Net use skyrockets," http;//www.canoe.ca, (accessed July 26 2001).

8. Mallory Jensen, "Emerging Alternatives: A Brief History of Weblogs" *Columbia Journalism Review* (2003), www.cjr/org/issues/2003/05/blog-jensen. asp,,(accessed 21 May, 2006).

9. Ibid.

11 The Interview

1. *Webster's Encyclopedic Dictionary of the English Language* (New York: Lexicon Publications, 1988): 506.

2. Paul Fitzgerald and Lynda Embrey-Wahl, "Dealing With the Media: CEO's perceptions," *Health Progress* 67:2 (March 1986): 22–25.

3. McKercher and Cumming, 83. Efforts at source control most often come from politicians, although business people and activists are also suspect. In general, control attempts come from people who have a partisan stance on an issue and view the media as another weapon in a battle for public opinion.

4. Eugene Webb and Terry Salancik, "The Interview, or the only wheel in town," *Journalism Monographs* No. 2 (November 1996), quoted in McKercher and Cumming, 83.

5. Quoted in Henry, 114–15.

6. Henry, 114–15.

7. Dave Knesel, *Free Publicity—A Step by Step Guide* (New York: Sterling Publishing, 1982).

8. Peter Hannaford, *Talking Back to the Media* (New York: Facts on File, 1986): 44.

9. Michael Klepper, *Getting Your Message Out* (New Jersey: Prentice-Hall, 1984): 135.

10. Hannaford, 60.

11. CBC Marketplace, 29 December, 1992.

12. Jack O'Dwyer, *Jack O'Dwyer's Newsletter,* cited in Ted Klein and Fred Danzig *Free Publicity: How to make media work for you* (New York: Charles Scribner's Sons, 1985) 138.

13. Ipsos Reid, 2003 Canadian Media Relations Review.

14. For example, see the Simon Fraser University guidelines "The Ten Commandments," cited *in The Sources Hotlink Special Edition.*

15. Natalie Webster, "Build Confidence with Media Training," *PR Journal* 48:2.

16. Klein and Danzig, 20.

17. Arie Kopelman, executive with Doyle Dane Bernbach advertising/public relations agency, cited in Klein and Danzig, 35.

12 The Interview Continued: Questions and Answers

1. Steve Rukavina, "Diary of a Replacement Host," http://www.sask.cbc.ca/archivesl, (accessed 8 September 2001).

2. See, for example, Jill Mahoney, "A bereaved community's fury lands on a reporter's shoulders," *Globe and Mail,* 26 June 1999.

3. McKercher and Cumming, 82.

4. McKercher and Cumming, 82.

5. McKercher and Cumming, 82.

6. McKercher and Cumming, 85.

7. CBC-TV's *The Fifth Estate* lost a libel case for $1 million plus legal expenses when a physician claimed the program had "excluded and distorted information to falsely depict him as uncaring, unprincipled, indifferent and neglectful about a product," (Jennifer O'Neill "Loss of $200,000 libel suit could kill CBC show," *The Ottawa Citizen,* 29 December 1999, A7). Among the factors which led to the ruling of libel was a segment in which the doctor could not read a document without his glasses:

> He had not been given prior notice that he would be questioned about the document and looking at it without his glasses made him appear nervous, uncertain, and hesitant, raising suspicion and suggesting guilt.

The Fifth Estate has been broadcasting for 25 years, has won many journalism awards for its investigations, and had a deserved reputation for thoroughness, toughness and fairness. The doctor who sued, however, thought he was simply providing information as a technical expert; in the words of the judge, "He felt he had given an interview based on science and was now being portrayed as a villain who defended a drug killing tens of thousands of people."

8. Bill Fox, *Spinwars: Politics and the News Media,* 13–22.

9. "Read All About It," *FFWD; Calgary's News and Entertainment Weekly,* 5 May 2002, http://www.ffwdweekly.com/Intro/arc2002.htm, (accessed 27 June 2002).

13 Evaluation and Revision

1. Memo from author to Dr. James Howell, Medical Officer of Health and CEO of the Edmonton Board of Health, 1991.

2. The issue of bias in media was most famously shown in the 1984 federal election. Prime Minister and Liberal leader John Turner appeared in a black-and-white photograph on the front page of the *Globe and Mail,* shot against a cloth background that had, for some reason, pictures of knives and forks on it. Of all the shots the photographer took that night, the one that was printed positioned Prime Minister Turner so that a knife and a fork appeared to be sprouting from his head, like horns; his expression gave the distinct impression he was snarling. Some of the *Globe's* own columnists complained in print that this photo, which appeared on the front page, was a cheap shot against the Liberal leader. A few days later, Conservative leader Brian Mulroney also had his picture taken, this time by the *Calgary Herald,* which also printed its photo on the front page, but in colour. The backdrop had gold crowns on a blue backdrop, and the smiling Mulroney appeared to have one of the crowns on his head. The choice of these photos communicated some bias to the readership.

3. Memo from Dagny Alston to members of Edmonton City Council/Senior Management Team, 1994.

4. Jim Rutenberg, "CNN Aims at Young Viewers As it Revamps News Format," the *New York Times,* 5 August 2001, A1.

14 Special Media, Special Cases

1. This quotation is popularly attributed to H.L. Mencken.

2. McKercher and Cumming, 268.

3. McKercher and Cumming, 277.

4. McKercher and Cumming, 282.

5. *CP Stylebook,* 244.

6. See, for example, 24 July 2006 news release from CAJ, "CAJ opposes advertising's growing influence on news coverage,"http://www.caj.org.

7. Tom Rosenstiel, "Yakety-Yak: The lost Art of Interviewing," Columbia Journalism Review 32:5 (January/February 1995).

15 The Fine Art of Complaining About the Media

1. Four separate and competing roles are suggested in the title of Finer D. Tonson and N. M. Bjorkman's article, "Ally, advocate, analyst, agenda-setter? Positions and perceptions of Swedish medical journalists," *Patient Educ Couns* 31:1 (Jan 1997): 71–78.

2. For the reader who wishes to follow this debate, please refer to David Taras, *Power and Betrayal in the Canadian Media* or Hackett and Zhao's *Sustaining Democracy: Journalism and the Politics of Objectivity.*

3. "The Editor-Error Question," *Columbia Review of Journalism.*

4. *CP Stylebook,* 13.

5. *CP Stylebook,* 15.

6. Quoted in Keane Shore, *Newspaper Ombudsmen in Canada* (Master's thesis, Carleton University School of Journalism and Communications; Resource Centre Ref. Journal 592): 18.

7. Quoted in *Columbia Review of Journalism* (September/October 1989), 5.

8. Shore, ii.

9. Susanne Craig, "Mulroney to head Sun media," *Globe and Mail,* 24 December 1999, A1.

THREE TOWARDS A GREATER UNDERSTANDING OF MEDIA

16 Emerging Trends in Media and Media Relations

1. Jack O'Dwyer, citing C-SPAN Chair, *O'Dwyer's PR Daily,* 6 June 2002: http://www.odwyerpr.com, (accessed 10 June 2002).

2. G. Sciadas, *Our Lives in Digital Times, Science* (Ottawa: Innovation and Electronic Information Division, Statistics Canada, 2006).

3. "Canadians choosing Internet over radio, TV," CTV website, http://ctv.ca/news, (accessed 31 July 2007).

4. Russell Smith, "Demeaning discourse: how bloggers lower the tone," *Globe and Mail,* 30 March 2006, GMR1.

5. Scott White, Canadian Press Executive Editor, speech at IABC Canada conference in Halifax, October 2005.

6. Bob Woodward, *The Secret Man* (New York: Simon and Schuster, 2005), 231–232.

7. Siri Agrell, "New breed of political ads simple, direct: U.S. Experts," *National Post,* 30 September 2006, A13.

8. Niall Cook, "Media Relations in the Social Media Era," *Communications World Bulletin,* January 2006: http://www.iabc.com/cw/private/cwb/2006/0106/socialmedia.htm, (accessed 11 February 2006.

9. Ipsos Reid, 3.

10. Ibid, 2.

11. The Project for Excellence in Journalism, *2006 Annual Report on the State of the News Media* (Washington 2006), 2.

12. Garry Norris and David Paddon, "CHUM offer a broadcast bombshell," *Winnipeg Free Press,.* 13 July 2006, B5.

13. For examples of international companies implementing CSR programs, please see Jared Diamond, Chapter 15 "Big Businesses and the Environment: Different Conditions, Different Outcomes," *Collapse: How Societies can Choose to Fail or Succeed* (Toronto: Penguin, 2005), 441–487.

14. Ibid, 484.

15. Project for Excellence in Journalism, 4.

16. "Note to Readers," *National Post* 16 September 2006, FP8.

17   Toward a Greater Understanding of Media, Communications and Technology

1. The Addison and Steele analogy is based on a *National Post* column. The author has tried to reach the *Post* in order to credit the author, but at the time of publication they had not responded to this request.

2. Thomas L. Friedman, *The World is Flat* (New York: Farrar, Strauss and Giroux 2006.)

3. "Rich and powerful believed to taint media," *Reginal Leader Post,* 16 June 2004, A10 (study available online from the Canadian Media Research Consortium).

4. Mary Ellen Schoonmaker, "A Beat Comes of Age," *Columbia Journalism Review* http://cjrarchives.org/issues/, (accessed May 21, 2006).

Bibliography

Books

Albrecht, Donna G. *Promoting Your Business with Free (or almost free) Publicity.* New Jersey: Prentice-Hall, 1997.

Angus Reid Group. *Canadian Media Review 1993: An Elite Survey of Editors and Journalists for Communications Professionals.* Toronto: Angus Reid Group, 1993.

Borden, Kay. *Bulletproof New Releases.* Georgia: Franklin-Sarrett Publishers, 1994.

Chakrapani, Chuck and Kenneth R. Deal. *Marketing Research: Methods of Canadian Practice.* Scarborough; Prentice-Hall, Canada, 1992.

Cogswell, David. *Chomsky for Beginners.* New York and London: Writers and Readers, 1996.

Covello, Vincent T., David B. McCallum, and Maria T. Pavlova, eds. *Effective Risk Communications: The Role and Responsibility of Government and Nongovernment Organizations.* New York: Plenum Press, 1989.

Davis, Covello, and Allen, eds. *Risk Communication: Proceedings of the National Conference on Risk Communication, held in Washington D.C. January 29–31.* Washington D.C.: The Conservation Foundation, 1987.

Desbarats, Peter. *A Guide to Canadian News Media.* Toronto: Harcourt Brace Jovanavich Canada, 1990.

Diamond, Jared. *Collapse: How Societies can Choose to Fail or Succeed.* (Toronto: Penguin, 2005).

Emery, Fred. *Watergate.* New York: Random House, 1994.

Fletcher, Tana and Julia Rockler. *Getting Publicity: A Do-It-Yourself Guide for Small Business.* Vancouver: International Self-Counsel Press, 1990.

Fox, Bill. *Spinwars: Politics and the News Media.* Toronto: Key Porter Books, 1999.

Frankfurt, Harry G. *On Bullshit.* Princeton: Princeton University Press, 2005.

Friedman, Thomas L. *The World is Flat.* New York: Farrar, Strauss and Giroux, 2006.

Hannaford, Peter. *Talking Back to the Media*. New York: Facts on File, 1986.

Henry, Rene. *Marketing Public Relations*. Ames, Iowa: Iowa State University Press, 1995.

Ipsos Reid. *Canadian Media Relations Review*. Toronto: Ipsos Reid, 23 November 2003.

Kasperson, Roger E. and Pieter Jan. M. Stallen. *Communicating Risk to the Public: International Perspectives*. Dordrecht, the Netherlands: Kluwer Academic Publishers, 1991.

Klein, Ted and Fred Danzig. *Free Publicity: How to make media work for you*. New York: Charles Scribner's Sons, 1985.

Klepper, Michael. *Getting Your Message Out*. New Jersey: Prentice-Hall, 1984.

Knesel, Dave. *Free Publicity—A step by step guide*. New York: Sterling Publishing, 1982.

Kotler, Philip and Gordon H.G. McDougall. *Principles of Marketing, Canadian Edition*. Scarborough: Prentice-Hall Canada Inc., 1983.

Lesley, Philip, ed. *Lesley's Public Relations Handbook*. Second edition. New Jersey: Prentice-Hall, 1978.

Levine, Allan. *Scrum Wars: The Prime Ministers and the Media*. Toronto: Dundurn Press, 1993.

Lindsay, Colin. *A Portrait of Seniors in Canada*. Second edition. Ottawa: Statistics Canada, 1997.

Martin, Robert. *Media Law*. Toronto: Irwin Law, 2003.

McKercher, Catherine and Carman Cumming. *The Canadian Reporter, News Writing and Reporting*. Second edition. Toronto: Harcourt Brace & Company, 1998.

The Project for Excellence in Journalism. *2006 Annual Report on the State of the News Media*. Washington, 2006.

Metzler, Ken. *Newsgathering*, Second edition. New Jersey: Prentice-Hall, 1986.

Salzman, Jason. *Making the News: A Guide for Non-profits and Activists*. Colorado: Westview Press, 1998.

Sciadas, G. *Our Lives in Digital Times*. Science. Ottawa: Innovation and Electronic Information Division, Statistics Canada, 2006.

Shiller, Ed. *The Canadian Guide to Managing the Media*. Second edition. Scarborough: Prentice-Hall, 1994.

Smith, Jeannette. *The Publicity Kit*. New York: John Wiley and Sons, 1991.

Taras, David. *Power and Betrayal in the Canadian Media*. Peterborough, Ontario: Broadview Press, 1999.

Tasko, Patty, ed. *The Canadian Press Stylebook: A Guide for Writers and Editors.* Toronto: The Canadian Press, 2006.

Ura, Mike. *Making the News: A Guide to Using the Media.* Vancouver: West Coast Environmental Law Research Foundation, 1980.

Wintonick, Peter and Mark Achbar. *Manufacturing Consent: Noam Chomsky and the Media.* Montreal: Black Rose Books, 1994.

Woodward, Bob. *The Secret Man.* New York: Simon and Schuster, 2005.

Periodicals: Journals

Adam, G. Stuart. "The Thicket of Rules North of The Border." *Media Studies Journal* 12:1 (Winter 1998): 24–30.

Barber and Rauhala. "The Canadian News Directors Study." *Canadian Journal of Communications* Vol. 30 (2005) 87.

Biggar, Brian. *PR Flacks and Media Hacks: Public Relations and the News Media.* Unpublished Master's thesis. Carleton University School of Journalism and Communications Resource Centre, 1995.

Biggart, Leo. "The Public's Use and Perceptions of Newspapers." *The Public Opinion Quarterly* 48:4 (Winter 1984): 709.

Carney, Bill. *The Value of Reactive Media Relations in Communicating Risk.* Unpublished, 1994. Available on request from the author.

Covello, Vincent. *Handbook on Risk Communication, presented by Dr. Vincent Covello, Director of the Center for Risk Communication in New York City.* Calgary: Risk Communications conference material, 1994.

Cranberg, Gilbert. "The editor-error equation." *The Columbia Journalism Review* 25 (March/April 1987): 40–42.

Diemer, Ulli. "Don't forget to write." *Sources Hot Link.* Toronto: Sources, n.d.

Dykstra, Robert. *The Hometown Paper and Viability of News in the Community Press.* Unpublished Master's thesis. Carleton University School of Journalism and Communications Resource Centre, Reference 775, 1998.

Fitzgerald, Paul and Lynda Embrey-Wahl. "Dealing With the Media: CEO's perceptions." *Health Progress* 67:2 (March 1986): 22–25.

Graber, Doris. "Seeing is remembering: How visuals contribute to learning from television." *Journal of Communications* 40:3 (Summer 1990): 134–55.

Hickley, Neil. "CJR Poll: Handling Corrections." *The Columbia Journalism Review* (July/August 1999): http://backissues.cjrarchives.org/year/99/4/poll.asp.

Jensen, Mallory. "Emerging Alternatives: A Brief History of Weblogs." *Columbia Journalism Review* (2003): http://www.cjr.org/issues/2003/5/blog-jensen.asp.

Joint Committee on Corporate Governance. *Beyond Compliance: Building a Governance Culture*. Final report, November 2001.

Klepper, Michael. "Surviving the Spotlight: Selecting a Media Trainer." *Communications World* 9:10 (October 1992): 16–17.

Lindemann, Walter K. "Content Analysis." *Public Relations Journal* (July 1993): 24–26.

Ma, Jianming and Kai Hildebrandt. "Canadian Press Coverage of the Ethnic Chinese Community: A Content Analysis of the Toronto Star and the Vancouver Sun, 1979–1990." *Canadian Journal of Communications* 18 (1993) 479–96.

Morton, Linda. "How Newspapers Choose the Releases they Use." *Public Relations Review* 18:1 (Spring 1992): 47–51.

Morton, P. and J. Warren. "Acceptance Characteristics of Hometown press Releases." *Public Relations Review* 18:4 (Winter 1992): 385–90.

Owen, Anne and James Karrh. "Video News Releases: Effects on Viewer Recall and Attitudes." *Public Relations Review* 22:4 (Winter 1996): 364–77.

Porter, Bruce. "The Scanlon Spin." *Columbia Journalism Review* 29 (September/October 1989): 49–54.

"Positive messages about PR outweigh negatives." *Communications World* (December 1992): 28.

Predy, Gerry, Bill Carney, and Joy Edwards. "Effectiveness of Recorded Messages to Communicate the Risk of Acquiring Hantavirus Pulmonary Syndrome." *Canadian Journal of Public Health* 88:4 (July/August 1997): 275–76.

Robinson, John P. and Mark R. Levy. "News Media and the Informed Public: A 1990's Update." *Journal of Communications* 46:2 (Spring 1996): 129–35.

Robinson, Michael J. and Andrew Kohut. "Believability and the Press." *Public Opinion Quarterly* 52 (Summer 1988): 174–89.

Rosentiel, Tom. "Yakety-Yak: The Lost Art of Interviewing." *Columbia Journalism Review* 32:5 (January/February 1995): 23–27.

Rowse, Arthur E. "How to Build Support for War." *Columbia Journalism Review* 31 (September/October 1992): 28–29.

Sauvegeau, Florin. "Surveying Attitudes," *Media Magazine* (Winter 2000). http://www.caj/mediamag/winter2000/media2000–15.html. (accessed 26 July 2001.)

Shore, Keane. *Newspaper Ombudsmen in Canada.* Unpublished Master's thesis. Carleton University School for Journalism and Communications Resource Centre, Ref. Journal 592: 1991.

Sumpter, Randy and James W. Tankard Jr. "The Spin Doctor: An Alternative Model of Public Relations." *The Public Relations Review* 20:1 (Spring 1994): 19–27.

Tonson, Finer D. and N.M. Bjorkman. "Ally, advocate, analyst, agenda-setter? Positions and perceptions of Swedish medical journalists." *Patient Educ. Couns.* 30:1 (January 1997): 71–81.

Walter, Lynne and Timothy Walters. "Environment of Confidence: Daily Newspaper Use of Press Releases." *Public Relations Review* 18:1 (Spring 1992): 31–46.

Webster, Natalie. "Build Confidence with Media Training." *PR Journal* 48:2 (February 1992).

Periodicals: Newspapers and Internet articles

Agrell, Siri. "New breed of political ads simple, direct: U.S. Experts." *National Post,* 30 September 2006: A13

Akin, David. "Albertans more wired than most: Survey." *National Post,* 30 December 1999: C1.

Calman-Alves, Rosental. "Many newspaper sites still cling to once-a-day publish cycle." *USC Annenberg Online Journalism Review:* http://ojr.org/ojr/workplace/1090395903.php.

Cook, Niall. "Media Relations in the Social Media Era." *Communications World Bulletin,* January 2006: http://www.iabc.com/cw/private/cwb/2006/0106/socialmedia.htm.

Craig, Susanne. "Striking unions for Herald meeting." *Globe and Mail,* 15 November 1999: B3.

Craig, Susanne. "Mulroney to head Sun Media." *Globe and Mail,* December 1999: A1.

Dunn, Katherine. "The Lies the Good Guys Tell." *Globe and Mail,* n.d.

Mahoney, Jill. "A bereaved community's fury lands on a reporter's shoulders." *Globe and Mail,* 26 June 1999.

Mahoney, Jill. "Libraries turn new page to thrive in digital age." *Globe and Mail,* 10 January 2007: A1.

McGee, Patrick. "Did I really hear that?" http://www.prcanada.ca/CRISIS/DISFLUT.HTM.

"More radio listeners tuning in to CBC." *Regina Leader Post,* 1 August 2003: A10

Near, Paul. *The Edmontonians.* February 1994.

"News Bias assessed." *Edmonton Journal,* 6 December 1992: F1.

Norris, Garry and Paddon, David. "CHUM offers a broadcast bombshell." *Winnipeg Free Press,* 13 July 2006: B5.

"Note to Readers." *National Post,* 16 September 2006.

Ochman, B.L.."Press Releases are a Colossal Waste of Time: Mail the Media a Letter." *Communications World* Online. http://www.iabc.com/cw/private/cwb/2004/0604/waste.htm.

O'Neil, Jennifer. "Loss of $200,000 libel suit could kill CBC show." *Ottawa Citizen,* 29 December 1999: A7.

Proudfoot, Shannon. "Internet blogs prompt rise in libel suits." *Regina Leader Post,* 18 March 2006: D12.

"Post forcing shift in advertising revenue: buyers." *National Post,* 30 October 1999: D4.

"Rich and powerful believed to taint media." *Regina Leader Post,* 16 June 2004.

Schoonmake, Mary Ellen. "A Beat Comes of Age." *Columbia Journalism Review.* http://cjrarchives.org/issues/.

Smith, Russell. "Demeaning discourse: how bloggers lower the tone." *Globe and Mail,* 30 March 2006: GMR1.

"A small business in career upgrading." *Globe and Mail,* 14 November 1999: D6.

"Read All About It." *FFWD; Calgary's News and Entertainment Weekly,* 5 May 2002: http://www.ffwdweekly.com/Intro/arc2002.htm

Thompson, Jane L. and Ellen Himelfarb. "TV that's so bad it's good." *National Post,* 13 February 1999: 13–14.

Weeks, Carley. "More and more Canadians are getting connected." *Regina Leader Post,* 21 July 2006: D12.

Index

radio
  ability to adapt of, xx, 215, 226
  audience, xx, 42, 43
  CBC, 43, 55, 70, 132, 165
  and community service, 138, 199
  competition with tv, 203, 226, 240
  in crisis situations, 202
  and file of stories, 81, 90
  making direct contact with, 129, 131
  and newsgathering, 61–62, 68, 70
  and PSAs, 140–41
  stations in Edmonton, xx, 55–56
  what it offers, 42–44, 56
  where leads come from, 52, 62, 101. *See also* talk
    radio and tv
Rain Man, 24–25
raising awareness, 4–5
Reagan, Ronald, 20
Red Cross, 88
Regina Leader Post, 11, 60
regional publications, 50
reporters. *See* journalists/reporters
research
  by communicators on target audience, 15, 89–92,
    136, 137
  on effectiveness of media contact, 122, 125
  on Internet, 63, 90, 92, 204, 213–14
  as part of media relations plan, 18–19, 76, 89–92
  by reporters, 63, 204, 213–14
Rimstead, Paul, 221
Ringle, Ken, 32
rip and read journalism, 101
risk communications, 18–19
Rushdie, Salman, 127

sales techniques for delivering message, 13–14
Salzman, Jason, 126
satellite radio, 43–44
scandals, reporting of, 2, 6–7, 17, 186
scheduling
  interviews, 78, 150–51
  news stories, 61–62
scrums, 124, 174
sensationalism, 10, 47
September 11 terrorist attacks, 184, 202, 203
single overriding communications objective (SOCO),
    156–57
situational analysis, 85–87
Slobodian, Linda, 35
Smales, Andrew, 145
society and communications revolution, 223–24
SOCO (single overriding communications objective),
    156–57

soft news, 41, 44, 198
soundbites, 164
Sounds Like Canada (radio show), 43
source control, 148, 153–155. *See also* message control
sources·
  blogs as, 204, 216–18, 219
  communicator's choice of, 18–20
  on Internet, xix, 204
  "not for attribution," 175
  verifying, 67, 77, 216–17, 218, 219
  who public accepts as credible, 18–20, 154–55, 219
Southam, 48
specialist information officers
  in crisis situations, 202
  difficulty with media, 178, 180
  in government, 196–97
  in private sector, 94
  scheduling, 78, 150–51
  and survey of reliability, 18–19
  training, 193
specialty media
  audience of, 136, 137, 142, 191
  business media, 192–94
  entertainment, 197–199
  Internet, 203–04
  magazines, 50
  newspapers, 47, 53, 55
  radio, 43, 55–56
  sports, 199–200
  tv, 45, 52–53, 132
  wire services, 51–52
spin
  as deception, xxi, 25–27
  to hide scandal, 17, 186
  history, 25–26
  as shield for bad news, 109, 158
  on websites, 143
spokespersons
  choosing, 94, 193
  policies and procedures on, 93, 94
  scheduling for interviews, 150–51. *See also*
    communicators
sponsorships, 138–40, 199
sports, 64, 215
sports reporters, 194, 199–200
staff
  and accessibility to media, 76, 78, 94
  co-ordinating media relations, 193–94
  in government, 194, 195–97
  and organizing media events, 127–28, 140
  showing sensitivity towards, 203
  as sources, 19–20
Star Wars, 198